CHINESE CIVILIZATION

An Introduction

CHINESE CIVILIZATION

AN INTRODUCTION

by

Werner Eichhorn

Translated by Janet Seligman

FABER AND FABER
24 Russell Square
London

Originally published in Germany as
'Kulturgeschichte Chinas: Eine Einführung'
This translation first published in 1969
by Faber and Faber Limited
24 Russell Square London WC1
Printed in Great Britain by
R. MacLehose and Company Limited
The University Press, Glasgow

SBN: 571 08525 3

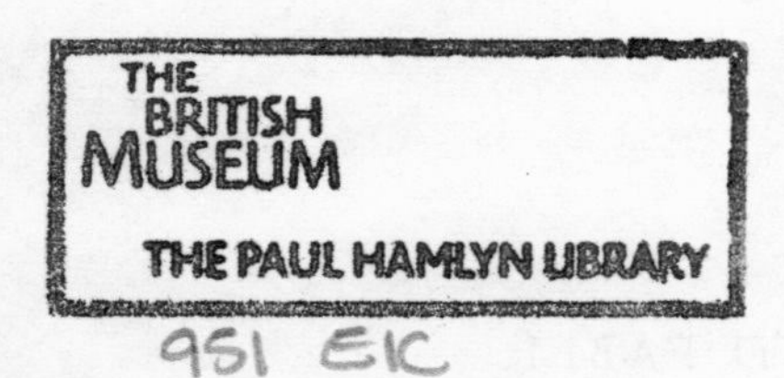

ACKNOWLEDGMENTS FOR THIS EDITION

Acknowledgments are due to the following for permission to quote translations of various works: George Allen and Unwin Ltd. (*The Book of Songs*, *The Analects*, *The Way and Its Power*, and *Taoism and Buddhism*, translated by Arthur Waley); George Allen and Unwin Ltd. and Robert Payne (*The White Pony*, edited by Robert Payne); Jonathan Cape Ltd. (*Tu Fu: The Autobiography of a Chinese Poet*, translated by Florence Ayscough); Constable and Co. Ltd. (*170 Chinese Poems*, translated by Arthur Waley); and the Harvard University Press (*The Mirror of Good Government*, vol. I of *The Chronicle of the Three Kingdoms*, translated by Achilles Fang).

Foreword

It is not the purpose of this work to provide an all-round picture of Chinese civilization. Its emphasis is principally on the intellectual aspect of civilization, while the material aspect, although not entirely excluded, has been treated much less fully.

The author's concern has been, in the main, to select and describe those facts in each separate phase of Chinese history that have seemed to him to be of special cultural importance. This has meant that individual aspects of Chinese civilization make their appearance at the moment when, in the author's opinion, they are in the forefront of events. As a result, their historical origins and subsequent development are often treated rather briefly, or may even merely be implied.

The author is also fully aware that the material he has selected to a large extent depended on his own subjective judgment and may therefore occasionally, perhaps, call for fuller justification and explanation. Since, however, the book is directed not so much at specialist sinologues as at a wider public — reasons of space-saving apart — explanations of this kind have been restricted to what seemed absolutely essential.

Moreover, it can hardly be expected that a scholar will have an equal command in every branch of the gigantic domain of Chinese civilization, however wide his knowledge. This is the reason for the somewhat unequal division of the material — which some people may find disturbing — and for the fact that a number of important subjects like the great encyclopaedias, astronomy and mathematics are only touched on, while others may not even be mentioned. This does not mean that the author had nothing more to say on them. But they did appear to him to occupy a less prominent position within his conception of the work as a whole, and they have consequently been relegated to the background. Some, he believed, deserved to be kept back for special, more exhaustive treatment.

However, in spite of these gaps, the author hopes that he has provided the interested non-specialist and the beginner in Chinese studies with a survey of the most important basic features, and a delineation, of Chinese civilization in its historical development. If the work stimulates further enquiry into the subject, as well as discussion and fruitful criticism, the author's essential purpose in writing it will have been achieved.

WERNER EICHHORN

Contents

TRANSLATOR'S NOTE

The Translation of Quotations from the Chinese

Where standard translations already exist, a translator normally uses them. As is well known, however, Chinese is an exceptionally difficult language, the study of which by western scholars is a continuing process. While much of the present author's material is new and unknown in English, some of the classical texts quoted were translated into English many years ago and have not been re-translated since. Some, moreover, were the work of men who were not linguistic scholars. Their renderings are therefore sometimes archaic in expression and inaccurate in the light of modern scholarship. For this reason, the translator has in many instances translated extracts from Chinese works from the author's German translations (of the Chinese originals). In cases where an existing English translation largely agreed with the author's version, the English translation has been used. In certain cases, the English versions which appear in the following pages are composite renderings. Standard English versions — even if in part discredited by modern scholarship — are mentioned in the Notes, since they may be the only sources available to the English reader who, although anxious to pursue the references further, is not a Chinese linguist.

NOTE ON PRONOUNCING WORDS TRANSCRIBED FROM THE CHINESE

The following are rough phonetic approximations:

a as *a* in *father*
ai as *I*
ao as ow in *now*
e and *eh* as *e* in *bet*
ei as *ay* in *bay*
ê as *u* in *run*
i as *i* in *tin*
ia as *ya*
iao as *eow* in *meow*
ie and *ieh* as *ye* in *yet*
ih as *e* in *her*
o as *o* in *orange*
ou as *ou* in *soul*
u as *u* in *rude*
ua as *wa* in *waft*
ui as *way*
uo as *wo* in *wobble*
ŭ as *u* in *fur*
ü as *ü* in German *über*
üa as *ua* in French *tuable*
üeh as *ue* in French *suette*
ch as *j* in *joy*
ch' as *ch* in *church*
j as *wr* in *wren*
hs as *sh* in *she*
k as *k* in *skid*
k' as *k* in *kid*
p as *p* in *spot*
p' as *p* in *pot*
t as *t* in *stall*
t' as *t* in *tall*
ts and *tz* as *dz* in *adze*
ts' and *tz'* as *ts* in *cats*

The consonants *f*, *h*, *l*, *m*, *n*, *ng*, *s*, *sh*, w and *y* sound as in English.

CHINESE DYNASTIES

Shang (Yin)	1766–1123 B.C.
Chou	1122–247 B.C.
Ch'in	221–207 B.C.
Han or Western Han	206 B.C.–8 A.D.
Later or Eastern Han	25–220
Three Kingdoms (San Kuo):	
Shu-Han	221–264
Wei	220–264
Wu	222–279
Western Chin	265–316
Eastern Chin	317–419

(separation between north and south)

NORTH		SOUTH	
Toba-Wei	386–534	Sung or Liu-Sung	420–478
Western Wei (Toba)	535–556	Ch'i	479–501
Eastern Wei (Toba)	534–543	Liang	502–556
Northern Ch'i	550–577	Ch'ên	557–589

Sui	581–618
T'ang	618–906
Five short-lived dynasties (Wu-tai)	907–960
Sung	960–1126
Southern Sung	1127–1279
(in the north at the same period)	
Liao (Kitan Tartars)	916–1119
Chin (Golden Tartars)	1115–1234
Yüan (Mongolian)	1260–1367
Ming	1368–1643
Ch'ing (Manchu)	1644–1911
Republic	1912–

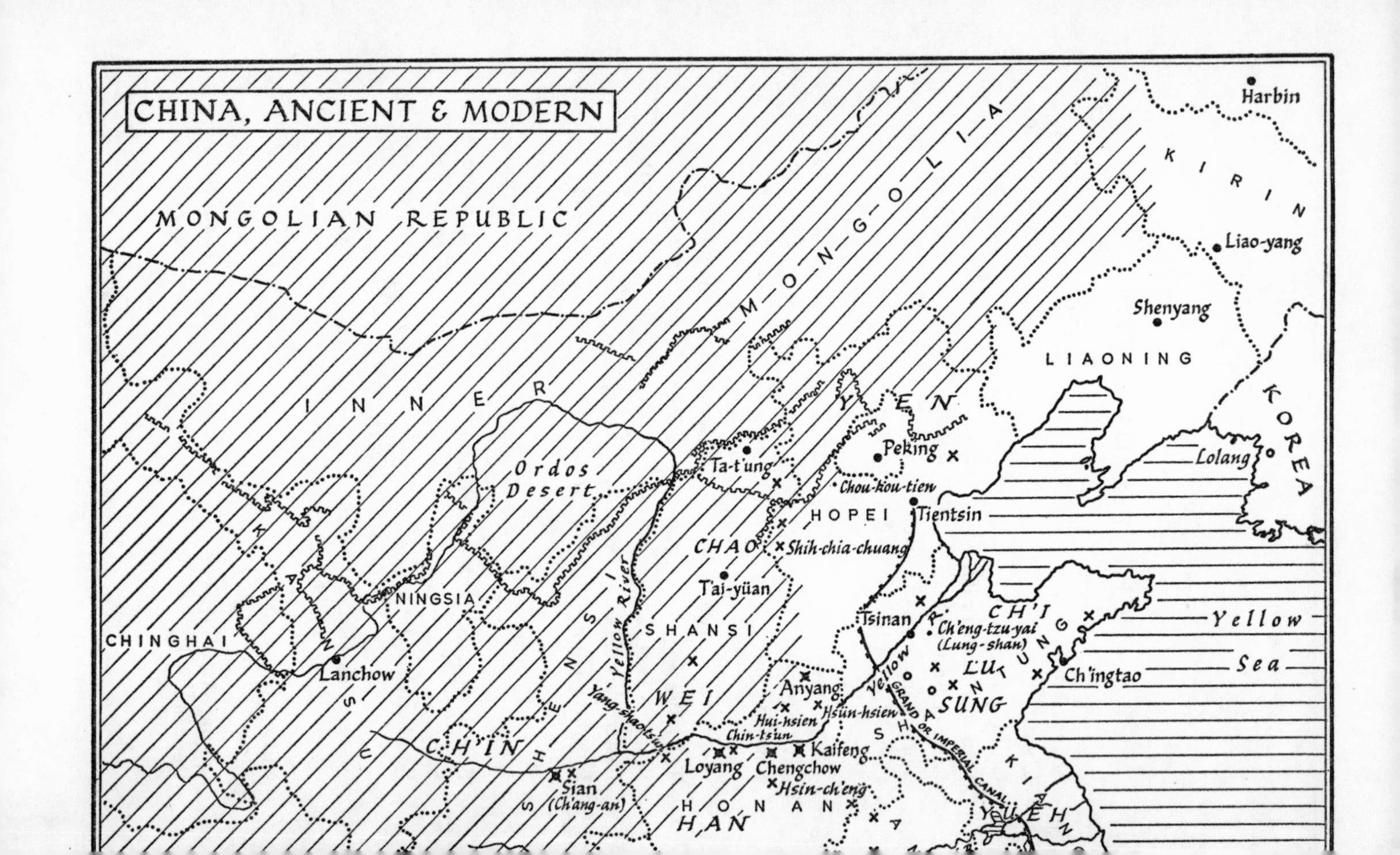

CHINA, ANCIENT & MODERN
MONGOLIAN REPUBLIC
MONGOLIA
INNER
KIRIN
Harbin
Liao-yang
Shenyang
LIAONING
KOREA
Lolang
YEN
Peking
Chou-kou-tien
Tientsin
HOPEI
Ta-t'ung
CHAO
Shih-chia-chuang
T'ai-yüan
SHANSI
Ordos Desert
NINGSIA
CHINGHAI
Lanchow
Yellow River
Yang-shao-ts'un
WEI
CHIN
SHENSI
Sian (Ch'ang-an)
Loyang
Chengchow
Kaifeng
Hsin-ch'eng
Chin-ts'un
Hui-hsien
Hsün-hsien
Anyang
HONAN
HAN
Tsinan
Ch'eng-tzu-yai (Lung-shan)
CH'I
LU
SUNG
SHANTUNG
Ch'ingtao
Yellow R.
GRAND OR IMPERIAL CANAL
KIANGSU
YÜEH
Yellow Sea

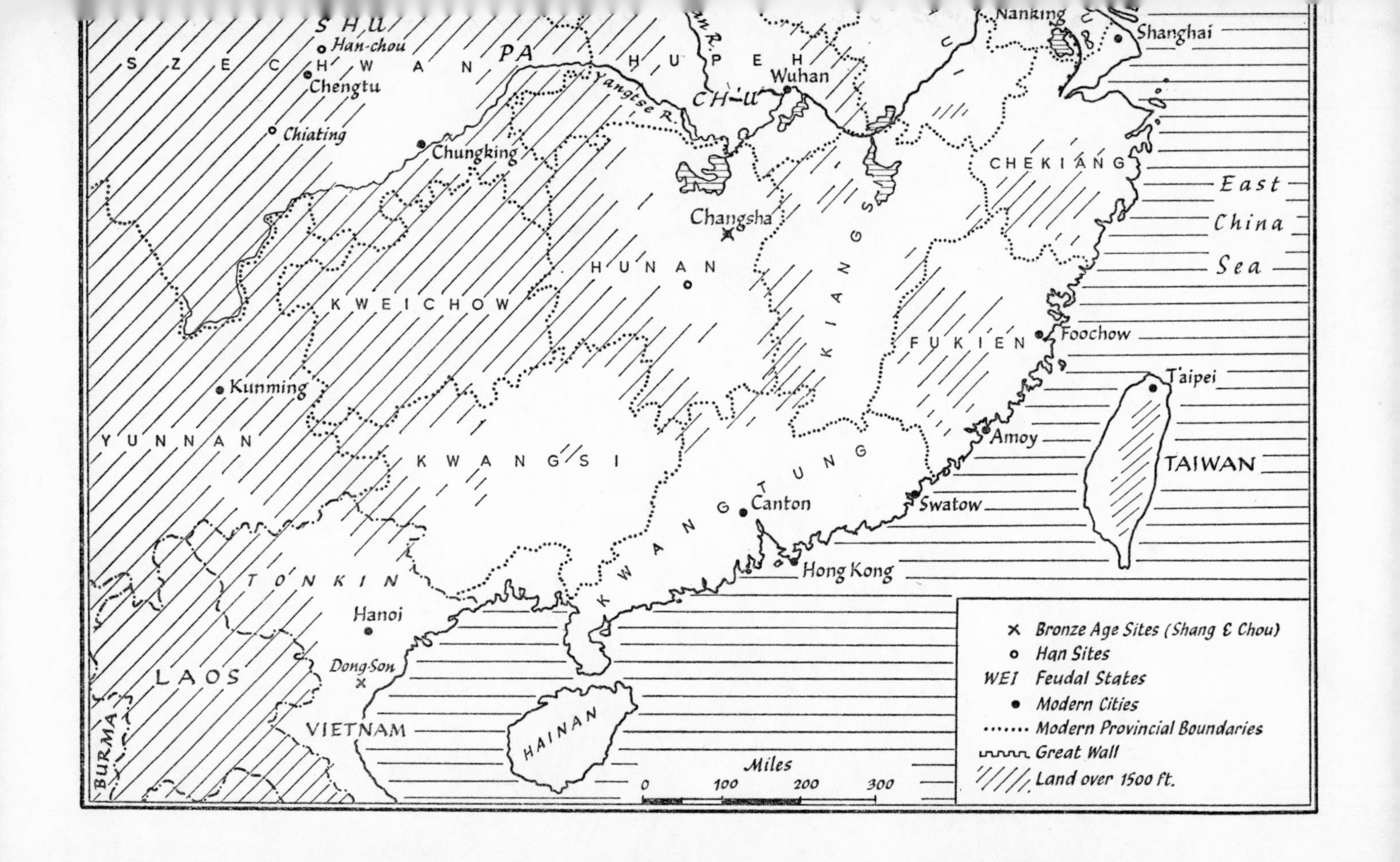
SZECHWAN
SHU
Han-chou
Chengtu
Chiating
Chungking
PA
HUPEH
Wuhan
CH'U
Yangtse R.
Nanking
Shanghai
CHEKIANG
East China Sea
Changsha
HUNAN
KIANGSI
KWEICHOW
FUKIEN
Foochow
Taipei
TAIWAN
Amoy
Kunming
YUNNAN
KWANGSI
KWANGTUNG
Canton
Swatow
Hong Kong
TONKIN
Hanoi
Dong-Son
LAOS
VIETNAM
BURMA
HAINAN
Miles
0 100 200 300
Bronze Age Sites (Shang & Chou)
Han Sites
WEI Feudal States
Modern Cities
Modern Provincial Boundaries
Great Wall
Land over 1500 ft.

I

The Beginnings of Chinese Civilization (i)

PREHISTORY, THE YANGSHAO EPOCH AND THE 'HSIA DYNASTY'

The skulls and skeletal remains found scattered round the campfire of *Sinanthropus pekinensis* and excavated between 1927 and 1951 near Chou-k'ou-tien in the vicinity of Peking, together with other finds made in the central Yangtze valley and in Kuangsi, Honan and Szechuan, can lead, it would seem, to only one conclusion. That is, that the terrain of China was already populated in the earliest days of the human race — which, in this instance, means by about 500,000 B.C. We may further assume that settlement here was extremely sparse, in contrast to the Mongolian desert (the Gobi), which had not yet dried out and appears to have afforded primitive man significantly better means of subsistence. As Mongolia grew increasingly cool and desolate, a large-scale migration south-eastwards of members of a primitive hunting and agricultural community seems to have begun.

Those migrants, who may have reached the plains of northern China towards the end of the Stone Age — several millennia after *Sinanthropus* — thus show cultural similarities to the civilizations which followed the Late Stone Age in the region of Lake Baikal. When they arrived in North China they completed the transition to a primitive agricultural economy. Evidence for this exists in the form of an archaic hoe, which was found with some stone tools and pottery and the bones of horses, cattle and sheep in the course of excavations in the vicinity of Lin-hsi, near Jehol. We may infer from this, and from other finds, that an established community who tilled the soil and kept animals was by then already settled on the loess deposits and extended from somewhere near Kansu to the Gulf of Liaotung.

A new civilization, whose distinguishing artefacts were heavy, finely polished stone implements and red ceramics with black-painted decoration, may have begun to displace the ancient Gobi civilizations in about 5000 B.C. or earlier. The bearers of this culture belonged to a race which, as has been established by finds of New Stone Age skeletons, differed considerably from those of the Gobi cultures. The latter are known as Tunguses (Mongolians) and the former as Sinae (Chinese), and it is they who are regarded as the true forbears of the present-day northern Chinese.

This painted, red ware clearly comes from the eastern spur of a long band of civilization which extends west as far as the Black Sea, although it is impossible to decide with any certainty where it originated or by what stages it spread. It is a characteristic of the wares that they were made by hand only and not on a wheel. The site of one of the principal finds is in Kansu; another, which has achieved great fame in the history of Chinese archaeology, is near Yangshao in Honan, where in 1921 successful excavations were carried out by the Swedish geologist J. Gunnar Andersson. This phase of civilization is usually called the Yangshao Epoch after the site.

The latter years of the 'epoch', from about 2200 B.C., coincide with the so-called Hsia dynasty, which has been a subject of controversy on many grounds. In traditional Chinese histories, it is usually placed as the first of the dynasties, and it is dated from traditional texts to 2205–1766 B.C. From other sources, the dates 1989–1558 B.C. have been calculated; but these are no more secure than the first.

On the basis of the excavations, it is possible to make a series of statements regarding the Yangshao civilization. Settlements of this period followed the courses of rivers and were situated on high ground out of the reach of floods, as is often still the case in present-day Honan, Shansi and Kansu. The people lived in houses consisting of hollows in the ground which they covered with a wooden framework. There was an opening in the middle of the roof to allow the smoke from the hearth of unfired clay to escape. Near the houses were cellars in which food-supplies were stored. The houses were round or square, with a door on the south side.

Burial-places were at some distance from the settlements. They have been found to contain utensils of all kinds made of clay and stone, from which we may conclude that the settlers believed in some kind of after-life. The dead were usually buried lying full-length on their backs, though graves have also been discovered in which the bodies had been buried face downwards. There are also a few graves in which the bodies had been placed in a crouching position, and children's graves containing clay sarcophagi.

As is shown by the numerous finds of agricultural implements, the settlers presumably lived mainly by tilling the soil. Their method was most primitive, and no manure was used, so that after a few years, when the soil was exhausted, another piece of land had to be put to work. Millet, sorghum and rice were cultivated. Pigs and dogs were the most widespread of the domestic animals. Cattle were kept mainly in Kansu. Other finds, however, prove that the settlers were also huntsmen and fishermen.

There are many observations in early Chinese literature which show that all kinds of ideas about conditions of life in this primitive Chinese society were current even in antiquity. It was assumed, for example, that, prior to the agricultural period, there had been a period when the settlers lived simply by hunting and gathering their food. Thus we read in a work of the third century B.C. called after Han Fei, the most celebrated representative of the Legalist school, 'In ancient times, the men did not plough, for the fruits of plants and trees were sufficient to feed them. The women did not weave, for the skins of beasts were sufficient to clothe them.'[1] In a work called after the philosopher Mo Ti, who lived in the fifth century B.C., we read: '. . . The people of ancient times . . . lived on high ground and dwelt in caves . . . Their garments were the skins of animals and their belts long grass. They ate simply and lived in segregation.'[2]

Another passage from the first work mentioned shows that

there was no belief that man had from the beginning been 'lord of the earth': 'In the age of antiquity, human beings were few while the beasts were numerous. Mankind was unable to become lord of the birds, four-footed beasts, insects, and serpents. But there appeared a great and holy man who plaited the twigs of trees to make a nest, in which he escaped dangers without number. This pleased the people so greatly that they made him king.'[3]

Modern Chinese writers like to point to this prehistoric era as the golden age of the first commune, in which there was as yet no private ownership. At that time, so it is assumed, mankind consisted of small communities under 'elected chieftains', who enjoyed no special privileges; and the 'means of production' — stone, bones and wood — were owned in common by the whole group.

Scholars are particularly fond of quoting in this connection a passage from the *Li Chi* (*Records of Rites*) attributed to Confucius:

> At the time when men still followed the Great Way [*ta-tao*, a concept which will be discussed later], all under Heaven was owned in common. Men were chosen for their ability and talent. Their teaching was reliable and they cultivated harmony. People of ancient times treated not only their nearest relatives as relatives and not only their own children as children. They cared for the aged until the end. There was employment for the strong and the young were given the opportunity to grow up. Widows, orphans, those left on their own, and invalids were all provided for. Men had their work and women their shelter. They accumulated provisions because they did not wish anything to be thrown away, but they were not supposed to amass goods for themselves. They toiled because they did not wish goods to be anything but the result of their own efforts. But they were not supposed to do this for the sake of personal advantage. Therefore selfish schemes did not arise and robbers, thieves and rebels were not in evidence. They went out without shutting the door. This was called the Great Community.[4]

Without going into the background of this 'ideal community', which was geared to totally different conditions, I should like to express the view that it would hardly have been reasonable for the less powerful members of the primitive commune to champion their right to common property in opposition to the chieftains. These men could scarcely have been comparable with the kindly, ideal sages of the later Chinese world who radiated mildness and wisdom. They were certainly brutal customers who used their physical superiority robustly to set aside any claim to private ownership made by the weaker members of the group. Nor may we assume that the 'output' created by 'communal labour' with 'communally owned stone tools' was apportioned according to modern laws of social justice. I therefore incline to the view that these primitive Chinese communities already contained all the seeds of the social system which later ripened into that 'feudalism' which is so much out of favour today.

Another much discussed phase of social evolution is matriarchy, or, more properly, the period in Chinese society when maternal rights operated. This did not mean that women or mothers enjoyed supremacy, but rather that the customs and rights usually connected with a father-son succession were at one time linked up with a mother-daughter succession. So that, for example, the woman did not follow her husband into her in-laws' community, but, instead, the man moved into his wife's social group. In a society of hunters and gatherers of food, the female element, tied as women were to the home, obviously possessed greater stability than the men, who were constantly on the move.

In an attempt to prove that a kind of dim memory of this matriarchal phase survived into later times, it is usual to quote a passage from the *Lü-shih ch'un-ch'iu* (*Spring and Autumn Annals of Lü Pu-wei*), a work of the third century B.C.: 'Formerly, in the most ancient times, there were no princes. The common people lived and dwelt together in groups. The mother (or mothers) were known, but not the father (or fathers). There were no relationships between kinsfolk.'[5] This last sentence presumably means that within a group of this kind there were no distinct families.

Although this is a literary statement and may be explained as a mere theoretical supposition about these primitive conditions, we also possess more concrete evidence relating to a matriarchal period in China. Thus, for example, the written characters for the eight earliest clan names all contain the component 'woman' and therefore relate not to a male but to a female first ancestor.

A feature of this matriarchal society was that marriages between members of the same group were forbidden. It was required that the men should come of a different group from their wives. As a result, a kind of firm arrangement for the exchange of partners probably grew up between two given groups (or clans), which regularly provided one another with spouses and together formed a line of descent.

This may have been the basis of another phenomenon which continued to exercise an influence in certain later cult forms. Let us assume that a man from group A moved over into his wife's group, B. His son then returned to group A as the husband of a woman of that group and had no further direct association with his father. The situation was, however, different for *his* son, who, in his turn, passed from A to B: there he came across his grandfather, with whom a bond developed based on the latter's memories of his youth, training and so on in group A. Thus it happened that a much closer relationship grew up between grandfather and grandson than between father and son, a peculiarity which we shall encounter again much later on in the ancestor-worship of the Chinese.[6]

Another manifestation which was in some way linked to the matriarchal phase of Chinese society was the totem cult. This was founded on the belief that the ancestor of the tribe was not a man but an animal, a plant or a natural phenomenon, such as thunder, lightning, or rain. Thus we read, for example, in the *Shih Chi*, the earliest general history of China: 'One day the mother of Hsieh (ancestor of the Shang dynasty) and two companions went bathing. On her way she saw a dark-coloured bird. The bird laid an egg. She took the egg and swallowed it. Afterwards she became pregnant and bore Hsieh.'[7] And the same event is mentioned in the *Shih Ching* (*Book of Songs*): 'Heaven appointed a dark-coloured bird. It descended and brought forth the Shang.'[8]

In such observations, which occur frequently in ancient

literature, we can catch the legendary echo of ancient clan totems. And just as we may conclude from the passage quoted that the Shang clan had a bird totem, we gather from other sources that Hsia had a plant and stone totem.

Worship of the totem was of vital importance in holding the clan together, and resulted in marriage within the same totem group being forbidden.

Later, when the matriarchal gave way to the patriarchal period, the woman following her husband into another totem group remained committed to her original totem. Her daughter was the first to come under the new totem. *Mutatis mutandis* the procedure described above was repeated and here again a close relationship sprang up between grandmother and granddaughter, since both venerated the same totem.

Another feature of the totem cult was the tabooing of the name of the totem. The custom of later times whereby it was forbidden to write or pronounce the father's personal name in the family circle or the ruler's name in public life — a prohibition that was extended to the names of the nearest ancestors — may have been a continuation of this practice. It probably started when the special temple names for use in ancestor-worship began to be given to the dead rulers.

The transition from a matriarchal to a patriarchal society was naturally only a gradual one and was no doubt associated with fundamental changes in the economic system. By the beginning of the so-called Hsia dynasty, however, this process had gone so far that the leadership of the Hsia people — whatever, indeed, this may mean — was no longer based on some form of election of 'the ablest' but was passing from father to son, that is to say, was being handed down in typical patriarchal succession. Nevertheless, it appears that the paramount influence of women in certain spheres of public life, probably the religious in particular, persisted for a long time to come. It was not until the Chou period that women were relegated to their familiar position in the background of society.

It is unfortunately impossible to speak with authority about the religion of the Hsia people. All the *Shih Chi* tells us about the first ruler, the legendary Yü, is that he venerated demons (meaning, presumably, the spirits of the dead) and gods. Furthermore, the account of the Hsia dynasty given in this work was compiled at quite a different period and is full of anachronisms. But the existence of grave-goods and the fact that the totem was venerated do enable us to conclude that some form of cult of the dead existed, although it would probably be rash to think of this in terms of the ancestor-worship of later years. Also, since the Hsia people consisted mainly of agricultural groups, nature-spirits and gods may have been worshipped which were linked with the yield of the earth, and particularly the sun and moon.

If the tradition recorded in the *Shu Ching* (*Book of History*) is to be believed, the position of the Hsia rulers came to assume some of the features of a tyranny based on sun-worship. The last of them, indeed, is made to cry: 'At the time when the sun ceases and dies, I also, and all of you with me, will perish.'[9] This is taken to mean that the ruler considered his position to be as exalted and secure as that of the sun. He may possibly have seen himself as the representative of the sun.

The broad, flat jade discs with holes in the middle which were found in the Yangshao deposit may prove the existence of sun-worship among the Hsia. The similarity of these discs to later symbols of the sun has caused many people to regard them as sun-symbols — but perhaps wrongly.

II

The Beginnings of Chinese Civilization (ii)

THE LUNGSHAN AND ANYANG PERIODS

The so-called Hsia dynasty falls, as already stated, at the end of an epoch fixed by excavations and named Yangshao after the principal archaeological site.

In 1928, in the vicinity of Ch'êng Tzŭ-yai in north-west Shantung (but south of the mouths of the Huang-ho), remains of a civilization were found which differs markedly from that excavated near Yangshao; at sites where they are in contact with the Yangshao remains, they lie above them — a clear indication that they are more recent. This civilization is called Lungshan — after the actual site of the excavations.

One of its principal features is an unpainted, plain black ceramic ware, made with a potter's wheel and considerably finer than that of Yangshao. Particularly outstanding among such ware is a type of vessel standing on three feet, the shape of which resembles female breasts; they are apparently indeed conceived as such and have a magical significance. These vessels are not found anywhere except in Honan and Shantung provinces. The shape is an earlier form of that of some of the bronze vessels of the Shang dynasty.

Even more important is the finding of bones (shoulder-blades of cattle, deer and an animal which has not yet been identified), which had been heated and used for oracular purposes. These may be regarded as the most remarkable feature of the Shang civilization.

Walls made of stamped earth which had originally encircled a large settlement or town, were also found near Lungshan. Among domestic animals, the horse has been identified for the first time.

All this closely links the Lungshan civilization with a site, now world-famous, near Anyang in North Honan, in the vicinity of Hsiao-t'un. Since about 1900 some hundreds of oracle-bones have been dug up there. Most of them are tortoise shells and on to some have been scratched characters belonging to an earlier form of the Chinese script that we know. Most have since been deciphered.

Bronze vessels were also found here. The fineness of their execution indicates that the technique of casting had already reached an advanced stage of development. This means that Lungshan and Anyang may perhaps, between them, be regarded as the cradle of both Chinese script and metal work.

With the finds made near Anyang, Chinese history begins to be comprehensible, for a great many facts may be deduced from the oracle inscriptions. Here we encounter the earliest independent and characteristic civilization to develop on Chinese soil; for the phases of civilization briefly outlined above must be regarded as phases common to the evolution of mankind as a whole.

The excavations near Anyang have revealed the remains of an ancient capital, while the texts on the oracle-bones bring us right into the middle of the Shang dynasty — traditionally placed after the Hsia — and, in fact, into the reign of the Shang king, P'an-kêng. By the old reckoning this corresponds to 1401–1374 B.C.; by a more recent one to about 1315–1287 B.C.

The Shang dynasty thus becomes the first era of Chinese history for which there is documentary evidence. It is reckoned to have lasted from 1766 to 1154 B.C., or from 1558 to 1102 B.C. During later periods it was usually called the Yin dynasty, after one of its last capitals.

III

The Shang (Yin) Dynasty

We must assume that the transition from the Hsia to the Shang was accompanied by violent conflicts, from which the Shang emerged victorious. They were greatly superior to the other tribes of the region, probably not only in the military but also particularly in the religious and economic fields.

It is possible that the differences began with one of the Hsia tribes called Ko ('wild runner-bean'), which may indicate that clan connections spread very wide. The following account occurs in the works of Mêng-tzŭ, written over a thousand years after the events described:

> T'ang [the leader of Shang] lived in Po and had Ko [in present-day Honan] as his neighbour. The chieftain of Ko lived a disorderly life and made no sacrifices. T'ang sent a man to ask why he did not sacrifice. The reply was: Because I cannot keep beasts for sacrifice. T'ang sent him oxen and sheep. The Ko chieftain ate them but made no sacrifice. So T'ang sent to question him again. He replied that he could save no millet. T'ang then sent the people of Po, his capital, to Ko to plough . . . The Ko chieftain, however, led his people against them, took from them all the provisions they had brought with them and killed those who would not give them up; one of these was a boy who was carrying the supplies of meat (for the leaders).[10]

This became the pretext for war.

In this we can recognize at a glance the typical programme for colonization: the people's backwardness (religious) is exposed, 'peaceful' penetration ensues and is followed by military conquest.

It is also possible to draw conclusions about the structure of the Shang state which was thus brought into being. There was — and this is corroborated by excavations — an upper class consisting of the conquerors and a lower class consisting of the people whom they had colonized. The latter was used by the upper class for all rough work, especially for tilling the fields and tending cattle. The upper classes kept possession of the arms which they used to compel the others to obedience. They were also the bearers of culture, which at that time was expressed mostly in religious practices.

We ought probably to imagine that the people of the time felt their lives to have been threatened from all sides by unknown, incalculable and mysterious forces, whose anger it was necessary to avert by sacrifice and all kinds of magical procedures, and whose favour had to be bought in the same way. To confront these forces, they needed a number of spokesmen and protectors in the persons of eminent men of the community, who in some way lived on after death and entered into communication with them.

It appears to have been the policy of the Shang to concentrate these unknown forces and all magical powers in their own family, which means, of course, particularly in the deceased members of the family, and thus to create a monopoly for themselves. We shall see later how this idea of basing political power on good relations with the forces which rule the universe was taken over by later dynasties and became a permanent foundation of sovereignty in China.

As the Shang period progressed, this came to mean, in practical terms, that each ruler became a god (*ti*) when he died. A ruler usually had a principal wife and a secondary one — later more than one — and the principal wives too were deified. They were particularly associated with illnesses, epidemics and the like, while prayers for offspring were also addressed to the female ancestor of the royal family.

It seems probable that over and above these dead and deified rulers there stood some kind of supreme god (Shang-ti), although he has so far not been identified with any certainty. It may be that this power comprised the most important ancestors of the

Shang clan. At all events, its assistance could be obtained only by the intercession of the deified Shang rulers.

At the time when the texts on the oracle-bones begin, this system was fully developed and we learn many details about it. The supreme god had at his beck and call a troop of servants in the shape of sun, moon, stars, clouds, winds, thunder and rain and another four servants representing the four quarters of the heavens, to whom the centre was added later, making five; all these were remembered in special sacrifices, and most of them continued to figure in the sacrificial services of later dynasties.

It is a fair assumption that the Shang took the nature gods of the Hsia clans and placed them under the supreme command of a god who was himself also appointed the personal protector of the Shang and the principal members of their clan.

The harvest, for example, depended upon the favour of Shang-ti and, particularly, on whether he sent rain when it was needed. The climate of northern China is said to have been warmer and drier then than it is today. The main hazard threatening the harvests was therefore prolonged drought. One text from an oracle-bone, for example, reads thus: 'Oracle of the day Kuei-ch'ou (or: on the day Kuei, hour Ch'ou?). Favourable oracle concerning the weather for the next ten days.' And the oracle was borne out as follows: 'On the day Chia-yin (i.e., the next day), round about the time of the great meal, continuous rain from the north. On the day I-mao (i.e., three days later), about the time of the small meal, clear weather. On the day Ping-shên (i.e., the fourth day), about the time of the middle meal, heavy rain from the south.' [11]

Assuming that the translation is correct, we might also deduce that, like us, the Shang had three meals a day. But it must be borne in mind that 'meal' can also indicate a measurement of time, something like the 'length of a meal'.

It also emerges that the Shang named the days after cyclical signs, in which they combined the signs for the so-called ten heavenly stems and for the twelve double hours (watches) of the day. This system which comprised a sixty-day cycle is supposed to have been invented by the legendary secretary of the mythical

'Yellow Emperor' (Huang-ti). The Shang also divided time into ten-day periods. At the end of each decade the oracle was consulted about the following ten days.

Since many names of stars appear in texts on oracle-bones and there is also frequent mention of eclipses of the sun and the moon, we may take it that great attention was paid to astronomical phenomena. It is thought that certain flat jade discs with strange inward-curving rims which have been found are some kind of instrument for determining the position of the stars. The relationship of the planet Jupiter to the yearly cycle was known and it is held that the expression 'Jupiter work', meaning work on the land, originated in the Shang period.

The year was divided into twelve lunar periods, with extra periods interpolated, perhaps irregularly, and very probably named after an important event which occurred in the course of each. This is an early example of that tendency to combine astronomy and history which is characteristic of China.

Work on the land probably provided the main source of food for the Shang community and naturally depended on the labours of cultivation being performed at the right time. It is therefore obvious that the science of the calendar and the correct determination of time were among the most important instruments of power of the Shang clan. Later dynasties from time to time established their own calendars, the acceptance of which usually indicated adherence to the dynasty or subjugation to it.

The Shang state in its earliest days should probably be envisaged as a number of settlements on arable land, all ruled by one clan. These settlements were bounded on one side by wooded hills and on the other by the broad rushy banks of the river. Thanks to their superior methods of cultivation, and later largely because they possessed bronze weapons, the Shang gradually extended their domination in the manner described above. In the end they controlled the whole of the region of the mouths of the Huang-ho and the country upstream to beyond the mouth of the Wei river, as well as a part of the Wei valley, the region of Huai river, parts of the region of the Han river and the country north of the lower Yangtze. But we must suppose that in inaccessible regions a number of other tribes and clans managed wholly or partially to preserve their independence.

We must also imagine the Shang king as in many ways resembling a great landowner, whose major preoccupation was the yield of the harvest and whose most pressing concern was to increase his domestic stock. His growing territories were clearly divided into demesnes which were managed by overseers (*tsai*). From time to time the king himself went on journeys of inspection. The overseers for their part were subordinate to a minister (*ch'ing-shih*) in the capital; he had a staff of scribes and messengers at his disposal which must be regarded as the nucleus of the highly complex official system of later dynasties.

As well as the royal demesnes there were a number of other demesnes or counties, whose landlords went to court from time to time or received the visit of the ruler and his entourage. In the early days, the landlords of these demesnes were probably always members of the royal family. For this reason the words which originally stood for degrees of relationship came in the course of development to stand for the ranks of nobility. Those who had distinguished themselves in shooting with bow and arrow at the target (*hou*) were often rewarded with counties (*hou*) on the border, where they found good opportunities for exercising their skill. Clan solidarity was probably maintained by frequent convivial drinking bouts.

Agriculture must have developed significantly under the Shang. From the frequent changes in the site of the capital during the first years of the dynasty, we may deduce that at first a primitive form of exhaust farming was employed, which made it necessary, after a certain time when the soil was exhausted, to annex new lands. As time went on, however, methods of agriculture and the appropriate implements were improved. The main crops were millet and rice; wheat was less extensively cultivated and was used to make an alcoholic drink for the religious festivals. The cultivation of silk was highly developed, as can be gathered from the sacrifice offered to the silk-worm goddess.

Moreover, the number of utensils and implements — especially, in the later years of the Shang period, bronze implements —

multiplied and made it increasingly difficult to keep on moving from one agricultural area to another. The result of all this was that when King P'an-kêng, 'following the commandment of his ancestors', transferred his capital to Yin, he encountered serious resistance from his subjects. In fact, Yin was the place which (doubtless because of its strategically secure position) remained the capital for the longest period. We hear of only one more removal, under the fourth king from the last who again favoured a site on the north bank of the Huang-ho. As against this, a total of thirteen removals are recorded in the period preceding P'an-kêng.

Not only did the sovereign divinity (Shang-ti) and his lieutenants support and direct the Shang kings in their military enterprises against their neighbours, but he seems also on occasion to have used the power of his divine magic to force the latter to voluntary submission. An echo of this idea recurs in later periods of Chinese history when it was believed that the emperor alone could, by virtue of the long-range influence of his imposing majesty, bring the barbarians to their knees and make them pay their tributes. We shall see later on that similar beliefs were still active at the time of the first contacts between the Manchu emperor and the western powers. Another consequence of the belief was that when, in later periods, political moves were made against the frontier peoples, greater reliance was sometimes placed on the ruling house's position of religious superiority in the universe than on military preparedness.

A number of different ways and means were used to forge links between the gods and the members of the Shang clan. There are, to begin with, a series of fragments of oracle texts which can only be interpreted as meaning that the gods moved about in person among men. One says, for example, 'Question to the oracle: Will Ti come down into the capital . . . ' or 'Oracle of the day Kuei-ssŭ. Reception (of the gods). When the sacrifice had ended the Ti-mother entered the town. Misfortune.' This misfortune may have been the outbreak of an epidemic. It is uncertain what in fact is meant here. There is a hint, however, in the *Kuo-yü* (*Conversations from the States*), a work written some thousand years later, of the belief that in early antiquity there had been a period of decadence of some kind, in which men and gods had intermingled.[12] During the Shang period moreover and also later, until about the second century B.C., the gods were thought of as human beings, but human beings who were larger than life and who were seldom or never seen. Occasionally, however, their footprints were found. But, whatever the truth of this, it is a fair assumption that for the man of the Shang period there was nothing 'supra-natural' about the gods in themselves and that he could on occasion legitimately expect to encounter them. Such encounters quite certainly took place in dreams, which were not infrequently mentioned in the bone-inscriptions. The first doubts about the reality of dreams and attempts to explain them rationally do not emerge until much later, in about the third century B.C.

One of the means of entering into contact with the gods was, in all probability, writing, which may even have been invented for this very purpose. Gods possess a deeper insight into things and relationships than men. It sufficed, therefore, to indicate one's meaning in broad outline and to express oneself in the briefest manner.

The most important means of communication between men and gods was, however, the oracle. The broad shoulder-blades of cattle and the shells of tortoises, procured for the purpose principally from the Yangtze valley, were employed. Before being used they were flattened, polished and incised. When touched with a small glowing bronze rod, each of these incisions delivered an oracle. From the cracks thus produced, which were often distinguished by numbers in the inscriptions, the oracle was interpreted as 'yes' or 'no', 'favourable' or 'unfavourable'.

Everything, without exception, was decided by oracle: when field labours and campaigns should begin, what sacrifices should consist of — in short, every issue of any importance for the Shang people. The Shang king made no decision himself; this was always left to the ancestors and their chief, Shang-ti. This meant that the sovereign position of the Shang rulers rested principally on their close relationship with the gods; all intercourse and intelligence with the gods depended on them or was at least controlled by them. For although the king was regarded as the high priest, who presided at the questioning of the oracle, himself executed the dances which constituted prayers for rain, interpreted dreams, and in general fulfilled all the functions of a religious leader, he nevertheless had at his side in the execution of his duties a highly organized clergy, made up of the officials mentioned earlier. There was no distinction between religious and administrative functions. In later times the functions of the religious assistants at the great state ceremonies continued to be carried out by specially appointed experts from the higher ranks of officialdom.

The first of these were the priestly scribes (*shih*). They were in charge of the whole business of writing. They were responsible for the inscriptions on the oracle-bones which were all preserved and represent a kind of state archive of relations with the divine world. We must also suppose that they wrote down too the most outstanding events of the day. Later on, when religious beliefs had changed, they became official historians and the character *shih* came simply to mean 'history'. It appears that during the Shang period, the importance of their function made it usual to select them from members of the royal family.

Besides the *shih* there were those who 'invoked' (*chu*) or were responsible for spoken intercourse with the gods. They also continue to appear in all the later dynasties.

In addition to the *shih* and the *chu*, there was an extremely numerous priesthood, known as *wu*. The *wu* were Shamans, who must also be regarded as an 'international' phenomenon of the ancient world. Most of the *wu* were probably women, although male *wu* became increasingly numerous later on. Aided by magical practices (dances), they had the power of embodying gods and dead persons, who, it was believed, in some way — usually, probably, through sexual union — literally took possession of the persons of the mediums and uttered instructions, counsels and oracles through their mouths. It is perhaps fair to deduce from this that even at that time it was believed that man did not consist of 'one piece' but that there was some element that could free itself and enter into relationship with others across great distances. What this meant in detail, however, remains uncertain, although it seems that no sharp, definitive line of demarcation was drawn between life and death. It is likely that death meant only that a mysterious sphere of great magical power had been entered, and the dead in their comfortable graves had therefore to be supplied with all the necessities of life. Intimate intercourse with them, or with the part which was freed from the body, lay, therefore, within the bounds of possibility.

Survival of this kind was not, of course, the lot of all members of the Shang society; rather, in the main, only of those in whom the life of the community was, so to speak, concentrated: the kings, owners of demesnes and others such — in short, only those to whom sacrifices were made after death. The accepted view was that subjects, like the 'workers' in insect communities, existed only through and for their overlords, and this led naturally to the conclusion that they had no choice but to be destroyed with them too. The mass sacrifice of men, some of them dead but probably including some still alive, who were buried with the dead Shang kings is not therefore a sign of unusual cruelty but the logical consequence of a primitive feudalism. The persons thus sacrificed were probably individuals whose existence depended so closely on the deceased that there was in any case no question of their surviving.

Persons who could enter into relationships with the dead rulers in so intimate a manner as the *wu* must obviously have made a great impression upon those around them. This very fact must have made it seem advisable to have them under control. The *wu* priesthood, both male and female, was therefore fairly numerous at court; the top ministerial posts were probably also sometimes filled from their ranks. The position of a king on his way to deification might therefore be equal to that of a super *wu*.

The *wu* had many functions over and above that of conjuring spirits. They played a large part in treating the sick, which at that time probably mainly consisted of various kinds of exorcism, prayers for health and sacrifices of rice, to expel the influences which had given rise to the disease. Perhaps their most exalted task was to ward off and drive out any magical influences which might harm the royal house (these probably often took the form of poisonous creatures which had found their way into the palace). They can therefore be regarded as the king's magical bodyguard. As such, they are likely to have formed a kind of secret police, too, since their magic arts enabled them to uncover elements hostile to the state.

The *wu*, whose chief practice seems to have consisted in the execution of wild, ecstatic dances, also introduced an overtly orgiastic character into the religious life of the Shang period. This was particularly in evidence at the celebration of the great state festivals, which may have taken place annually. Thus later accounts by religious opponents contain reports of fertility celebrations in which unclothed men and women pursued one another in and out of 'forests of hanging meat and pools of wine'. The great state-sacrifices — to which the whole people including the landlords of the demesnes contributed, and which thus represented a kind of economic conspectus of the Shang state — were in all probability wild orgies of eating and drinking in which all, both living and dead, took part, and where the greater part of the year's agricultural produce was consumed. One of the reasons why the last Shang king lost his subjects' sympathy may have been that, owing to increased demands for supplies, he tried to introduce a form of state granary system.

Another function of the *wu* was rain-making. This too was mostly done by dancing, but also by certain methods of self-torture. The underlying intention was to induce the deity embodied in a cloud to let fall his seed, the rain. The imaginative association between the cloud with its rain and sexual intercourse has persisted into modern times in Chinese literature.

We have no clear picture of the social structure of the Shang people. There was the king, his family and the numerous priest-officials — this much is fairly plain; but here certainty ends since it is extremely difficult to know what interpretation to put on the 'mass of the people' named on the bone-inscriptions. It appears, however, that there was another social group comprising warriors required for the military expeditions — possibly annual events — against the border territories. These 'wars' were probably no more than plundering campaigns conducted each autumn. They may also have been to a small extent the means of procuring labour by force for the far-flung agricultural lands and cattle-herds of the ruling clan.

The oracle-inscriptions show that most of the people who were pressed into labouring for the Shang came from the west and were of Tibetan origin. This may have contributed to the state of growing ethnic antagonism within the Shang people which finally flared up at the end of the dynasty.

Figures of between 4,000 and 5,000 men have been given for the strength of the established army. Numbers so far discovered for prisoners-of-war do not, however, exceed between 50 and 60. But these may not give a correct impression, for one oracle-inscription mentions 2,656 enemy slain. This figure, however, may refer not only to those killed in battle but may also include prisoners who were afterwards sacrificed to the ancestors. This custom, known as *hsien-fu* ('offering prisoners in the ancestral temple') persisted through the dynasties, though in a form that gradually became more humane.

Those who survived capture and sacrifice had, it seems likely, to perform the most degrading tasks — as is the lot of prisoners today — and, as it were, work their way up by the hardest route until they had justified their existence. Whether this practice and the methods of colonization described above entitle us to follow Chinese Communist scholars in labelling the Shang community a 'slave state', seems to me to be extremely doubtful and greatly to exaggerate the situation. Although we must accept the fact that there existed two classes of widely divergent social position, it is not really possible to describe them simply as 'slave-owners' and 'slaves'.

One of the privileges of the upper class was hunting. Men no longer went hunting to obtain food but found it a means of enjoyment. Wild pigs, wild horses, tigers and elephants were among the quarry. The result of this privilege was that, in all probability under the Shang and certainly in the succeeding periods, meat-eating was confined to the aristocratic upper class. The difference between the two social classes was, of course, also expressed in dress and in every detail of life and custom.

The craftsmen who cast bronze, made pottery and all kinds of implements from bone, stone and jade, were concentrated in the towns and must have formed another fairly large social group. Nothing is known about their social standing. But it should perhaps be assumed that it roughly corresponded to what we understand by serfdom. We read, for example, in texts relating to the subsequent period, that princes exchanged craftsmen as though they were gifts. By this period the secrets of the various types of craft were probably already being passed down from one generation to the next within large or small family groups.

Bronze is a special case. Its emergence in Anyang remains at the present time as completely hedged round with unresolved questions as is the emergence of writing. A single glance at the numerous and complicated forms of the vessels is sufficient proof of the astonishingly high level of the casting techniques. As far as their quality is concerned, the Shang bronzes are equalled only by the works of the best bronze casters of the present day.

As far as I know, no single agricultural implement of that time made of bronze has yet been found. All such tools were presumably made only of wood and stone. A number of bronze weapons have, however, survived.

This shows that bronze was the very material with which the city-dwelling aristocracy secured its superiority over the people of the surrounding countryside. The great numbers of bronze vessels, tripods and such-like to which archaeological finds bear witness, may in one sense have been no more than a kind of reserve of raw material, for these objects could in emergency be melted down to make weapons.

As has already been indicated, the Shang civilization rested on the domination by an upper class armed with metal weapons of a highly evolved class of craftsmen and a lower class of husbandmen and cattle-raisers who were still at Stone Age level. The structure of this upper class was again strictly hierarchical and culminated in the supreme representative of the ancestor cult who passed the counsels of his deified forbears on down the scale. The country-folk living in small settlements, though, probably venerated nature gods, especially gods of fertility, who occupied some kind of subordinate position in relation to the ancestors of the ruling family.

IV

The Chou Dynasty

1. THE WESTERN CHOU

The Chou, with the valley of the Wei river as the focal point of their dominion, were the most powerful opponents of the Shang in the west. Like the Shang, they were a group of clans with many branches, in which the Chi clan occupied some kind of position of leadership.

The ancestor of the Chou may have been a contemporary of the founder of the Shang dynasty and have settled somewhere near the middle reaches of the Ching river in western Shansi. He was later venerated as a divine hero and protector of crops, and was named 'Prince Millet' (Hou-chi).

Driven by pressure from Tibetan (?) tribes, one of his descendants escaped to the south and founded a settlement or town near the Ch'i mountains in the vicinity of the valley of the river Wei. The settlement was called Chou and the family group named after it, as was the dynasty they later founded.

The name Chou is found in oracle-inscriptions of the time of the Shang king, Wu-ting (1324–1266 or 1274–1216 B.C.), where the Chou even appear as allies of the Shang.

By absorbing and subjugating the surrounding tribes (perhaps Tibetans), however, the Chou so greatly increased in strength that, by the time of the fourth king from the last, they were already serious rivals to the Shang. Under the last ruler of that dynasty, struggles broke out which at first went badly for the Chou. Their leader, King Wên, was taken prisoner but was eventually set free.

His successor, King Wu, founded a new capital, Fêng, near

present-day Sian (Shensi) and, when the Shang were greatly weakened by violent warfare against the eastern border tribes (Koreans?), seized the opportunity of fighting a decisive battle for it.

But the Shang were by no means finished and continued to form as strong a group of clans in the east as ever. The brother of King Wu, the so-called Duke of Chou (Chou-kung), who ruled on behalf of his young nephew, the second Chou king, was the first to found the new dynasty on a firm basis, to disperse and divide the Shang people and to set a new ruling class in the saddle.

In the year 770 B.C., as a result of continual threats from nomadic peoples from the north, the capital of the Chou state was moved westwards to Loyang (Honan). Thus began the so-called Eastern Chou dynasty.

New Gods

The Chou, to all appearances, saw clearly from the first that the struggle against the existing dynasty could not be decided by arms alone. Shang domination was based on the divine ancestors who declared their will through a blood-member of the family. It was therefore imperative to destroy the religious standing of the Shang.

It appears that the Chou also made an early attempt to insinuate themselves into the family tree of the ruling clan by tracing their descent back to the highly legendary emperor K'u, from whom the Shang were alleged to have been descended. The ancestresses of both Chou and Shang, so the story went, had been wives of this emperor. The tale was further slanted to suggest that the ancestress of the Chou was the first wife of this gentleman while the Shang's ancestress had only been the second. This in itself arouses the suspicion that the whole legend of their ancestry was an invention of the Chou.

Although this may have lent the Chou claim to domination, a certain legality within the living generation, the religious, magico-mystical background of the Shang dynasty was by no means destroyed as a result. For, as we have already seen, the true ancestor of the Shang was no human spouse but the dark-hued totem bird. In order to meet this difficulty, the Chou now seem to have introduced a version of these supra-natural origins that was extremely novel for the times.

We may first briefly recall one of the characteristics of the matriarchal, totemistic phase. It is very likely that at that time no importance was attributed to male intercourse with the mothers of children: it may even have been held to have had no causal connection with their birth. Children were not the product of intercourse with a man but of the mother's relationship with the totem, to which a kind of magical power of procreation may well have been attributed.

It was probably not until the patriarchal period that the view that the bearing of children was traceable to intercourse with a human father became prevalent. In other words, the procreative power of the totem was now transferred to the male member or members of the clan; and with this, the religious point of departure was reached, from which the Shang finally arrived at the idea that when the outstanding men of the clan had departed from the generation of the living, they represented this magical power in all its purity and thus, as we have said, became gods.

Now the ancestral legend of the Chou shows that their conceptions were no longer those of the matriarchal period but that they already viewed the situation in the light of the patriarchal phase. According to this legend, the Chou ancestress conceived the ancestor by treading in the foot-print of a giant which she chanced upon while walking in open country.

This, however, established the fact that the first ancestor of the Chou was not one of those totem creatures— which had probably in the meantime lost much of their virtue as objects of faith — but was one of the new anthropomorphic gods, a fact which could not fail to make its effect on mentalities conditioned by the Shang ancestral gods.

It is a sign of the patriarchal situation that the mother sees this conception as irregular, and exposes the newly-born boy in an attempt to be rid of him. Not until the child has escaped in the most miraculous fashion from every kind of danger does the mother recognize him.[1]

It is also noteworthy that the giant, or more properly, the god, did not have direct physical relations with the mother but as it were influenced her from a distance, so that his impingement did not in fact call the legality of the father-son situation into question. One might say that he animated the growing life in the mother but was not its true begetter.

We shall see later how this situation was afterwards reduced to a fixed formula and given a place in a great system of universal connections — in that a certain god, known as Kan-shêng-ti (life-inspiring god), was involved in the birth of every founder of a dynasty.

The god who participated in so mysterious a way in the creation of the Chou ancestor is something fundamentally new. *T'ien*, the old character used to denote him, represents the figure of a man with a strongly marked head. Since it does not occur with this meaning among the characters on the oracle-bones, it can be certainly regarded as an invention of the Chou. It shows beyond doubt that the god was visualized in human form.

We can scarcely suppose that this being was one of the deified Shang ancestors. It is also clear from the legend we have recounted that it was not a 'deified' head of a Chou clan, for the intervention of one of these would certainly have jeopardized the legality of the child.

The possibilities, therefore, narrow down to the one that this T'ien belongs to the group of cloud-gods and spirits of the various parts of the world whom we have already encountered as the servants and messengers of the sovereign divinity of the Shang. He bears every mark of representing a collective personification of these spirits. At all events, he is not associated solely and exclusively with the Shang clan but can, as we have seen above, also turn his attention and favours to other clans. In comparison with the sovereign divinity of the Shang, he certainly represents a superior, objective authority. He thus had to be treated with much greater circumspection and the wild orgies of eating, drinking, dancing and fraternization between god and man became inappropriate as far as he was concerned. For this reason, the new religion of the Chou possesses an overtly puritan character.

The lower part of the character *t'ien* is the same as the character for 'large'; it shows, that is, the figure of a man who is taller than the average — as represented by a horizontal mark. The character is closed at the top by another horizontal line which indicates that what is being described reaches higher than anything else. Thus *t'ien* also contains the meaning 'heaven', or the highest part of the world.

Unfortunately, we have no certain indication of how far upwards the world of the Shang extended. There is, however, a tradition that the Shang king sought to combat the growing belief in the heavenly god, T'ien, fostered by the religious propaganda of the Chou, by having a leather bag filled with blood hung up and shooting at it with arrows, an operation he called 'shooting T'ien'.[2] We may perhaps conclude from this that the 'high' gods of the Shang were still within arrow-shot.

The arrows aimed at T'ien failed to find their mark, as is proved by the victory of the Chou over the Shang. And we may even conjecture that, together with the new god, new concepts of space (infiltrating from the west?) were emerging.

After the overthrow of the Shang, their sovereign divinity, Shang-ti, was, doubtless for political reasons, divorced from the company of the other ancestral gods and united with T'ien to become a new god, Huang-t'ien-shang-ti (highly august-heaven-sovereign divinity). He persisted in this form through the centuries until very recent times as the sovereign divinity in the Chinese state religion.

Just as the ancestral gods of the Shang had been accompanied by their deified spouses, so this one, imagined as a male god of heaven, was partnered by a female divinity. The being in question was a collective personification of the fertility and earth-gods mentioned above, to whom the name Hou-t'u (Princess Earth) was given. This name does not appear in the oracle-bone inscriptions either.

It was believed that it was the influence of the god of heaven upon the earth-gods which brought all things forth. But man was now adduced as the agent who worked in the fields and converted this influence into fact. And at this point we again encounter the Chou ancestor, Hou-chi, the hero of cultivation, who should probably be regarded as the principal character in this process of mediation.

Thus we see that, at any rate from the Chou period onwards, the concept of the divine in Chinese civilization took the form of the triple aspect of heaven, earth and man.[3] And, indeed, this continued into later periods when the gods and superhuman beings recognized by the state were similarly divided into three groups. The fact that Buddhism could not properly be fitted into this scheme meant that, although it was the most widespread and, for a time, the really dominant religion of China, it never lost the character of a foreign import. We shall discuss the position of Taoism later.

Mutability of the Divine Mandate

Whereas in the old order of things the Shang king — conquered or not — could justifiably assert that only he had the right to receive and pass on the instructions (*ming*) of the superior arbiters of mankind, his ancestral gods, a new kind of sovereign divinity was now created who was empowered to give a summary mandate (*ming*) to anyone he chose.

And this, so the Chou argued, was supported by precedent. Before the Chou there had been the Hsia dynasty; their increasing decadence excited T'ien's anger to such a pitch that he removed the mandate (*ming*) from them and gave it to the Shang. The same action was, however, now being repeated between the Shang and the new dynastic clan of the Chou; though this does re-awaken the suspicion which we mentioned earlier that the Hsia dynasty may be basically a mere fabrication concocted by the Chou in order to legalize their seizure of power.

In the speeches and statements of the Chou which have survived (though certainly in part in radically revised form) in the *Shu Ching* (*Book of History*), it is constantly being pointed out that the mission of T'ien 'is not for ever', that 'T'ien cannot be trusted blindly', and that the 'T'ien mandate (*t'ien-ming*) is not easy to establish'.

As an obvious consequence, one of the chief problems confronting ancient Chinese speculation was the question as to what fitted a claimant to receive the *t'ien-ming*. And in this connection we encounter the conception *tê*, which, for lack of a more apposite word, is usually rendered as 'virtue'. *Tê* is another character which does not appear before the Chou period. It is possible that it was originally a sign for the quality which is acquired, or the relationship with the domain of the gods which results, when the 'god who inspires life' (Kan-shêng-tï) enters into relations with the mother of the future founder of a dynasty. It appears that the conception *tê* came into existence at the same time as that of *hsiao*, which denotes the bond between parents and children and is usually translated as 'filial piety'. Just as the ruler must have *tê* in respect of the sovereign divinity, so he must have *hsiao* in respect of his ancestors.

There is, however, a difference between the two concepts. Just as it was necessary to be prepared for changes with the T'ien, so there is no universally valid scheme (*shu-ching*) for *tê*. *Tê* was just as little to be relied upon as was the T'ien mandate. In contrast to this, *hsiao* in Chinese ethics is one of the most constant concepts imaginable.

The creation of these two concepts is a natural consequence of separating the sovereign divinity from the other ancestral gods and of making him independent. Such a differentiation was unnecessary under the old conditions of the Shang period. The people's attitude to all the ancestral gods, including the sovereign divinity, was the same. In the clan also there was, in the main, only a relationship from generation to generation and not from parents to children.

The Family System and Duty to the Ancestors

In spite of the importance of Huang-t'ien-shang-ti for the emergence of the dynasty, duty to the ancestors did not in any way diminish in importance. Quite the contrary, the Chou now enlarged it into a thoroughly well organized system and it became the distinguishing mark of the ruling social class.

Whereas the rituals for the gods of heaven and those of the

earth who produced the harvests were a concession to the humble people of the neighbourhood, and took place, so to speak, outside on the fringes, duty to the ancestors was now, as ever, the central point in the religion of the aristocratic family.

All those who had an ancestor-cult were thereby bound to a certain attitude towards their like which was called *li* (ritual) and was laid down precisely, to the smallest detail. This meant in other words that they needed to justify their actions only to their forbears, whereas those who had no ancestral temple were subject to an extremely strict criminal law. Ancestor-worship and punishment by mutilation were the marks of two different social classes. This was expressed in the words: 'The rules of ceremony (*li*) do not go down to the common people. The penal statutes do not go up to great officers (that is, to the aristocrats).'[4]

The reform of ancestor-worship by the Chou meant that relations between the living and the dead members of the family were subject to fixed formulae and that there was no more orgiastic intercourse between the two in the form of the Shamanist practices which had been common among the Shang. The following verdict occurs in the *Li Chi* (*Records of Rites*): 'The Chou people honoured the *li* and had a liking for public proofs of favour. They served the (ancestral) spirits and the (heavenly) gods with piety but kept both at a (respectful) distance.'[5]

We have already indicated that the Shang were a clan community which was on the point of breaking up into families. It is significant that the Shang kings did not come to the throne by a father-to-son succession but that, instead, the rule passed from one brother to the next. It was only when none of the king's brothers were left that the throne passed to a son. Of thirty successions to the throne during the Shang period, fourteen passed from brother to brother. When the succession passed to a son, that is to say, to a new generation, it did not necessarily pass to the son of the eldest brother nor, probably, to the son of the 'principal wife' either. It may have been the Chou who also introduced a system of precedence for the wives, but there is no agreement on this point among Chinese scholars.

The Chou system brought rigid organization into the clan

group and differentiated between the members according to main and collateral lines, or 'high' and 'low'. The unit of the family group within the clan was now established, too, although, in the opinion of the scholar Hu Hou-hsüan, its existence can be traced as far back as the Shang period.[6]

The family comprised the man and his wife and the four generations preceding them: in other words, father, grandfather, great-grandfather and great-great-grandfather, as well as several generations downwards — extending in theory to the great-great-grandson. Limited in the past and the future, this family group was also bounded on both sides in the present. It ends with the 'outer' or 'peripheral' relatives. Something of the organization of the family group found expression in finely nuanced regulations for mourning, which laid down the duration and outward signs of mourning in the minutest detail. The terminology denoting the phases of mourning later served in Chinese law to indicate degrees of kinship.

The main line (father — eldest legitimate son) now branched to give collateral lines headed by the brothers of the eldest son (the heir); and their innumerable sons form the heads of further collateral lines. This apparently means that the family group decreased in size in proportion to its distance from the main line and finally ended in families consisting of only two generations, father and son.

All these families together, however, form a clan or ancestral community which culminates retrospectively in the first ancestor or founder of the whole line. The following rule applies to such groups:

> Those (people) who have the same clan-name form an ancestral community (*tsung*). It is for them that the legal conception of clan solidarity exists. They are bound together by means of the clan-name and must not break away from it. They are stitched together by family meals (clan celebrations) and must not stay away. Even when a hundred generations have passed, members of the same clan must not intermarry. This is the way of the Chou.[7]

As long as the families belonging to a clan lived near to one another in one region, the clan celebrations mentioned in this passage remained an extremely important means of keeping them together. They are described in many songs in the *Shih Ching*. One runs:

> Set out your dishes and meat-stands,
> Drink wine to your fill;
> All you brothers are here together,
> Peaceful, happy and mild.

They also strike a religious note:

> For the spirits are listening
> Whether we are all friendly and at peace.[8]

It is not difficult to recognize in the regulations concerning marriage the continuing influence of the custom mentioned above of exchanging spouses between two matriarchal or patriarchal groups.

As regards the state as a whole, the system looked something like this: the kings succeeded one another by generations, the eldest son of the principal wife always becoming king of the new generation. All, however, offered sacrifices to the first ancestor, that is to say, the founder of the whole house or of the dynasty. This was called the 'great ancestral community' (*ta-tsung*). Alongside these the younger sons of the principal wife and the sons of the subsidiary wives became hereditary feudal princes and, as such, formed a series of 'small ancestral communities' (*hsiao-tsung*). The same process occurred within these communities and the younger sons of the feudal princes became ministers, dignitaries and suchlike, with hereditary junior fiefs. Their younger sons in turn formed the lower nobility, designated by the word *shih*, which later took on the two meanings 'warrior' and 'scholar'. In the course of the Chou dynasty they acquired great political significance — we shall encounter them frequently further on. The younger sons of the *shih*, however, constituted 'the mass of the people' (*shu-jên*) and, since, as we have seen, they had no part in the ancestor cult or the *li*, they were subject to criminal law.[9]

This shows that the ancient Chinese world saw itself as the continually multiplying posterity of a common first ancestor or, as it was often expressed, as 'a great family'. This Supreme Ancestor was above all the ancestor of the Chou, the Hou-chi (Prince Millet) whom we have mentioned before. One of the songs of the *Shih Ching* marks his position as the deified ancestor:

> Hou-chi, august one,
> You resemble the God of Heaven.
> It is thanks to you alone
> That we stand up in multitudes.
> You gave us wheat and barley,
> For God decreed there should be food for all,
> Not briefly, not in a narrow area,
> But throughout the empire and for all time.[10]

The strongly religious note of this song is most obvious.

As other large clan groups came to be absorbed into the empire, it soon became necessary to reform the genealogical tree and to extend it to include the clan heads of the new groups. And so at last the mythical Yellow Emperor (Huang-ti) was reached and he long maintained his position at the head of a family tree which had sprung in the main from political considerations.

To belong to the recognized genealogical tree meant entering the sphere of *li* (ritual) and thus gaining the right to be treated in accordance with specific procedures. A result of this in the epoch of the feudal states which emerged as the Chou continued in power, was that the Chou spoke openly of 'we', the Chou, in contrast to the 'barbarians' around them, whom there was no obligation to treat with consideration. This attitude became in time one of the basic features of the Chinese mentality and has persisted to the present day.

The system as a whole produced another trait of the Chinese world, which was expressed, probably at the time of the Chou, in the sentence: 'In men let us in all circumstances prefer the old. But in vessels and tools, let us seek not the old but only the new.'[11] Worship of youth, such as makes its appearance among Europeans after every political reverse and is undoubtedly a sign of the 'ageing' of a people rather than of its youth, has played no part in China, except during one short period of its history and perhaps at the present time. The intellectual and emotional current of the Chinese world has always set primarily towards the older generation.

Just as the clan had been re-organized, so now was ancestor worship re-organized. An extremely important article specified that only the legal son and heir had the right of offering sacrifices to his father and to the other direct ancestors — a fact which leaves no doubt that there were other rights which went with that of sacrifice.

Whereas under the Shang probably every ancestor who had distinguished himself in any way was remembered in sacrifices, the Chou made a selection based on the structure of the family group and its social position. As it says in the *Li Chi*: '. . . the king has seven ancestral tablets . . . A feudal prince has five ancestral tablets . . .' and so on, down to the *shih*, whose ancestor worship was confined solely to the deceased father.[12] Since, however, the *shih* quickly increased in numbers and at the same time probably also diminished in social status, things soon developed in such a way that only those *shih* who served a more exalted personage and thus possessed land and a fixed income were able to maintain an ancestor-worship. To the others, the same applied as to the common people: 'The common people (*shu-jên*) have no ancestor worship. Their dead are called ghosts (or demons, *kuei*).' Sacrifices were occasionally offered to them in the back room of the house.

But sacrifice was not permanently assured even to the ancestors of the higher classes. The situation deloped under the Chou in the following manner: only the Supreme Ancestor, Hou-chi, and the two founding kings, Wên-wang and Wu-wang, continued to receive sacrifices throughout the whole period of the dynasty. In addition, each king sacrificed to his direct forbears back to the fourth generation, which produced the above-mentioned seven ancestors of the royal family to whom sacrifices were offered. The ancestors beyond the fourth generation, though, were by degrees 'removed' according to a sliding system and ended up, at least theoretically, in the same position as the dead of the common people, as untended ghosts (*kuei*). The same, of course, applied, with appropriate down-grading, to the ancestors of the other ranks of the upper class of the Chou.

The obvious result was that the Chinese world soon came to be peopled with vast numbers of untended spirits who often made their presence felt in an extremely unpleasant manner. Thus we read in the *Tso Chuan*: 'When a ghost has a place to go to [provided for it by ancestral sacrifices], it does not becomes a spirit to torment the living.' [13]

It was for this reason that among the regular state sacrificial ceremonies of later dynasties there also appeared a short sacrifice for uncared-for emperors, kings, deserving ministers, generals and others of former generations. Furthermore, all ancestral spirits who in life had acquired great merit in the performance of their official duties and so on were given the opportunity of finding a niche as local or city-gods in some capacity or other.

Another trait of Chou ancestor-worship is reminiscent of the Shamanist practices of the Shang and shows how these too were puritanized. This is the so-called 'putting up the corpse', which is the custom by which the deceased father is impersonated at the ancestral ceremonies by his grandson. We have already seen that the grandfather-grandson relationship may perhaps have had its roots in the matriarchal era. The way in which the ancestors were ranged in the temple in two categories, *chao* (shining) and *mu* (venerable) — a distinction which led to endless discussions — was probably also connected with this habit of missing out a generation.

The impersonator of the dead man, who, it was believed, literally embodied the deceased in his own person, did not comport himself at all in the ecstatic manner of the Shamans. On the contrary, his appearance was extremely dignified and calm, as befitted the solemn nature of the Chou ancestor-worship. A verse in the *Shih Ching* runs as follows:

> The wild-duck are on the Ching;
> The ducal Dead [impersonator of a former Duke or
> ruler] reposes and is at peace.

Your wine is clear,
Your food smells good.
The Dead One quietly drinks;
Blessings are in the making.[14]

It was important that in spite of raised voices and drunkenness at the ceremony everything should proceed in an orderly fashion:

A gentle light surround you, Prince,
And high renown for ever!
Good will ever thrive,
The ducal Dead proclaims it.
What is the message that he sends?
'Dishes and food are clean and good,
And the help our friends have given us
Is strictly according to commands and full of honour.'[15]

This custom by which a living man impersonated the deceased persisted throughout the whole of Chinese antiquity and into the Han period. But it seems that here again — if not at the beginning, certainly in the course of later developments — social hierarchies played their part. We read in the elucidations of the Kung-yang commentary on the *Lü-shih ch'un-ch'iu (Spring and Autumn Annals of Lü Pu-wei)* that on the occasion of the great state ceremonies the dead emperor was impersonated by his minister, the dead feudal prince by his first dignitary, and so on; it is, indeed, possible that at the Chou court on the occasion of the state ancestral ceremonies six impersonators appeared for the six dead emperors as well as a special impersonator for Hou-chi. Only among the lower nobility, whose families had played no very outstanding part in public life, was the dead father impersonated by the grandson.[16]

However much the formal element of ritual may later have come to predominate in these ancestral ceremonies, they were at first determined by a deep religious feeling, of which we can derive some conception by reading in the *Li Chi* how pious sons prepared themselves spiritually for the ceremony. They began many days in advance to think constantly of the dead person, to visualize him: '. . . how he sat and lingered, how he laughed and spoke, what were his aims and purposes, what he delighted in, and what things gave him joy.'[17] They performed the ceremonial ritual itself in a state of deep absorption; so much so that their faces broke into a smile every time they caught sight of an object which had once pleased the father.

This short account will, I hope, show what enormous religious energy worship of the ancestors released. The non-ancestral gods were treated much more coolly in contrast. We shall now also understand why, in consequence of this continual commerce with the family dead, an attitude towards death itself arose in the Chinese world which was entirely different from that of Europeans, for whom death means a terrible and irrevocable departure from the world of the living.

The Feudal System

A feudal system was also in existence and was related to the system we have described. The *Li Chi* contains a short account of its basic features: 'As soon as the region under Heaven had a legally established king, the king divided the land and set up the (feudal) provinces (*kuo*). He founded a capital and fixed the boundaries of the domains (*i*). He established ancestral temples and opportunities for gradually removing the ancestral tablets and he sacrificed accordingly.'[18] In the commentary on this passage, the following is quoted from the 'Royal Regulations' (in the *Li Chi*): 'If a great officer or a *shih* owns land, he establishes an ancestor-cult; but if he is not a landowner, he only makes occasional, vegetable (?) offerings.' There was thus a link between ancestor-worship and agrarian ownership, or, in other words, the position of the ruling class was based on these two elements. For this reason, the Shang clans which did not yield to the Chou became separated from both and moved to other parts. This separation automatically made them *shu-jên* or common people.

Another manifestation of the same thing was the fact that temples to the nature-gods were set up opposite the ancestral temples. The combination of the two was the sign of sovereignty over the surrounding territory. The bases upon which the Chinese cities were founded were not, therefore, economic; they rose up round the landowner's temples to his ancestors and to the nature-gods. Thus again it says in the *Shih Ching*: 'Building began with the city-wall and the rooms for the worship of ancestors, and with that it was finished.'[19] As well as valuable ritual vessels, arms were stored in the ancestral temple and all important political business was transacted there.

The city was the centre from which the land was administered and supervised — especially the complicated arrangements for irrigation. It was the political centre (*kuo*) and seat of the overlord. Now, just as all the lands within his fief belonged to him, so also did the people who lived on these lands and worked them. The country-dwellers were strictly prohibited from leaving the fields they worked and moving to other regions at will. Nor were the craftsmen who had put up the buildings of the city permitted to move at their pleasure. The old records relating to fiefs, which have come down to us in the form of inscriptions on tripods and sacrificial drinking vessels, mention everything which belonged to a fief: common people (*shu-jên*), overseers and slaves, carts and horses, soldiers and fields. One of the misdeeds for which the Chou reproached the Shang was that they took in fugitives and did not hand them over.

Thus the demesne (*i*) came into existence in the first Chou period as the lowest economic and administrative unit of the feudal state. Unhappily we have few indications from which to draw conclusions as to the size of a city-demesne of this kind. In the *Tso Chuan* there is a vague statement: 'All that remained of the people of Wei, men and women, only amounted to 730 men; and when to these were added the people of Kung and T'ang, the number was only 5000.'[20] A demesne of the humblest kind was probably generally ruled by a member of the lowest nobility (*shih*). Several demesnes together formed a larger unit which was ruled by a 'minister' (*ch'ing-ta-fu*), who was in turn subject to a feudal prince (*chu-hou*). In the midst of the feudal principalities lay the imperial lands (*ta-i* or *pang-nei*).

The great plan for the formation of the empire can be seen

from a passage in the *Shu Ching*: 'The king has come as the viceroy of Shang-ti (i.e., the god at the centre of Heaven). He has set up his own domain in the centre of the land. Tan (i.e. Chou-kung, mentioned earlier) said: This great city (with the domains of the hinterland) has now been established, from now on he (the king) is the peer of the august one of Heaven . . .'[21] The lands of the feudal princes were grouped in a circle round this central point. Beyond them lay a sphere comprising territories which paid regular tribute and beyond these again lay lands which were drawn by the majesty of the king and the brilliance of his court and wished to cede themselves. Most distant of all were the lands of the barbarians who had neither culture nor a stable system.[22] This is another pattern which became an unchanging element in Chinese thought and has continued to have its effect up to the present day.

The fiefs came into being with the firm establishment of the Chou as the new dynasty and it was probably Chou-kung who systematized them and brought them into association with the clan organizations mentioned above. We may suppose him to have been the creator of the new ruling class and its division into ranks. It is therefore no wonder that later, when the system was renewed in an attempt to halt the dissolution of the empire, he was regarded as superhuman and a saint.

Fiefs were given in the first place to the leading members of the royal clan. We read that under the Western Chou, fifteen brothers of Wu-wang and forty men of the Chi clan were invested with lands (*kuo*) in fee. After them came the prominent leaders of allied clans, such as the Chiang, who had intermarried with the Chi. Fiefs were finally given to the descendants of celebrated leaders of the prehistoric eras and to the descendants of the Shang who had yielded to the Chou. This shows that steps were being taken to prevent too many members of the upper class being demoted to the ranks of the common people.

The actual granting of fiefs was undoubtedly the chief political function of the king, who, for the rest, interfered little with the internal affairs of the feudal lords. This function was indicated by the word *fêng*, which originally meant the low wall of earth with which the fief was surrounded. The ceremony of enfeoffment consisted in handing over a clod of earth from the soil of the fief and took place, significantly enough, in the temple of the ancestors. The record of the enfeoffment was inscribed on a bronze tripod, which likewise became one of the important symbols of feudal rule. The fief with its appurtenances remained theoretically the property of the king, as it says in the *Shih Ching*: 'Under Heaven is no land which is not the king's. Within the coasts of the four seas is no man who is not the king's servant.'[23]

In its first phase, the Chou dynasty thus appears as the rule of a clan aristocracy distributed among large and small demesnes and brought together by means of a reformed ancestor-worship under one many-branched family tree. The whole system was supported by an agricultural economy worked by a lower class destitute of rights. How this system operated and prospered is once again expressed in a song from the *Shih Ching*:

> Abundant is the year, with much millet, much rice;
> But we have tall granaries,
> To hold myriads, many myriads and millions of grain.
> We make wine, make sweet liquor,
> We offer it to ancestor, to ancestress,
> We use it to fulfil all the rites,
> To bring down blessings upon each and all.[24]

The religious basis of the whole thing is also clearly expressed in such statements as this: '. . . inferiors serve their superiors . . . and superiors perform their duties to the Spirits.'[25] The extent to which the various strata of society entered into communication with the divine world was the yardstick by which social degrees were fixed.

Emotional Life

As the above account will have shown, the emotional life of the ruling class in ancient China was largely absorbed by the solemnities of ancestor-worship and the parental relationship. The general ideal is best described in these words: 'My honour has been proved in celebrations of rites without number.' But in the *Shih Ching*, which, with the bronze-inscriptions, must be taken as the principal source for the period in question, there are a number of songs which give us a glimpse of those more private emotions which have to do with the relations between the sexes. Although in many cases these songs refer to the practices and customs of a social sphere below the level of the *shih* or lowest aristocracy, I would no more claim them as records of the true state of feeling of the lowest social classes than I would the folk-songs of the German Romantics. At best they represent the life of the country people as reflected in the sentiments of the *shih*, the section of the population which had the most contact with them. And it seems to me to be significant that the songs reveal the misconception, also prevalent in our own world, that the erotic relationships of the lower classes are much freer or, one might say, more 'natural' than those of the upper classes with their strict adherence to etiquette.

Another striking point is that by far the greater number of these love-songs are put into the mouths of women. Thus, for example, we read:

> That mad boy
> Will not speak with me.
> Yes, all because of you
> I leave my rice untouched.
>
> That mad boy
> Will not eat with me.
> Yes, it is all because of you
> That I cannot take my rest.[26]

Since we cannot suppose that all these songs were in fact written by women, I am inclined to believe that the man, absorbed as he was in the religious (aristocratic) enthusiasm of the ancestor-worship, was ashamed of such trivial and base emotions (base because they were shared with the meanest servants). He therefore expected the ladies to address to him those expressions of passionate adoration in which it is customary in the western world for men to celebrate their mistresses. And, if they did not exist naturally, it was probably just as well for the women to fan these sentiments into life as quickly as they could, since they were from the beginning economically entirely dependent on the man — as this poem about marriage shows:

> Thick grows the tarragon
> In the centre of that slope.
> I have seen my lord;
> He was pleased and courteous to boot.
>
> Thick grows the tarragon
> In the middle of that island.
> I have seen my lord,
> And my heart is glad.
>
> Thick grows the tarragon
> In the centre of that mound.
> I have seen my lrod;
> He gave me a hundred strings of cowries.
>
> Unsteady is the osier boat;
> It plunges, it bobs.
> But now that I have seen my lord
> My heart is at rest.[27]

The way to marriage, moreover, was not through mutual affection but, now as later, through the decision of parents and intermediaries:

> How does one cut an axe-handle?
> Without an axe it is impossible.
> How does one take a wife?
> Without a matchmaker she cannot be got.[27a]

The marriage took place in the bridegroom's house. Its principal feature was the presentation of the young woman in the temple of the ancestors. A little later she paid a visit to her parents, doubtless to assure them that all was in order.

Finally, another song tells us what were then regarded as the marks of feminine beauty:

Hands white as rush-down,
Skin like lard,
Neck long and white as the tree-grub.
Teeth like melon seeds,
Lovely head, beautiful brows.
Oh, the sweet smile dimpling,
The lovely eyes so black and white.[28]

— a type that was hardly suited to the harsh working life of the lower classes!

The Lower Classes

If the songs of the *Shih Ching* provide us with no real insight into the lives of the non-aristocratic lower classes, we do, however, learn a good deal from the bronze-inscriptions. One, for example, makes it clear that persons of the lower classes had a price and could presumably be exchanged or bought. We read that a horse and a bundle of silk equalled the capacity of five human labourers (*fu*) in value; that the capacity of one labourer represented a value of twenty *lo* or *lieh* (= a handful, an ancient unit of money).[29] Both men and women also appear on surviving lists of gifts. They were in fact all the family property of the aristocratic clans and were passed down by one generation to the next.

But there were sub-divisions even in this lowest social class of Chou society. The lowest of all were probably the horse and cattle herdsmen, and they, like the husbandman and his fields, could be given away or sold with their animals. The servants in the houses of the nobility represented a higher social class. This class was exceptionally large and was sub-divided in accordance with a great many different functions. Many overseers and assistant overseers were chosen from its ranks. The organization of the servants at the seat of the feudal prince and at the royal court developed into the officialdom of later times and was to some extent already departmentalized in respect of the servants' functions in the palace, the capital city and in the province (that is, in the outlying estates).

The servant classes were mainly recruited from prisoners-of-war. The bronze-inscriptions give us information about the military booty of the time. It consisted mostly of men, horses, carts, cattle and sheep. Records show that captives could number as many as 3,081. Leaders were listed separately. The left ears or the heads of the enemy dead were cut off and brought home, since the booty was shared out according to the number of these trophies.

The military formed a special class also derived from the lower strata, although it was under the command of the nobility and their followers. The core of the ancient armies was the wagon unit. This consisted of a baggage wagon, in which all the arms and implements were transported, three armoured officers (*shih*) — these were the people who were really responsible for the fighting — and seventy-two (?) men; in addition there were ten cooks, five men to look after clothing and equipment, five grooms and five men to gather firewood and water. There were also heavy battle wagons with crews of twenty-five (three *shih* and twenty-two men). A baggage wagon and a battle wagon formed another, and larger, unit of a hundred men in all.[30] All the men were of the lower classes and the majority were presumably former prisoners-of-war. In times of peace they probably provided some kind of police and surveillance service.

The craftsmen formed yet another group; of these, many had originally been taken over from the Shang capital. This applies especially to the bronze-casters, whose wares — although they did not, perhaps, achieve the high quality of the Shang bronzes — included new forms of bells, vessels, weapons and suchlike. As against this, great progress is apparent in clothing and architecture as well as in the building of boats, wagons and bridges. The craftsmen were presumably subdivided in accordance with the materials they worked, into woodworkers, jade-workers, potters and so on.

As has already been said, each fief was an economic unit and, as such, possessed craftsmen to make all the utensils needed. There seems, nevertheless, to have been a certain amount of trading already, as appears from these words spoken by Kung-sun Ch'iao, an aristocrat of the Chêng state:

In earlier days my ancestor, Duke Hsüan, left the royal domains of the Chou with a merchant. They cultivated a piece of land in partnership and lived there together. They made a treaty of friendship binding themselves and their descendants. The treaty said: You will never rebel against me and I will never extort your goods from you at fixed prices or coerce you into delivering them. If you sell valuable commodities in my markets and make profits, I shall not mind. Thanks to this covenant, mutual security exists between us and the merchant's descendants and stands the test admirably.[31]

These observations refer to conditions before 806 B.C. and show that there may have been wholesale merchants even in those days; later, when social conditions had changed, they were to become extremely important. The observations do suggest, though, that in general the sovereign dealt with such merchants in an utterly despotic manner.

However great these merchants' resources may have been, from the social point of view they belonged to the lower class. As we have seen, nobility was tied to ancestor-worship and ancestor-worship to land-ownership. At this time, however, ownership of land could be acquired only through enfeoffment and not by purchase.

2. THE EASTERN CHOU

The Eastern Chou dynasty (770–249 B.C.) is usually divided into two phases, although these do not quite cover the total period.

The first is called the Ch'un-ch'iu (spring-autumn) period (722–481 B.C.). The name originates from the fact that the excerpts (?) attributed to Confucius from the *Chronicle of the Lu State** fall within this period. These excerpts are very short: 'Duke Yin, first year, spring, first month of the king (this means that the Lu state followed the official calendar of the Chou). Third month, the duke (of Lu) and I-fu from the state of Chu made a treaty in Mieh. Summer, fifth month, the earl of Chêng conquered Tuan in Yen . . .', and so on.

* Ch'un-ch'iu.

Such records would clearly be most inadequate were they not elucidated by three commentaries, among which the *Tso Chuan* occupies a special position, since it is most probably based to a large extent on ancient historical material. Unfortunately, however, it was written in the period following the Ch'un-ch'iu epoch and from the point of view of the Confucian ritualist school. It is therefore to be assumed that it often presents matters one-sidedly and is not free of anachronisms.

The second period is known as the Chan-kuo epoch (403–221 B.C.), and is also marked by a literary work, the *Chan-kuo ts'ê* (*Intrigues of the Warring States*). This consists of records of the political plans of the states of the period.

Such a division into two periods is fully justified historically, for they do in fact represent two different phases of intellectual, social and economic development.

The Ch'un-ch'iu Period

The outstanding feature of this epoch is the shift of power from the central royal domain to the feudal princes. By about 632 B.C. the Chou king was almost entirely dependent upon the feudal princes, who, since the beginning of the period, had been caught up in violent warfare and political intrigues. Whereas when differences had arisen in earlier times, they had bowed to the king's decision, they now disregarded his judgment, and at every opportunity intervened unbidden in the affairs of the royal house, where there were frequent quarrels over the inheritance. The king was simply summoned to appear or participate at gatherings of the princes; he often even felt himself obliged to make begging visits to them, which the *Tso Chuan* glosses over with the words 'he set out on a hunting trip to . . .' New countries with vast territories, such as Ch'u and Wu south of the Yangtze, which had hitherto been considered 'barbarian' now entered the Chou union of states.

The dynasty was clearly at an end and the god of heaven (T'ien) could have given another clan the mandate to rule. As events fell out, however, one feudal prince would show himself for a time to be more powerful than the others but was no match for them when they formed an alliance. The effect of this was that, as long as he remained on top, he acted as the self-appointed protector of the royal house. These gentlemen were called *pa* ('rising potentate', the sign also means 'changing moon'). There was a constant succession of them throughout the whole of the Ch'un-ch'iu period.

However powerless the king may have been in their hands, he still possessed a certain prestige among the lesser feudal princes, who were inclined to join his cause rather than that of the *pa*, since the latter obviously owed their position to their desire to put an end to the small feudal states. The king, moreover, represented now — as he had always done — the main line in the general worship of ancestors and was thus also the head of the religion which predominated in aristocratic circles.

The Weakening of Religious Faith

Political conditions were vividly reflected in the spiritual life of the time. The principal source is again the *Shih Ching*. Heaven expressed its displeasure with the human predicament by means of natural catastrophes, among which lack of rain appears to have had the most disastrous effect. The king seeks to excuse himself:

> . . . Alas!
> What blame belongs to the man of today?
> Heaven sends down ruin and death.
> Famine comes repeatedly.
> And yet there is no god to whom we have not sacrificed,
> No beast we would not willingly have offered . . .'
> Alas, Hou-chi, our ancestor is weak,
> And God no longer condescends . . .'
>
> Terrible is the drought,
> With nothing to end it.
> It burns us with its fiery heat,
> No place to give us shelter.
> The great appointment (*ta-ming*) nears its end . . .[32]

The fact that sacrifice was unavailing shows that the sovereign divinity had turned away and took no interest in the fate of men. He was 'unmerciful', 'unjust' and so on. Of the ancestors it was also asked: 'Has our ancestor no feeling for mankind that he looks on unmoved at our suffering?'

And so the idea must have spread that gods, ancestral spirits and superhuman beings did not possess the powers attributed to them, or at least did not use them, when needed, in favour of mankind. The result of this was that religious belief began to lose much of its potency and rational ideas sprang up which sought to blame not anonymous, divine powers but human beings themselves for current misfortunes. This, in its turn, suggested that, if conditions were to be changed, reliance should no longer be placed on religious or magic practices but on men's own capacities. The *pa* in their aspirations to power therefore made less use of religious propaganda designed to undermine the dynasty and more of well-equipped armies.

Times had changed since the Chou had liquidated the Shang by their superiority in the religious field and we read in the *Tso Chuan* for the year 644 B.C. the following words from a passage (that may, however, be an interpolation): 'Fortune and misfortune depend upon men'; in other words, they are not sent by the gods. And before this, for the year 706, the same work expresses opinions which reveal a marked change in the basic religious attitude. It says for example: 'The people are the master (or host) of the gods. For this reason the sage kings first set the people to rights and only when this was completed did they turn their attention to the gods.' And in another passage it says that when a country is flourishing attention is paid to the word of the people but when it is in decline men turn to the gods.

What is here called the 'people' (*min*) is not, however, what we usually understand by the word. It is highly probable that it meant only the social groups which were able to make themselves felt politically and these did not extend beyond the lower aristocracy (*shih*).

Meanwhile, the lower aristocracy had itself undergone a change. As time passed it had naturally become increasingly difficult to find land for all the younger sons of the family groups and clans; thus, between the aristocratic upper class and the common working people (*shu-jên*), a kind of nobles' proletariat had formed possessing neither land nor revenue but remaining distinct from the lowest social classes. A large number of these impoverished *shih* found employment as superior servants and became overseers, stewards, officers, scribes and so on. Most of them had occupations which demanded a certain degree of education and knowledge.

Soon, however, the *shih* multiplied to such an extent that the possibility of obtaining one of these positions became increasingly rare. It came to such a pitch that many of them had to wander about looking for employment at the princely courts and houses of the rich nobility. One of these *shih* who had to search for employment and who has since become famed throughout the world was Confucius (K'ung-tzŭ, or Master K'ung). His descent can be traced to the princely house of Sung (an old state in Honan), whose rulers were descendants of the Shang kings. His father was an officer in the service of the state of Lu (south Shantung). Significantly enough, Confucius began his career as an overseer of granaries and herds.

Changes in Important Concepts

Hand in hand with the weakening of religious belief went changes in a number of other ideas in one way or another connected with it. First among these was the concept *tê* (virtue), which, as we have already seen, was closely related to the divine appointment (*t'ien-ming*). In order to preserve it, it would in fact only have been necessary to reactivate the quality of *tê* in some way by associating it with the occupant of the throne at the time. But since the heavenly appointment was, so to speak, in a state of suspense, it was naturally to be expected that the quality of *tê* should also be found in other noblemen, principally, of course, in the *pa* potentates. *Tê* was no longer confined to the imperial clan.

In these changed conditions, the possession of *tê* was revealed in exterior appearance. *Tê* was the counterpart or the cause of the majestic, imposing bearing of the man who observed the ritual (*li*): 'Reverent, thoughtful, majestic in bearing — such is the possessor of tê.'[33] '*Tê* walks upright and all lands obey.' says the *Shih Ching* of one of the *pa* princes, who were, indeed, the next claimants to the heavenly appointment.

The so-called 'cruel' kings of the first Chou period had presumably endeavoured whenever possible to prevent the princes from amassing power and wealth. The result of this was that the princes accused the king of neglecting *tê* (virtue). And in the Ch'un-ch'iu period the 'prestigious (adjective from *tê*) demeanour' of a ruler probably meant that the latter was entirely taken up with kingly deportment and intervened as little as possible in current affairs. This was regarded as unworthy 'courting of favour'.

> You, who call yourself ruler
> Do not know the lofty gait of virtue
> What you acquire by cunning and skill
> Will be preserved in the warehouse.

Tê was, as it finally emerged, a comprehensive term used to denote all the qualities or the bearing of a ruler which aroused the respect and willing obedience of his subjects and so upheld his power. But now, in contrast to this good *tê*, with its state-preserving properties, there was also an 'evil *tê*', thanks to which bandits, enemies and corruption multiplied in a threatening manner. The word 'virtue' thus conveys something of the concept of *tê* in its final sense.

The concept of ritual (*li*) also underwent a change. As we have seen, this had a religious emotional angle, on the one hand, and, on the other, was an expression of the sovereignty of the nobility. Regular and orderly sacrifice indicated that the state was flourishing and secure. The emphasis was now on the formal, external side of ritual and this resulted in countless detailed regulations governing the precise enactment of the ceremonies. The distinction between the proprieties (*i*) and the actual ritual (*li*) meant in itself that the latter, constituting as it did the basic principle of the aristocratic way of life, became increasingly an object of abstract, philosophical speculation. In contrast to this, voices were now also raised denouncing ritual as a mere pretext for demanding higher tributes and extra services.

It appears that there was already considerable doubt as to whether the rites furnished an adequate principle of state organization. In the *Tso Chuan*, for the year 536 B.C., there occurs the first mention of a book of criminal law by Tzŭ-ch'an minister of the state of Chêng; it probably did not apply only to the lowest social classes. It was soon followed by other works of the same kind, which shows that the controversy as to whether there should be ritual or law was in full spate. As was only to be expected, the first champions of legality met with violent opposition. The principal argument against them was that the Former Kings had not ruled by laws, that the application of laws diminished the respect of the people for the nobility, and that laws would bring confusion into the old, hallowed order. Tzŭ-ch'an's answer was simple: he was concerned only to save present-day mankind. He could have indicated that ritual was in decline and frequently disregarded. Thus a prince was known to have refused to mourn his father and another went hunting immediately after the death of his mother; petty potentates imitated the ceremonial of the royal court and offered sacrifices which were the prerogative of the king.

Confucius

Confucius lived from 551 to 479 B.C. and came, as has been stated, from the social group of the *shih*. There was at this time among the *shih* a kind of tradition of specialization which had originated in the fact that every impoverished *shih* who had succeeded in obtaining an official position endeavoured to secure it for his family, instructing only his son and heir (or his sons) in the necessary professional knowledge. There were thus specialists in oracular procedure, calligraphy, the ritual, use of arms and so on. Since his father was an officer, it was doubtless intended that Confucius should learn the craft of arms. It appears, however, that he did not do so, but devoted himself to the study of ritual and its close ally, music, and to the writing of history, the nature of numbers (?) and the old odes and songs, all of which, clearly, were non-military disciplines. This obviously represented a clean break with the habit of specialization. The advantage of the innovation was apparently that it offered the individual impoverished *shih* wider possibilities of employment. At the same time, this infringement of the monopoly of the specialists created the conditions for competition, of which men of the lower classes also began gradually to take advantage. The slogan under which the innovation was heralded in literature was 'to the able according to his deserts'. The word for 'able' (*hsien*) originally meant those who had proved themselves the best shots at archery contests or out hunting. It now came to denote special excellence in the civil professions listed above.

This appreciation of ability ran parallel with the traditional principle of 'kith and kin', to which nepotism is the nearest approximation. It was not until later, in the philosophical system of Mo Ti, that advancement for the able became a revolutionary slogan, directed against the hereditary aristocracy. The Confucian *hsien* (man of ability) always remained within the framework of tradition. Thus it says in the *Lun Yü* (*The Analects*), one of the main sources of the teaching of Confucius:

> . . . A Man who
> Treats his betters as betters,
> Wears an air of respect,*
> Who in serving father and mother
> Knows how to put his whole strength,
> Who in the service of his prince will lay
> down his life,
> Who in intercourse with friends is true to
> his word —
>
> others may say of him that he still lacks
> education, but I for my part should certainly
> call him an educated man.[34]

* Or perhaps 'takes beauty lightly'.

It should be noted that religious attitudes no longer find a place in this brief sketch of the desirable ethical personality and that the notion 'intercourse with friends' transcends the principle of kinship. The mention of princely service shows that this attitude applied to persons outside the ruling clans of the high aristocracy, since, for those within it, princely and filial duty were one and the same. Duty to the family is mentioned before duty to the prince precisely because it only came to be regarded as a separate obligation as the clan system began to loose its hold. This passage shows plainly that the Confucian ethic was in the main addressed to a middle class situated between the high aristocracy and the common people.

The outstanding mark of the success of the studies inaugurated by Confucius was the fact that, thanks to the knowledge they had acquired, many of his pupils were able to obtain high and lucrative positions. It is doubtful, however, whether he himself ever occupied high office. There is, it is true, one story which says that in about 497 B.C. he was a kind of deputy-minister in the state of Lu. The position of the prince of Lu was greatly weakened at that time and was threatened by rising leaders of noble clans who were already setting up cities (that is to say, centres of government) for themselves. As a remedy for this state of affairs, Confucius doubtless had in mind a return to the system inaugurated by Chou-kung. This idea may also have been suggested by the fact that the princes of Lu belonged to a direct collateral line of the house of Chou and were therefore very closely related to it in the matter of ancestor-worship. It is thus not surprising that Confucius was a confirmed champion of state organization based on ritual, since this secured the position of the aristocracy; and was an opponent of the Legalists, especially since he belonged to the social class which would be the next to be affected by the criminal laws. One of his first measures as minister of state is, therefore, said to have been to have executed a certain Shao-chêng Mao because he 'gathered followers, incited them by speeches which condoned evil' and in this way 'subverting good, gave prominence only to his private opinion.'[35] Shao-chêng Mao was in all probability a Legalist, one of those innovators so much disliked by the *shih*. It may, all the same, be doubted whether the passage in fact recounts a historical event, for the biographies of Confucius are known to contain a mixture of fact and fiction.

When he spoke of ritual (*li*), however, Confucius meant only its true essence and not the visible outward trappings: '... Ritual, ritual! Does it mean no more than presents of jade and silk [i.e. ritual utensils and vestments]? Music, music! Does it mean no more than bells and drums?'[36] This opens the door to regarding *li* as a philosophical abstraction and the basic principle of an ethical attitude, as is expressed in the following passage, in which Yen Hui asks for details of the ruler's submission to ritual: 'The Master said, "Look at nothing in defiance of ritual, speak of nothing in defiance of ritual, never stir hand or foot in defiance of ritual." '[37] *Li* may properly be summed up in, for example, the expression: above is above and below below or, in other words, that the prince is the prince and the servant the servant, that 'policy is not decided by Ministers . . . commoners do not discuss public affairs . . . all orders concerning ritual, music and punitive expeditions are issued by the Son of Heaven [i.e., the Chou King] himself'.[38]

Li represents for Confucius primarily a principle of order, according to which every man and every object has its appointed place in a great orderly whole. This gave rise in his school to a doctrine known by the slogan, 'rectification of terms'. In contrast to the Taoist concept of the mutability of terms or appointments, Confucius seems to have been of the opinion that appointments (*ming*) were clearly defined mandates (*ming*) which had been fixed once and for all and which bound the possessor to an appropriate attitude. A prince must bear himself like a prince (that is to say, as laid down by the *li*). If he did not do so, he was no prince.

An anecdote recounted in the *Lun Yü* will serve as an illustration of this idea: Fan Ch'ih asked the Master to teach him about farming. The Master said, 'You had much better consult some old farmer.' He asked to be taught about gardening. The Master said, 'You had much better go to some old vegetable-gardener.' When Fan Ch'ih had gone out, the Master said, 'Fan is no gentleman! If those above them love ritual, then among the common people none will dare to be disrespectful. If those above them love right, then among the common people none will dare to be disobedient. If those above them love good faith, then among the common people none will dare depart from the facts. If a gentleman is like that, the common people will flock to him from all sides with their babies strapped to their backs. What need has he to practise farming?' In order to remain a member of the upper class, a man must not debase himself by doing manual work. The man who did such work came under the designation *hsiao-jên* ('common man', or literally 'small man').[39]

One result of 'rectifying the terms' was that the top officials of the government became the objects of criticism from their underlings. The *Ch'un-ch'iu* is supposed to be full of such criticism, allegedly from Confucius himself. Similar chronicles, however, were undoubtedly kept in other states too and were not Confucius's own innovation. They certainly in part represent some kind of statement of account, showing how the states stood in relation to other states with regard to the organization of honours, ritual and suchlike, and they may have provided a basis for conduct on occasions when one prince visited another. It is inadmissible to regard the *Ch'un-ch'iu* as in any way illustrating the doctrine of the 'rectification of terms'.

Li (ritual) is closely associated in the thought of Confucius with the conception *jên*, which is usually translated as 'humanity'. The character consists of the signs for 'human being' and for 'two', and so means the relationship of one human being to another. But here again the human beings in question are not just anyone but only members of the upper classes, for it says in the *Lun Yü*: '. . . It is possible to be a gentleman [*chün-tzŭ*, i.e. a worthy member of the upper classes] and yet lack humanity. But there has never yet existed a commoner having humanity.'[40] *Jên* is the benevolent and gracious attitude of the superior to the underling, as appears from an utterance of Confucius recorded in the work of a later philosopher (Han Fei-tzŭ): 'To be sure, according to the rules of propriety, the Son of Heaven loves (that is, shows *jên* towards) All-under-Heaven, the feudal lords love people within their respective domains, High Officials love their official duties, and scholars and warriors (*shih*) love their families (*chia*)'.[41] *Chia* means a number of people under one roof and was in earlier times a working unit of some ten men organized on a patriarchal basis — as can be shown from inscriptions on ancient bronzes. It was not until later that the sign took on the sense of a family (of the lower classes?).

Just as *li* (ritual) may be said to represent the existential side of the old ancestor-worship, so *jên* corresponds to the emotional side. In addition, the concept was now made to embrace all the elements likely to make the application of laws seem unnecessary. Thus *jên* is linked with wisdom and education, which, as a rule, could only be acquired by members of the upper class. Humanity, in Confucius's view, extended from 'the wise men at the top' — among whom, of course, the king stood supreme — down to the 'stupid ones at the bottom', but individuals of the intermediate classes could move up by dint of study and willing acceptance of instruction (the main substitute for laws). *Jên* also includes love for one's children, bravery, respect, magnanimity, trust and so on. The basic emotional substance of this concept, however, is a combination of all the feelings which were directed towards the preservation of the clan system as it existed in the first Chou period. We probably come nearest to the core of Confucianism if we think of it as a rationally enlightened form of ancestor-worship.

A problem which has been much discussed concerns Confucius's attitude towards religion. There is a passage in the *Lun Yü* in which the Master declined to speak of marvels, gods and spirits, and which is widely quoted in this connection. Nevertheless, it appears that he believed in 'heaven' and subscribed to the view, which, to judge from various remarks in the *Tso Chuan*, was universally held at the time, that, by meting out reward and punishment, heaven intervened in the destiny of men. It says in the *Lun Yü*: 'Death and life are the decree (*ming*) of Heaven; wealth and rank depend upon the will of Heaven (*t'ien*).'[42] Thus the concept *ming* (heavenly decree), which has already been mentioned many times, now occurs in a sense which more or less corresponds to our word 'destiny'. And heaven now no longer means the old heavenly god of the Chou. '. . . Heaven does not speak; yet the four seasons run their course thereby, the hundred creatures, each after its kind, are born thereby. Heaven does no speaking.'[43] According to this statement, heaven is something which controls the course of human life and of nature.

The last quotation also indicates that we are approaching an area of thought which finds its full expression in the concept of *t'ien-tao* ('way of heaven', 'course of nature') and leads on to Taoism. That certain of the basic ideas of this system existed at the time (probably shortly before 400 B.C.) when the *Lun Yü* was being written can be shown from several allusions in this work.

This leads on again to the concept *i*, 'change', probably primarily in the sense of oscillation between opposite poles. This idea was perhaps engendered by the change of dynasty from Shang to Chou and was further stimulated by the increasingly obvious social and intellectual changes of the subsequent periods. The 'changes' are the subject of the *I-ching* (*Book of Changes*), which is said to have been written at least in part by Confucius. The work plausibly establishes the great points of transition. Change itself is conceived as a rhythmic progression repeating itself at intervals. From this the belief follows that the progression can be foretold — a fact which made the *I-ching* the classic work on oracles and prophecies. It is possible that Confucius regarded knowledge of the course of destiny, or the art of prophecy, as one of the qualities in his conception of the ideal gentleman (*chün-tzŭ*), for the *Lun Yü* records the following utterance: '. . . He who does not understand the will of Heaven (*ming*) cannot be regarded as a gentleman (*chün-tzŭ*).'[44] The study of numbers mentioned earlier probably meant juggling with the numbers which occur in the *I-ching*.

Confucius's attitude to the spirits (of the ancestors) was one of awe certainly, but also one of aloofness. The point is made by the answer he gave to one of his pupils. '. . . Till you have learnt to serve men, how can you serve ghosts?' Tzŭ-lu then ventured upon a question about the dead. The Master said, 'Till you know about the living, how are you to know about the dead?'[45]

The gods and spirits of the ancestors are replaced in Confucius's vision of the world by the 'former' or 'sage' kings. 'Sage' (*shêng*) was originally a quality reserved exclusively for the bearer of the heavenly appointment. But it now began to be dissociated from this concept and we shall see that in later writings, when Confucius had become the hero of legend, the epithet 'sage' was applied to virtually no one but Confucius himself. Confucius understood it to mean an ideal man who had from birth possessed all knowledge and all wisdom, without having to study or receive instruction. He expressly disclaimed the quality for himself.

The 'sage-kings' who occur in his teachings are the legendary emperors Yao, Shun and Yü. These figures possibly appear in this sense for the first time in the literature of the end of Ch'un-ch'iu period. The extracts referring to them in the *Shu Ching* must definitely be regarded as having been written at a later period, in fact at the time now under discussion.

Confucius primarily regarded the sage-kings as merely holders of high ethical and political ideals: '. . . Greatest, as lord and ruler, was Yao. Sublime, indeed, was he. "There is no greatness like the greatness of Heaven", yet Yao could copy it. So boundless was it that the people could find no name for it; yet sublime were his achievements . . .'[46]

Associated with the concept of the ideal ruler was the doctrine that a generation (that is, thirty years) after the appearance of such a sage, humanity (*jên*) would achieve a universal breakthrough and an era of general perfection would dawn.

The sage-kings were for Confucius simply ideal figures taken from the ambiance of the ancestral temple. It must therefore also be borne in mind that (at least in theory) they represent all the ancestors of the ruling class. They precede the Emperor K'u in the family tree. But when they acquired that position is a question which, together with others connected with it, still awaits solution.

Mo Ti

Another outstanding representative of the intellectual life of the period was Mo Ti (or Motse). His dates, although uncertain, lie between about 479 and 381 B.C. so that he should, in fact, be regarded as belonging to the following period. According to one reading, he was a subject of the state of Lu and in his youth devoted himself to the studies inaugurated by Confucius. It is clear that he belonged to a social class below that of the aristocratic proletariat. He may have come from a family of small independent peasants.

There is, unfortunately, no space here to show how continually improving methods of cultivation enabled these peasants to move away from the old conditions of feudal serfdom to a system of fixed tributes and services and private ownership of land. It is certain, however, that in Mo Ti's time there already existed a class of independent, or almost independent, peasants who cultivated their land in the summer and in the winter worked at pottery, spinning or similar crafts.

One of Mo Ti's utterances will perhaps tell us enough about this side of his personality. He says of himself:

> . . . I have thought of becoming a farmer and feeding all the people in the world . . . But when a farmer's produce is divided among the world, each person cannot get even one *sheng* of grain . . . I have thought of becoming a weaver and clothing all the people in the world . . . But when a weaver's goods are divided among the world, each person cannot get even a foot of cloth . . . I have thought of putting on an armour and carrying a weapon to come to the feudal lord's rescue . . . Now it is evident that one soldier cannot hold out against a regular army. I concluded that none of these is as good as to familiarize myself with the Tao of the ancient sage-kings, and discover their principles, and to understand the word of the sages and be clear about their expressions; and with these to persuade the rulers and then the common people and those who have to go on foot. When the rulers adopt my principles their states will be in good order . . . Therefore I think though I do not plough and feed the hungry or weave and clothe the cold, I have greater merit than those who plough and feed, and weave and clothe.[47]

The people against whom Mo Ti's polemics were in this instance directed are early members of the so-called agricultural school (*nung-chia*) about which the ancient texts unfortunately only offer scattered information. This school, which must, all the same, have had many followers in ancient times, centred round the God-peasant (Shên-nung), traditionally the inventor of agricultural implements. It is possible that Shên-nung had been adopted at the beginning of the Chan-kuo period in that legendary era of pre-history which gradually developed from a genealogical tree composed of aristocratic clans into a pseudo-historical register of the principal saints of recognized religious or ideological groups. The school held autarchical and sometimes anarchical beliefs. One of their ideals was that each man should himself produce everything he needed. But there also emerged from their ranks a number of soil and agricultural experts whose knowledge helped materially to increase agricultural yields. Fragments of this knowledge are also found in the extant works of other schools.

Mo Ti also based his work on the 'former sage-kings', Yao, Shun and Yü. But these figures had by now been to a large extent stripped of the elements connecting them with the ancestral temple and were looked upon as ordinary human beings. It appears that the personages in question were master-craftsmen or labour heroes of ancient times. 'The sage-kings built houses and palaces for the comfort of the living, not as architectural show-pieces; they made garments, belts and shoes . . .' '. . . Shun cultivated land at Mount Li and made pottery near Ho-pin . . .'[48]

The most popular sage of the Mo school was, however, Yü. He is the model of the self-sacrificing leader who wears himself to the bone and physically exhausts himself in hard unremitting labour for his people. Mo Ti and his pupils strove to embody this ideal by a simple ascetic way of life and untiring activity for the good of the community. This naturally produced a similar attitude towards them in their followers. Thus the communities of the Moists were pervaded by the spirit of willingness to make reciprocal sacrifices — the leader for his followers and the followers for the leader.

Mo Ti's position as leader was passed on to his disciples in a manner which has not yet been explained. (Perhaps it was a form of reincarnation?) Thus we read: 'They (the Moists) consider the grand master (Chü-tzŭ) to be the sage (i.e., the bearer of authority). They all desire to act as his impersonator (i.e. at certain ceremonies which have already been touched upon). They hope by this means to succeed to his qualities.'[49] The *Huai-nan tzŭ* records of Mo Ti that 'he had 180 devoted followers, all of whom he could command to go through fire and tread upon swords. (Certain) death could not persuade them to turn back.'[50]

The Moist communities were thus the source of a tendency which has persisted throughout Chinese history for the lower classes to band together, either openly or secretly, into societies, guilds and the like in order to further or protect their religious or economic interests. Significantly enough, histories of Chinese secret societies usually begin with a reference to Mo Ti.

Associations of this sort commonly had a religious background. That also came within the scope of Moist teaching. There is a passage in the work attributed to Mo Ti which sets out to prove the existence of spirits, ghosts and gods. Doubt as to their existence was regarded by Mo Ti as one of the causes of the evil and confused conditions of the time. It is also probable that religious indifference, as we find it in Confucianism, was confined to certain 'enlightened' strata of society, whereas the lower classes, from which Mo Ti came, were 'believers'. Mo Ti rightly ridicules the fact that Confucianists supported ritual while doubting the existence of spirits when he says that it was as though one were to 'perform the ceremonials of hospitality when expecting no guest' or to make 'fishing nets when there are no fish.'[51]

The question of the existence of ghosts was identical with the problem, much discussed at the time, of whether the dead were in a state of consciousness or not. Mo Ti maintained unhesitatingly that they were. He adduced a number of historical examples in which men who had been unjustly executed died saying: 'If man has no consciousness after death, then everything is over; but if I keep my consciousness you will know all about it'. The dead then in fact return — sometimes in the form of animals — to take their revenge.

Spirits keep the living under constant surveillance, wherever they may be — in a 'deep gorge', a 'dense forest' or a 'dark cavern'. They see everything and, depending on how men and women behave, promptly mete out reward or punishment. Neither birth nor riches, power nor weapons protect the evildoer from vengeance. It is possible to regard the spirits as a religiously grounded substitute for the systems of popular surveillance based on collective responsibility which came into being around the third century B.C. These should perhaps be interpreted as a mark of the victory of the 'atheist' Legalists over the 'believers'. The practical value of religious faith is expressed in the reply which Mo Ti made to a doubter: 'Of two servants of whom one works only when he sees the master but the other works even when he does not see the master, which is the better?'[52] Since the believer feels that he is constantly watched by spirits who are usually invisible, he will regulate his conduct accordingly.

Mo Ti distinguishes between the spirits of heaven, the spirits of mountains and rivers and the spirits of dead people, a distinction which corresponds with the division into heaven, earth and mankind which has already been mentioned. Heaven occupies a special position in his system too in that it is the special influence on the emperor: 'When the Son of Heaven practices virtue Heaven rewards, when the Son of Heaven does evil Heaven punishes. When the Son of Heaven is smitten by disease and calamities he fasts and bathes and sacrifices wine and millet to Heaven and to the spirits. Heaven can then remove the evil.'[53] The purpose of heaven is primarily to carry through the basic aims of the Moist teaching, 'universal love' and 'mutual benefit for all', from which it can be seen that heaven loves and aids all men without discrimination. Moism probably provides the first instance of the concept of equality before heaven. 'All states in the world, large or small, are the domain of Heaven, and all people, young or old, honourable or humble, are its subjects . . .'[54] Mo Ti is here abolishing the position of social and religious superiority enjoyed by the upper classes, though not their political leadership. Mo Ti also believed in an established special order in the will of heaven, which finds its expression in lawfulness (*i*), without which nothing can exist.

Lawfulness consists in heaven ruling the king, the king the feudal princes, the *shih* the people, and so on.

Mo Ti did, however, with the greatest severity, oppose the social barriers of the Confucian clan society and clan rule. Thus 'humanity' was replaced in Mo Ti's system by 'universal love'. '. . . The way of universal love . . . is to regard the land of others as one's own, the family-group (*chia*) of others as one's own, the persons of others as one's self. Then the feudal lords would love one another and there would be no more war; the heads of families would love one another and there would be no more usurpation of one another's (land and people); men would love one another and there would be no more enmity.'[55] In contrast to this, the clan system of Confucianism is criticized thus: 'As he loves only his own family and not other families, the thief steals from other families to profit his own family.'[56] Mo Ti's teaching leads to a kind of system of reciprocity: 'If a man loves others, others will love him. If a man helps others, others will help him. If a man hates others, he will be hated'[57] — and so on. The members of the Mo Ti communities were thus committed to every kind of mutual aid and we may certainly suppose that up to a point collective ownership operated.

Mo Ti's attitude of opposition to clan barriers is apparent in every branch of his teaching. In the chapters on 'promoting the able', attention is particularly drawn to the fact that the sage-kings chose their assistants for their ability and not on the basis of kinship. He deplores the fact that the king, the princes and the great ones of his day permit none but their nearest relatives to rise to positions of honour and wealth.

According to Mo Ti, history itself began when the 'ablest man' (*hsien*) on earth ended the anarchical chaos in which every man followed his own idea of lawfulness and a state of universal conflict existed, and was chosen by heaven for his surpassing ability and made the son of heaven. His main activity then consisted of selecting other 'able men' and setting them up as princes; these in turn picked out the able from among their subjects — and so on. This, clearly, is the clan system shifted to a basis of ability. In practice the system meant that inferiors told their superiors all that they happened to hear, both good and bad, and the superiors decided what was to be believed and what rejected. The inferiors were then obliged to yield unconditionally to the judgment from above. In other words, Mo Ti's ideal resembled the idea advanced in our own day in the guise of 'Führerprinzip'.

Mo Ti's basic attitude led him also to oppose any extravagance connected with ritual (*li*), especially magnificent burials, long periods of mourning, costly ritual utensils and so on. This was one of the principal issues in the polemical disputes between Confucians and Moists. Another consequence of Mo Ti's advocacy of a simple, functional way of life for everyone was the ultimate rejection of music, which had played a major part in the ancestor-worship of the noble clans. 'There are three things that the people worry about, namely, that the hungry cannot be fed, that the cold cannot be clothed, and that the tired cannot get rest. Music is unnecessary.'[58] The following anecdote is characteristic:

> Motse asked a Confucianist why the Confucianists made music. He replied, 'Music is made for music's sake.' Motse said, 'You have not yet answered me. Suppose I asked, why build houses. And you answered, it is to keep off the cold in winter and the heat in summer, and to separate men from women. Then you would have told me the reason for building houses. But what would it mean if you answered, "Houses are built for houses' sakes" '.[59]

Mo Ti was, furthermore, a confirmed opponent of wars of aggression. The main reason for this was, no doubt, that he had come to know war from an entirely different angle from, for example, the author of the *Tso Chuan*. The *Tso Chuan* often gives the impression that the conflicts between the princes of the Ch'un-ch'iu period were merely extremely chivalrous tournaments or 'knock-out' engagements fought according to the rules of honour. In the works of Mo Ti, however, we read that a powerful state on principle joined battle only with a weaker one and that the aggressor then: 'laid waste the harvest, felled the timber trees, razed the city walls, blocked the irrigation ditches, burned down the ancestral temples, slaughtered the sacrificial animals, killed the men who opposed him, led the rest of the population away in chains and coerced both men and women into slavery.'[60] War for Mo Ti is merely murder and crime on a large scale. He was, however, a realist and for this reason maintained that the aggressor should be repulsed and means of defence be provided. And so we have the paradoxical situation that the ancient Chinese art of warfare originated from a pacifist school and that the Moist communities were usually well organized and well trained as battle units. So fanatical was their spirit of solidarity that the ordinary people often followed their leaders to their death of their own accord.

One particular feature of these communities may be mentioned in conclusion. Many of them came under the influence of an intellectual movement of which the basic belief was that periods of misfortune — when wars, plagues and natural catastrophes were rife — alternated with periods of universal harmony (*t'ai-p'ing*). The origins of this doctrine and the religious forms it assumed have already been described. Its effect was to make of the leaders of these communities great magicians able, because of their special relationships with the world of spirits and some power over it, to lead their followers, who were bound to unconditional obedience, through the periods of misfortune into those of happiness and well-being. Communities of this kind in all probability already existed during the Chan-kuo period; but their first recorded appearance was during the vast uprising of the 'Yellow Turbans' towards the end of the second century A.D.

V

The Chan-kuo Period

The states of the Chan-kuo period — some the products of the conflicts and intrigues of the Ch'un-ch'iu era, some, such as Shu-Pa and Yüeh, making their first appearance in the historical arena — may properly be regarded as nation-states. The different territories built frontier defences which effectively prevented all passage from one to the other except at specified points, a measure probably originally adopted to curtail the migration of labourers.

We may also suppose that, in the outlying regions especially, indigenous peoples of different ethnic origins made a great impact upon the lower classes and that, as a further result, forms of speech began to differ more and more between the various states.

This applied in a lesser degree to the upper classes. The education of the aristocratic youth was largely uniform and this, together with the fact that they studied texts written in an essentially unvarying literary language, counteracted any tendency of the languages to diverge. Brisk diplomatic activity, marriages arranged for political purposes and ancestor-worship also enabled the upper class to retain a certain solidarity which transcended national frontiers. We have already seen that Confucius wished to make this the basis for the peaceful unification of the empire.

The *shih* were another international element. They appear to have migrated in large numbers from one state to another and to have gathered in the places where they were best received. They formed an important factor in the political interplay between the countries, and the princes vied with one another in attracting them to their courts. They were to be found as scholars in the newly emerging academies in which the most varied branches of study were pursued; as political advisers and intriguers; as wily tax-collectors and fanatical assassins. Regulations in the *Li Chi* relating to persons who abandon their hereditary ancestral ground and shift their national allegiance presumably refer to the *shih* and to this period.

Another feature of the period is the rise of a class of rich merchants. This was primarily the result of the growing exchange of products between the towns, where markets and artisans' quarters were coming into being, and the people living on the land. The harvest speculators also had a hand in this; in association with the 'alternation of periods' briefly described in the last chapter, the theory grew up among them that good and bad harvests alternated in accordance with a set rhythm. There was also a trade in rarities, precious stones and valuable works of art, which was pursued regardless of frontiers.

Wealth was the new force which was coming into being side by side with the clan aristocracy, whose power was based on possession of land and arms. States sometimes came under the sway of rich merchants. Such a case — and one which acquired a special historical significance — was that of the merchant Lü Pu-wei, who became minister in the western state of Ch'in.

The merchants seem to have held definite notions as to how political conditions could be reorganized. They were opposed to fixed boundaries between the countries and in favour of restoring the unitary state. This state was not, however, to be set up at the discretion of scholars with an ill-defined ethical and emotional outlook but in accordance with clear-cut laws applicable to all classes of society.

In pursuance of these ideas, attempts were made in Chan-kuo states both to concentrate political power in the hands of the ruler representing an authority beyond the reach of the law, and to improve the position of the people from the economic and military point of view. This was achieved, of course, at the expense of the petty feudal aristocracy, who, shorn of their feudal rights, became less and less distinguishable from ordinary landowners. Associated with this was the growing emancipation of the lower classes, which culminated in the peasants actually owning the farm land and being able to sell it as they wished. But a further development began simultaneously to manifest itself and quickly gathered momentum: the very peasants who had just gained their 'freedom' were robbed of their land when they were forced into debt and subjected to other means of compulsion. They were thus brought to a new state of dependence which soon became indistinguishable from the old.

This period also saw the emergence of a vast body of officials. They adopted a position between the court and the common people and took over the functions of the former feudal petty aristocracy. This class became the true domain of the *shih,* for whom it represented a position from which to establish a bureaucracy in opposition to the nobility.

1. THE BEGINNINGS OF TAOISM

The Chan-kuo period was the golden age of philosophical speculation in ancient China. A number of other schools emerged besides those which evolved from the two movements we have described, but we shall only give a brief outline of the most important of these. One of them venerated Lao-tzŭ as the chief among its founding fathers and became celebrated in the Han period under the name of Taoism (*tao-chia*).

The most celebrated work of this movement is the *Tao-tê ching* which was long regarded as having been written by Lao-tzŭ himself. The title means 'classical book of Tao and Tê' and was given to the work in about the sixth century A.D. Before that it occurs in the texts as the 'five thousand character writing' or the 'Lao-tzŭ book'. It has been translated into every civilized language and belongs today to the great literature of the world.

There is every probability that Lao-tzŭ was a historical personage. Beyond this, however, any statement about him must be regarded as extremely tentative. He may have been a contemporary of Confucius; he may have been an archivist at the Chou court; the *Tao-tê ching* may contain the basic tenets of his teaching. Since sinological research has now established beyond question that the work dates from the Chan-kuo period, it obviously cannot be the work of a man who lived in the Ch'un-ch'iu period. Nor, probably, was Lao-tzŭ ('aged master') a name, but a description which very old men were wont to apply to themselves in a foreign state. Lao does occur, though, as a family name in the region believed to have been Lao-tzŭ's home. But his real name is said to have been Li Êrh, his assumed literary name Tan or Po-yang. The situation could scarcely be more confused. He is said to have given the *Tao-tê ching* to the Keeper of the Pass as he left Chou.

Even more than Confucius, Lao-tzŭ became the hero of an ever-growing legend. This legend became a central feature of Taoism, which was formed of the confluence of a number of philosophical and religious currents.

We have no clear picture of any of these currents and even the one which I hope to outline, although it is based on recent publications relating to the beginnings of Taoism, leaves many questions open.

It begins with the philosopher Yang Chu, who we know lived at about the turn of the fourth and third century B.C. We have already seen that there existed in Moist communities a tradition of collective aid in necessity and assistance over periods of want. In contrast to this, Yang Chu stood for the preservation of the individual, with the slogan 'everything solely for the sake of my person'. This meant that he would refuse to enter a town threatened by war or to undertake military service, to such a point that he would not sacrifice a hair of his head to save the world.

We know that there was a similar trend in Confucianism in as much as a pious son held it his duty to return his body unharmed to the parents from whom he had received it. This was not one of the tenets of Yang Chu, who believed rather in the 'fullness of life', which meant preserving the individual's own life in all circumstances for the longest possible time. But it seems that he regarded one hundred years as the age that might be reached in natural circumstances.

In order to achieve this 'fullness of life', Yang Chu advocated the avoidance, as far as possible, of all affairs, the holding of all office and so on and withdrawal into a state of not-being-needed and not-being-noticed. In this he became the earliest advocate of a Taoist idea which later found a distinguished champion in Chuang-tzŭ; its main concern was that its adherents should stand aloof from public life.

A consequence of valuing the individual life as the highest good was that certain restrictions had to be imposed upon the desires, in order that life should not be endangered. This involved some degree of restraint in eating, sexual activity and so on, and caused numerous practices to be developed among the later Taoists.

No work by Yang Chu has survived. The chapter which appears under his name in the work called after the Taoist Lieh-tzŭ is certainly a forgery. In spite of the wide dissemination of his teachings, he probably did not found a school in the sense in which Confucius and Mo Ti did and had no disciples to collect his dicta. His opinions were, however, absorbed in various ways into the works of the later Taoists. Thus, for example, we read in the *Tao-tê ching*: 'The only reason that we suffer hurt is that we have bodies; if we had no bodies, how could we suffer?'[61] Or in the work called *Chuang-tzŭ*:

> There was a totally crippled man named Su . . . By tailoring, washing and sifting rice he was able to feed himself and his family. But when the government conscripted soldiers, he sauntered unconcernedly among the crowd. And when there were heavy public works to be done, he was not employed because of his infirmity. But when rations were distributed to invalids, he received a plentiful amount of corn and firewood. If a man whose body was so far removed from serviceable form could survive and live out his allotted span, how much truer must this be of those who abandon the all-applicable virtues (of the Confucians)![62]

And we read in the same work: 'To complete the span of years which Heaven allots and not to perish midway upon the path of life, that is the highest wisdom.' A line may be drawn from Yang Chu to the celebrated academy of scholars which had its seat near the Chi gate in the capital of the state of Ch'i (more or less corresponding to the northern part of Shantung). It is said that

King Hsüan (320–302 B.C.) thought highly of the learned *shih* who journeyed from place to place expounding their doctrines and invited them to his court. There he assembled a great number of them, so that all opinions were represented, and encouraged them to discuss among themselves.

It appears, however, that one group outnumbered the others. These were the scholars who, in later literature, were known as advocates of 'Huang-Lao'. It seems, moreover, that this gathering of scholars in the state of Ch'i did not originate in the reign of King Hsüan but was part of an older tradition which may have begun when Kuan Chung, the celebrated minister — thanks to whose clever counsels Duke Huan of Ch'i (685–643 B.C.?) became the first *pa* prince of the Ch'un-ch'iu period — arrived at court as an adventurer. The proponents of the Huang-Lao theories had probably also long been in the majority there and dominated the intellectual life of the capital.

The 'Huang' of this phrase is Huang-ti, the 'Yellow Emperor', whom we may probably regard as the first and most important 'sage' of this school. He is believed originally to have been identical with Shang-ti, who has been mentioned often already; he may have been given the attribute 'yellow', the colour of the centre, under the influence of the doctrine of the elements, which was also emerging in Ch'i. As far as dates are concerned, he may have come into vogue at about the same time as Shên-nung, the God-peasant, since the two are frequently mentioned together. The two schools associated with these sages have many features in common too, for the course of nature and the succession of the seasons were important points of departure in their teachings.

We possess an ancient sacrificial vessel from the state of Ch'i and of the period of King Wei (356–320 B.C.), the inscription on which names the 'high ancestor Huang-ti'. This indicates that at that period the Yellow Emperor was already regarded as a historical personage[63] and was probably the head of a line of ancestors recognized in Ch'i. Unfortunately no investigation has, as far as I know, yet been made into the question of when, exactly, this new family tree came into existence and what its relationship was to the Chou. Clearly it represents a move in a political game aimed at substituting another dynasty for the Chou.

'Lao' is, of course, the name of Lao-tzŭ. So that Huang-Lao is the name given to teachings which were later included under the title of Taoism. It is, unfortunately, impossible to say at what point in the pre-Han era this expression was coined. Later on, it seems, it was most often taken to mean the political brand of Taoism. It was in any case discredited after the failure of the uprising of the Yellow Turbans and replaced by the combination 'Lao-Chuang' (Lao-tzŭ and Chuang-tzŭ).

The earliest proponent of the Huang-Lao theories at the academy at the Chi gate at this time of whom we have a record was Sung Hsing (or K'êng), some of whose works have been preserved in extracts in the work named after the minister Kuan Chung. As matters stand now, it would appear that these chapters, the titles of which mean, roughly, 'art of the heart' and 'inner (or esoteric) instruction',[64] probably represent the earliest literary fragments of Taoism.

The connection of the philosophy of Sung Hsing with the thought of Yang Chu is evident from the fact that it also mainly revolves round the individual and his nature. Thus we read, for example:

> When a thing does not comply with my rule, even if it brings profit, I do not do it. When a thing does not suit me, even if it brings profit, I do not act in that way. When a thing does not lie in the way that has been shown me (Tao), even if it brings profit, I do not take it.

Or:

> Man by birth is certainly possessed of balance and fitness. That whereby he loses them is pleasure, anger, grief and calamity . . . Therefore for stopping anger there is nothing like the Songs, for discarding grief there is nothing like Music. For controlling Rites there is nothing like reverence, for controlling reverence there is nothing like impassivity. When the interior is passive and the exterior is reverent, then one can return to one's own true nature.

We can see how the teaching of Yang Chu has here been turned to apply to the inner nature of the individual. Music and ritual have here become merely the means of creating the poise and inner calm necessary to the 'well-being of the heart'.

> When one has been able to be fit in body and mentally serene, one will be of a stable mind. If a stable mind abides in one's midst then one's ears will be acute and one's eyes will be clear, the four limbs will be strong and one can become the abode of the minute parts.

The 'minute parts' (*ching*) is one of the most important concepts of Taoism and is expounded for the first time in these chapters of the *Kuan-tzŭ*. 'The small parts truly are the small parts of the breath.' There presumably existed an ancient theory that the smallest parts of the breath or the air constituted the essential foundation of the physical body and of the universe. The *Kuan-tzŭ* has this to say of them:

> Those of the things which possess the finest of breath, below they produce the five grains, above they are the stars. When they flow between Heaven and Earth they are called the spirits. When they are stored within their breasts, they are called the saints.

Conservation of the small parts in the human body soon became one of the most important means by which the Taoists sought to prolong life. Their practices were based upon certain breathing exercises and dietary rules, which are also found for the first time in the work of Sung Hsing:

> As to the way of feeding, if one over-fills, the belly is harmed and not strong. If one is over-fastidious the bones will rot and the blood will be stopped up. The mean between overfilling and overfastidiousness is called harmony completed. It is wherein the fine parts abide . . .

The *Kuan-tzŭ* also contains the sources of the Taoist doctrine concerning the macrocosm and microcosm, in as much as the inner structure of man corresponds to the outward structure of the state:

> The heart in the body occupies the same (central) position as the ruler (in the state). The functions of the nine orifices are the duties of the officials. When the heart keeps to its way, the nine orifices follow their appointed functions.

When, however, the heart yields to the fulfilment of its desires, confusion follows, just as though the ruler of a state were to take over the functions of his officials. This obviously leads on to the theory later advocated in political Taoism of the passivity of the ruler, as required by his position as mediator between the universe and mankind. This further developed into a grandiose system of correspondences between the basic structure of man and that of heaven and earth. Each part of the universe has its counterpart in man, on earth and in the stars. Each Taoist god has a place among the stars, on earth and in the human body.

The inner life must now achieve the proper relationship with that which lies outside it and must draw therefrom what is important and beneficial to the life of the individual. The *Kuan-tzŭ* has this to say:

> What can unify the humours so that they change is called the fine parts. What can unify matters so that they change is called wisdom . . . He who holds to unifying and is not negligent may command the myriad things, shine together with sun and moon and regulate together with heaven and earth.

The problem is ultimately resolved into the old question: how is it possible to draw from the universe (meaning heaven and earth) the powers which make the perfect ruler or saint; or, as it was formulated above: how do I induce the god of heaven to bestow his favour on me? By way of rejoinder we read: 'When the body is not upright and straight, virtue (*tê*) does not come.' The inner man must prepare himself to receive that which is to enter into him. 'When one empties oneself of desire, the spiritual will enter in and make its abode; when one sweeps away what is impure, the spiritual remains.' The appetites must therefore be banished in order, so to speak, to make room for the awaited spirit, which must also be offered an acceptable dwelling-place.

Here also we encounter the concept Tao (the way). The book says: 'The Tao of heaven is emptiness', and: 'Emptiness is the beginning of all things.' 'The Tao of earth is that which is at rest.' Tao can thus be expressed as the fundamental quality which heaven and earth have in common. 'Tao is between heaven and earth; nothing exists which could be larger and nothing which could be smaller', which means that Tao embraces all the possibilities of existence. 'The great Tao is such that one can indeed rest (in it) but cannot predicate it.' 'One must therefore know about the matter of not-speaking and not-doing, then will one know the secret threads of Tao.' Confucius's words quoted above about heaven not speaking should be compared with this passage. In this new relationship *tê* (virtue) is the action of Tao in mankind. 'If one receives it (Tao) as into a dwelling-place, it is called *tê* (virtue). There is therefore no space between Tao and *tê*.'

The extracts also contain a series of comments directed against the Legalists and the Confucians, as well as an obvious bias towards the pacifism of the Moists. They contain the rudiments and germ of almost all the elements of the later Taoist philosophy.

These fragments of Sung Hsing's works are written in verse. Some of them have, unfortunately, got out of order and they are riddled with all kinds of interpolations, so that it is frequently hard to establish what is the original text and what later addition. But the overriding difficulty is the fact that we are compelled to substitute for the original concepts terms used in the western conceptual system: although these may approximate to the Chinese, they are very far from being exact renderings.

2. SHÊN TAO AND CHUANG-TZŬ

One of the ideas discussed at the academy by the Chi gate was that of equality or the elimination of differences, which we have already discovered in connection with Mo Ti. The principal exponent of this idea was the academician Shên Tao, to whom is attributed the second chapter of Chuang-tzŭ's *The Identity of Contraries*.

That this chapter emanates from the academy by the Chi gate is demonstrated by, for example, the fact that Sung Hsing's metaphor of the body and its parts is quoted and reinterpreted. These now came to be regarded as a kind of anarchical community, in which each one had its natural place and no 'ruler' was appointed.

This chapter — which also contains a series of parables probably added later — is one of the most interesting in all ancient Chinese philosophy. The passage which provides the link with the one from Mo Ti quoted above occurs not, indeed, in this but in the preceding chapter. It runs: 'The blue of the sky, is that its real colour? Or does it merely seem so because it is so far away and has no end? When (P'êng, the giant bird, from the zenith of its flight across the sky) looks down, the (earthly world) will look just the same to him.'[66] This means that the diversity of things on earth will appear to him as one, just as for Mo Ti the social distinctions of human society lose their meaning against the background of heaven.

This idea is demonstrated in another nature parable at the beginning of the second chapter. It concerns the 'flute-music of heaven' (*t'ien-lai*). This music is engendered when the great breath of the universe, the wind, is caught in the numberless hollows, holes and clefts in rocks and trees and other things, and each of these apertures produces its own, individual note. In the face of these innumerable separate sounds, the wind presents an all-embracing, omnipresent unity which has no sound itself and is therefore silence. This brings us back to the important Taoist concept of no-sound or no-speech. The wind, therefore, is a metaphor for Tao, in which, in the same way, all things and all individualities are dissolved or made equal.

By the use of dialectic argument, Shên Tao endeavours to lead us away from this world of diversity and contrast into the universal sphere, or sphere of Tao. All beings can be seen as both object and subject. Our perceptions, however, have not an objective but a subjective origin, since the subject is that which lies nearest to each one of us. It may be expressed thus: 'The object grows from the ground of the subject, but the subject is grounded in the object.' Object and subject, therefore, have only a partial or temporary life (existence); indeed, they live (exist) only as long as the one allows the other to do so. This means that life and death, the possible and the impossible, right and wrong are simply the consequences of the standpoint we adopt, whether it be the subjective or objective: in themselves they are nothing.

The sage (*shêng-jên*), therefore, is not concerned with all this but regards it from the point of view of heaven (nature). The subject then also becomes the object and the object the subject and, in their relationship to being and not-being, they are one. Is there, then, a distinction between subject and object? Not to bring the opposing positions of subject and object into play is the 'pivotal point of Tao'. This point forms the centre of a great orbit and, while itself remaining unmoved, it can respond to every position of transition and change. 'Therefore the sage brings (men) into harmony by means of "yes" and "no" but himself reposes in the neutrality of heaven.' We have clearly left the Confucian world with its fixed positions — a prince is a prince, a servant a servant — behind us and have entered a world of perpetual change, in which everything can become everything else. Stability, however, has shifted from positions to relationships, connections and trends.

The practical consequence of this was that the sage sought to lose himself in Tao, that is to say to be dissolved in Tao and to become one with it. This was achieved by meditation and breathing exercises. And this chapter begins characteristically by showing us an adept in this state of 'union with Tao'. 'He leant (in a special position) against the (meditation-) table and sat down. He gazed heavenwards and his breath streamed slowly out. He was like one sundered from his bodily self.' There is more about breathing in the sixth chapter, which is by Chuang-tzŭ himself: 'For pure men (the perfect Taoist) draw breath from their uttermost depths (heels); the vulgar only from their throats.'

In the last resort, Shên Tao and Chuang-tzŭ, like Yang Chu, advocate the prolongation and safeguarding of life. In their opinion, this goal is to be reached by yielding to nature or by losing oneself in Tao, which is all-embracing and resolves all opposites and thus outlasts everything.

Death and life are also only points of transition on a great road (Tao), much like dreaming and waking. This is demonstrated in a celebrated anecdote which comes from Chuang-tzŭ's inner circle:

> Chuang-tzŭ dreamt he was a butterfly, fluttering hither and thither, to all intents and purposes a butterfly. He was conscious only of following his fancies as a butterfly, and was unconscious of Chuang-tzŭ. Suddenly, he awoke and was Chuang-tzŭ. Now he does not know whether he was then Chuang-tzŭ dreaming he was a butterfly, or whether he is now a butterfly dreaming he is Chuang-tzŭ.

Here we see ancient concepts which had their origin in the mind of the Shang reappearing in a different, philosophical context.

The theory of decline, which finds frequent expression in Taoist works, also occurs in this chapter:

> Knowledge in antiquity reached the highest point of perfection . . .They had no idea that matter (things) existed . . . In the next period they recognized that matter existed but they still set no limits to it. In the third period they recognized the limits but knew nothing of affirmation and negation. When in due course these appeared, Tao was lost. With the loss of Tao, one-sided preference (i.e. one-sided 'point-of-view') arose.

'Appearance' and 'loss' — do they in fact exist? The position here is the same as with the zither-playing of the celebrated music-master, Chao Wên. While he was playing he was committed to a single sequence of notes and lost the unison of sounds; when he was not playing he was in possession of this great unified harmony and did not hear individual notes.

Whereas decline is here presented as an increasing differentiation of perception, Chuang-tzŭ gives it an ontological twist. He explains in the following words his refusal to mourn his dead wife:

> At the beginning she had no life, nor had she form of any kind, nor even breath (i.e. finest substance). Only when she became separated from the great unformed mass did she become breath. The breath changed and became form. Form changed

and became life. Now another change has taken place — death. This is like the course of the seasons, spring and autumn, winter and summer. She is now at rest, slumbering in the great chamber (i.e. the universe), and shall I therefore mourn and weep?[67]

It is unfortunately beyond the scope of this book to follow all the trains of thought of this chapter in detail. But from what we have discussed, it is clear that at this period, at the turn of the third and second century B.C., Chinese philosophers were already concerned with problems fundamental to western philosophy, such as the descent from the universal to the particular and the ontological structure of things.

Chuang-tzŭ is believed to have lived from about 369 to 290 B.C.; his name was Chuang Chou and he came from a place in present-day Honan. He was one of the Taoist 'hermits'. Most of these may be thought of as well-to-do landowners for whom an official position was less essential than it was for the impoverished *shih*; instead, they were able to spend their lives quietly on their land communing with nature and pursuing Taoist studies.

The story is told of Chuang-tzŭ that he was fishing in the P'u river when two high officials of the King of Ch'u came and offered him a ministerial post. Without interrupting his fishing, he replied: 'I have heard that in Ch'u there is a sacred tortoise which has been dead now some three thousand years. And that the prince keeps his tortoise carefully in his ancestral temple. Now would this tortoise rather be killed ceremonially and officially and have its remains preserved and venerated, or be alive and wagging its tail in the mud?' 'It would rather be alive', came the prompt reply. 'Begone!' cried Chuang-tzŭ. 'I too would rather wag my tail in the mud.'[68] High honours after death are no reward for a life sacrificed to official functions.

With Chuang-tzŭ, ancient Chinese philosophy leaves behind the social and political atmosphere of Confucianism, and enters the realm of nature and the observation of the natural world. Nature is the source of the grandiose fables of Chuang-tzŭ, whose poetical powers assure the works attributed to him a place among the great works of world literature.

Like the one quoted above, many of the fables relate to Tao. One of the finest is *Ch'iu-shui* (*Autumn Floods*), which begins:

> It was the time of autumn floods. Hundreds of streams poured into the Huang-ho. So wide was the river that from one bank to the other it was impossible to tell a cow from a horse. This pleased the god of the Huang-ho and he thought there was nothing in the world greater than himself. He abandoned himself to the stream and journeyed eastwards to the Northern Sea. He turned towards the east and gazed. He saw no end to the water. His eyes roamed over the sea until, in the distance, he saw the sea-god; he sighed and said, 'I have heard a proverb which says that amongst a hundred ways one thinks one's own is best. This applies to me. I have also heard of people who say that Confucius's learning is commonplace and the bearing of his ideal heroes insignificant. I did not believe it. Now I see your immeasurable space. If I had not come to your abode I would surely have continued to look upon the followers of the great Tao as absurd eccentrics.'

The sea-god then expounds the spatial and temporal relativity of great and small and converts the river god to Taoism.

In spite of its universality and intangibility, Tao is no abstraction. It is rather the true reality of all things.

> A man from the eastern suburb asked Chuang-tzŭ, 'What you call Tao — where is it?' 'There is nowhere', replied Chuang-tzŭ, 'where it is not.' 'Tell me one place at any rate where it is', said Tung Kuo Tzŭ. 'It is in this ant,' replied Chuang-tzŭ. 'And how is it with even lower creatures?' asked Tung Kuo Tzŭ. 'It is in this blade of grass', said Chuang-tzŭ. 'Still lower?,' asked Tung Kuo Tzŭ, 'It is in this potsherd,' said Chuang-tzŭ. 'And does it then go lower yet?' asked Tung Kuo Tzŭ. 'It is in this heap of ordure,' said Chuang-tzŭ. And with that Tung Kuo Tzŭ gave up.[69]

It is also said of Tao:

> Tao is actual, and demonstrable but it is devoid both of action and of form. It may be transmitted, but cannot be received.

> It may be obtained, but cannot be seen. It has its own beginning and its own end, before heaven or earth existed, from everlasting to everlasting. It extends further back than the remotest antiquity and yet it is not old.[70]

It might then be said that Tao is a mysterious something which works and guides the continual change and mutation of all existing things. Its own basic nature, however, was paraphrased by Chuang-tzŭ in the expression *tzŭ-jan*, which may be approximately rendered as 'to be oneself as one is' or 'to be naturally as one is'. And this *tzŭ-jan* which is imparted to all beings through Tao appears, especially in the later interpretations of post-Christian commentators, to be the basic theme of Taoism as expounded by Chuang-tzŭ. He himself wrote: 'Unite your breath (finest substance) with the boundless (i.e. Tao), fall in with the natural character (*tzŭ-jan*) of living things, do not adopt points of view . . .'[71] and so on.

There is also a passage in the work of Chuang-tzŭ which neatly demonstrates the difference between the western attitude to nature, in which man seeks coercion and mastery, and the Chinese, in which the individual aspires to become one with nature. This is the story of the master-cook of the Prince of Liang (Wei). The man was carving an ox with such consummate skill that the performance resembled a rhythmic dance. He explained this by saying that he was a devotee of Tao and that this had taught him no longer to view the ox 'with his eyes, but to get his measure on the spiritual plane'. Now he was simply following its natural structure and the creature was of its own accord falling into its proper divisions. Although he had been using his knife for nineteen years and had carved many thousands of oxen with it, it was as sharp as though it had just been whetted. 'Excellent!' cried the Prince. 'From the words of this cook I have learnt the art of caring for living things.'[72]

This is one of the most important of Taoist practices and, as we can see, involves becoming one with the natural structure of living things. The more remote consequences were that faithful Taoists were not permitted to insult heaven by boorish and offensive behaviour nor to wound the earth by great drilling and digging operations. These were theories which retained considerable weight in the Chinese world until very recent times.

Chuang-tzŭ also used parables to conduct polemical battles against his opponents. In his opinion, one of the principal errors of other schools of thought was that they tried to improve nature by artificial means. A case in point was that of the wild horses who had hooves to enable them to tread on the snow and long thick coats to protect them against the cold. But a man came along who claimed special knowledge of handling horses. He branded the wild horses, trimmed their hooves and coats and set them to work. Of ten horses, two or three fell ill and died.[73]

There is humour in those parables in which Chuang-tzŭ comes out against all the efforts by which other schools attempted to safeguard and defend the states. A state, according to him, is like the coffer in which a careful man keeps his money. He fastens it with strong iron bands (i.e., ritual, the law and civic morality) and with locks (the military and the police). When a strong thief comes along he takes the whole coffer on his back and his only concern is that the bands and locks shall hold so that he may carry his booty to safety.[74] According to this theory, the greatly honoured sages and wise men of the Confucians and Moists had after all only worked to the advantage of the robbers.

Nor will it do to deny the thieves high moral qualities. For a man to dissemble his purpose as long as the coveted prize is in safe-keeping is like the wisdom of the sages. To be the first to break in is courage. To be the last out is justice. To seize the right moment to act is wisdom. To apportion a fair share of the booty to all is philanthropy.[75]

These theories obviously continue to be endorsed in our own day.

3. THE *TAO-TÊ CHING*

The problem of whether the early chapters (1–7) of Chuang-tzŭ's *The Identity of Contraries* date from before or after the *Tao-tê ching* still awaits solution. Either alternative is possible. Three-quarters of it consists of rhymed aphorisms (or sayings) which were collected by an author of the Chan-kuo period to form a coherent work. It is also uncertain to what extent the text has come down to us in its original arrangement and attempts have recently been made to restore this.

In the considerably later Chapter 33 of Chuang-tzŭ's book ('All below Heaven') Lao Tan, the alleged author of the *Tao-tê ching*, and another equally mysterious Taoist, Kuan Yin ('The keeper of the Pass'), are named as representatives of the same Taoist school. Its characteristic features are given as follows: 'They believed the soft, the weak and the humble to be the outside (of Tao), and the empty, which never causes harm to any being, they believed to be its core.' In particular the opinion is attributed to Kuan Yin that Tao moves like water, rests like a mirror and responds like an echo.

The contents of the *Tao-tê ching* are entirely consistent with these views. To be soft and weak is what principally matters in questions of life and survival.

> When he is born, man is soft and weak; in death he becomes stiff and hard. The ten thousand creatures and all plants and trees while they are alive are supple and soft, but when they are dead they become brittle and dry. Truly, what is stiff and hard is a 'companion of death'; what is soft and weak is a 'companion of life'.[76]

'Nothing under heaven is softer or more yielding than water; but when it attacks things hard and resistant there is not one of them that can prevail.'[77]

It is therefore essential, if a man desires to prolong his existence, to be weak and yielding. As these lines say:

> He who knows the male, yet cleaves to what
> is female
> Becomes like a ravine, receiving all things
> under heaven,
> And being such a ravine

He knows all the time a power that he never
calls upon in vain
This is returning to the state of infancy.[78]

The 'female' is, of course, self-abasing weakness. But, since it underlies everything, it contains all resources and powers, especially the power of rejuvenation. Everything which has moved upwards falls by nature back down to where the dark, primeval forces wait to ascend. This is also expressed in the *Tao-tê ching* in the injunction to 'apprehend the mother, but also know the son (sprung from her)'.[79]

This concept was also applied to questions of knowledge and ethics in this respect: that it was desirable, through an understanding of knowledge and of honourable behaviour, to recognize no-knowledge and shameful behaviour — meaning, in fact, that which precedes all knowledge and every ethical nuance.

The 'world ravine' (that is, the extreme depths of the world), the 'primeval beginning', the 'mother' and others are all designations of Tao. And in so far as Tao supplants the ancient sovereign divinity or, more properly, forms the primal ground, from which spring heaven and earth and all they hold — and this includes the gods — we have for the first time the idea that the reality of the divine is manifest in softness, lowliness or self-abasement and that the almighty is in fact the all-weakest.

In Tao the only motion is returning;
The only useful quality, weakness.[80]

Tao, the irreducibly simple basic material, disperses and becomes a plurality of entities charged with all kinds of functional qualities. All these entities, however, retain something of Tao, with the result that what is hard and unyielding in them shows a tendency to revert to the weak and soft. This tendency, which stems from the fact that the entities have retained some Tao, is the quality which in the *Tao-tê ching* is called *tê* (virtue).

This becomes the main theme of the second part of the work, where the following passage occurs:

When Tao is lost, then comes *tê*. When *tê* is lost, then comes

> *jên* ['humanity', a basic concept of the Confucian ethic]. When *jên* is lost, then comes *i* ['morality', one of the basic concepts of the school of Mo Ti]. When *i* is lost, then comes *li* [the ritual of the school of rites]. But *li* is the thin (husk) of loyalty and faith and the beginning of social disorder.[81]

This descending series, which to some extent represents the passage from soft universality to the limited and rigid and is but one example of several, shows that the compiler of the *Tao-tê ching* was familiar with the other intellectual trends of the Ch'un-ch'iu and Chan-kuo periods. There is in fact scarcely one on which this work does not contain some observation.

The styles adopted by the kings of the Chan-kuo states — 'the destitute', 'the imperfect' and suchlike — were now linked with this idea that lowliness and poverty were the true strength; for it was believed that they had assumed these styles because they regarded the commonplace and the mean as the true foundation of their exalted position. This belief is expressed by the following axiom:

> To remain whole, be twisted!
> To become straight, let yourself be bent.
> To become full, be hollow.
> Be tattered, that you may be renewed.[82]

or:

> How did the great rivers and seas get their
>   kingship over the hundred lesser streams?
> Through the merit of being lower than they; . . .[83]

and:

> Therefore the Sage
> In order to be above the people
> Must speak as though he were lower than the
>   people.
> In order to guide them
> He must put himself behind them.[84]

It is due to the great influence of this school in the intellectual life of China that the characters *wu wei* or 'inaction' — meaning to follow the great natural course of things and not to strike out in an autocratic spirit against it — were placed over the imperial throne like a guiding principle for all time. As it says in the *Tao-tê ching*: 'A state may be governed by rectification (of the terms), and a war may be waged by strategy, but the whole kingdom under Heaven may be obtained by letting-alone.' Therefore the sage says:

> So long as I 'do nothing' the people will of
> themselves be transformed.
> So long as I love quietude the people will of
> themselves go straight.
> So long as I act only by inactivity the people
> will of themselves become prosperous.
> So long as I have no wants the people will of themselves
> return to the 'state of the Uncarved Block'.[85]

According to the *Tao-tê ching* the best type of ruler is the one whose very existence is unknown to the people. By his wise non-intervention he so influences them that they believe that it is by their own efforts that all results are being achieved.

The ideal community is portrayed as a small country with few inhabitants, in which machines which could do the work of ten or a hundred men are not used, where all fear death and none wanders into distant lands, where the people have enough to eat from the food they have produced themselves and are adequately clothed by garments of their own making. The inhabitants can distinctly hear the cocks crowing and the dogs barking in the neighbouring country but never once in their lives do they meet the subjects of the neighbouring state.

There is unfortunately no space to show in detail how the political views of the Taoists made themselves felt in the history of the Chinese people.

4. OTHER TRENDS IN CHAN-KUO PHILOSOPHY

Soon after the death of Confucius, his disciples split into eight schools. I should like to say a few words about some of them.

First there was K'ung Chi, called Tzŭ-ssŭ, a grandson of Confucius and believed to have been the author of the small work, *Chung-yung* (*The Mean-in-Action*), though it too contains additions by later editors. In this work we read: 'To have no emotions of pleasure and anger and sorrow and joy surging up, this is to be described as the mean. To have these emotions surging up but all in tune, this is to be described as a state of harmony. This mean is the supreme foundation, this state of harmony the highway [*tao*], of all under Heaven.'[85a] It seems very probable that this is also a reflection of the swiftly changing social background of the time and that it is precisely to counteract it that it counsels adherence to the mean. 'The Master said, Mean and constancy, is it attainable? The people can (but) rarely remain in that state.'[86] This clearly refers to the social re-grouping taking place at the time.

A striking feature is the frequent occurrence of the word Tao. Yet this does not mean precisely the same thing as the Tao of the Taoists. 'That which Heaven entrusts to man [in fact, appoints, *ming*] is to be called his nature. The following out of this nature is to be called the Way [Tao]. The cultivation of the Way is to be called instruction in systematic truth (*chiao*). The Way, it may not be abandoned for a moment.' (Tzŭ-ssŭ, trsl. Hughes.) 'The Way is not far removed from men. If a man pursues a way which removes him from men, he cannot be in the Way.' (*ibid*) It is clear from this that no distinction is drawn between external and inner nature, which links this doctrine to that of the macrocosm-microcosm briefly mentioned above. But what binds the external and internal together is something called *ch'êng* (usually translated as 'reality'). '*Ch'êng*,' the book says 'is the Tao (that is, the way) of heaven and *ch'êng* is also the Tao of mankind.' *Ch'êng* is the beginning and end of all beings and without *ch'êng* no being would exist. Teaching can transform *ch'êng* in men into lucidity and enlightenment and thus gives mankind the opportunity of recognizing the inner, secret course of the exterior world. 'Through the Way (Tao) of the highest reality (*ch'êng*) men can foreknow. When a country is about to flourish, there are bound to be omens of good. When it is about to perish, there are bound to be omens of evil fortune.'

This is one of the basic concepts of the Chinese mind and it gave rise to a number of 'scientific' methods whereby exact observation of phenomena in the heavens, on earth and in mankind enabled men to foretell the path of history.

In the last years of the Ch'un-ch'iu and during the Chan-kuo periods there were innumerable speculations of this kind which culminated in the doctrine of the five elements of water, fire, wood, metal and earth. These are the driving forces behind the motions of the universe, whose course they govern in a specific sequence.

This doctrine is expounded (perhaps for the first time) in the chapter '*Hung-fan*' ('great plan') of the *Shu Ching* (*Book of History*). And in the work of the philosopher Hsün-tzŭ, there is a comment to the effect that it was begun by Tzŭ-ssŭ and continued by Mêng-tzŭ. This is the basis of the hypothesis recently advanced by Chinese scholars (Yang Jung-kuo) that the *Hung-fan* chapter should perhaps even be attributed to Tzŭ-ssŭ.

The five elements may be said to be the active bases of a vast system of groups of five which recur through the length and breadth of the universe. Thus there are the five sensations of taste (salt, bitter, sour, sharp and sweet), the five human activities (demeanour, speech, sight, hearing and thought), the five measurements of time (the planet Jupiter [year], the moon [month], the sun [day], the points of the zodiac [double hours?] and the calendar reckonings [?]), the five atmospheric influences (rain, sunshine, heat, cold and wind), the five basic principles of human society (humanity, lawfulness, observance of ritual, wisdom and belief) and so on. We can see here the efforts made by Chinese philosophers to reduce the whole universe — man and the world around him, the external and the internal, the high and the low — to a common denominator, in this case the number five. Now the system of which these groups are part is concentrated round the 'majestic peak', which more or less corresponds to what was earlier called the 'centre'. But it is, in the last analysis, the 'son of heaven', who is meant and it depends on personal qualities whether the people receive a share of the five forms of happiness (long life, wealth, health, love of virtue and a good end to life) or the six (!) misfortunes: a short life, illness, worry, poverty, wickedness and weakness. The *Chung-yung* goes on to say: 'Thus it is that the Way of the true monarch is rooted and grounded in his own personality and proves itself in the eyes of the people . . .' (Tzŭ-ssŭ, trsl. Hughes.) In order to form his personality, the ruler is recommended to study the founding kings of the Hsia, Shang and Chou dynasties, to ground himself in heaven and earth, to present himself before the spirits of the ancestors and to wait for the appearance of the saints, which happens once every five hundred years. 'To present oneself before the spirits of the ancestors and not to doubt, that is to understand Heaven. If one can wait five hundred years for a sage man without doubting (him), that is to understand man.' In the interpretation of later Confucians this means that, because of his central position in the universe, the emperor is responsible by his conduct for the bad harvests and natural catastrophes by which heaven and earth signal their disapproval. When such misfortunes occur the emperor must mend his ways accordingly. And it is advisable for him to give ear to the counsels of old and wise ministers.

It was also in the work of Tzŭ-ssŭ that Confucius first came to be regarded as a divinity. The principal saint of this school, he was in the end placed 'on an equal footing with sun and moon'.

It is more than likely that the basic features of the doctrine of the elements were not an invention of the period of Tzŭ-ssŭ, that is, the second half of the fifth century B.C., but date from remoter ages of Chinese antiquity. They may have originated at the time when the ordinary people were gradually becoming aware that good harvests were not due to the intercessions by the (five) feudal lords (duke, prince, earl, baron and overlord) with the gods, but were the fruits of the earth; or, as the *Lu-yü* (*Discourses of the Land of Lu*) says, 'it is the five elements which generate growth.'

The teaching of Tzŭ-ssŭ was carried further by Mêng-tzŭ (Mêng K'o) who later became, next to Confucius, the principal exponent of Confucianism. He lived from *c.* 372 to 289 B.C. His teaching takes up the thread of the phrase quoted above, that a man should be 'guided by his nature', in the sense that he must turn inwards to himself and his true nature if he wishes to recognize what is right and significant. 'If there is something inadequate in our conduct, then in all such cases we turn round and look into ourselves.'[88] The natural consequence of this view is that human nature is basically good and that it is only necessary for a man to delve deeply enough into his own nature in order to recognize the good. 'The power man has without learning is the true [intuitive] power (*liang-hêng*), the knowledge that he has without thinking is the true [intuitive] knowledge (*liang-chih*).'[88] This concept of intuitive knowledge, especially, plays an important part in later Chinese philosophy.

The basic principles of humanity (*jên*), lawfulness, observance of ritual and wisdom are to be sought in the primal impulses of our nature. Pity, for example, is the source of love of mankind, being ashamed the source of lawfulness, reverence the source of ritual and the feeling for right and wrong the source of wisdom. Mêng-tzŭ's abrogation of the distinction between the inner and the outer world emerges from such utterances as: 'He that goes to the bottom of his heart knows his own nature: and knowing his own nature he knows Heaven.'[89]

The fundamental good in human nature is overlaid, however, by all kinds of superficial emotions and appetites which we experience in everyday life. Like the Taoists, Mêng-tzŭ concludes that the heart should not be moved by doubt and that the appetites should be eliminated. He recommends holding fast to the 'breath of night', that is to say, to the underlying principle of the heart which remains uninfluenced by any daily event. Another concept which emerged in this connection he called 'the breath which contains man's true nature' and is more or less the equivalent of Tzŭ-ssŭ's reality (*ch'êng*).

To examine the other important points of Mêng-tzŭ's teaching would take us beyond the scope of this book. I would, however, like to mention the 'democratic ideas' which make their appearance in his work. 'The people [*min*] rank highest, the spirits of land and corn come next, and the lord weighs least.'[90] This view reflected greatly altered social conditions. The people (*min*) were the subjects who had been freed from the domination of the feudal lords. These ideas were frequently raised in later times, with the result that at periods when the monarchy wielded totalitarian power (Ming period), Mêng-tzŭ's tablet was temporarily removed from the Confucian temple.

Despite the comment of Hsün-tzŭ quoted above, Mêng-tzŭ only hinted at the doctrine of the elements. It is treated at length, however, by Ts'ou Yen, another distinguished member of the academy by the Chi gate and a scholar greatly renowned in his own time.

Ts'ou Yen was a younger contemporary of Mêng-tzŭ, who also for a time belonged to the same academy. Unfortunately not a single fragment of his numerous works have survived and we know his ideas only from short accounts in other works.

Ts'ou Yen linked the doctrine of the elements with the course of history by maintaining that the beginning of a new dynasty was indicated by the activity of one of the elements. So, for example, before the Yellow Emperor entered upon his rule a vast number of earthworms and mole-crickets suddenly appeared, announcing the activity of the element of earth. In Yü's time certain plants survived the winter, a sign that the element of wood was in the ascendant. At the beginning of the Shang dynasty metal knives appeared in the water and at the beginning of the Chou a flame-coloured bird with a flame-coloured letter appeared, which suggested that the elements of metal and fire were active. Water must surely be the next to become active. As soon as the right signs appeared, according to this belief, the time would be ripe for the empire to be united under one dynasty. And sure enought the Ch'in dynasty, which followed the Chan-kuo period, was placed under the influence of water. Later on, however, when it was felt that a place should be found for Confucius the uncrowned king, the system was upset.

Soon, also, two opposing theories gained currency. According to one, the elements followed in succession, mutually generating one another; according to the other they mutually eliminated one another.

From now on each dynasty ruled in the sign of one of the elements and only for as long as this element was active; periods differed for the individual elements, but on the average activity lasted for five hundred years. And so we read in Mêng-tzŭ: 'Every five hundred years a true king (i.e. one who will found a dynasty) will arise . . . Now over seven hundred years have gone by and this number has been exceeded . . .'[91] It was thus high time for a new imperial dynasty to emerge.

One consequence of this theory was that all unusual natural phenomena were carefully observed, recorded and interpreted in the light of the doctrine of the elements. And up to the most recent times Chinese official historical compilations have contained sections entitled 'transactions concerning the five elements' which give records of this kind.

The doctrine of the elements was also combined with the two principles, *yang* (light, male) and *yin* (dark, female) which alternated as the year ran its course. Ts'ou Yen and his disciples were therefore also known as the Yin-Yang school. This school may be regarded as the foundation of the typical Chinese philosophy, with its characteristic view of the interplay of the universe and the human world. Among the achievements of the Yin-Yang school, which soon attracted all the others into its magic circle, just as the agricultural school (*nung-chia*) briefly mentioned above had done, were the annual plans and almanacs with reminders for farmers, careful calculations of lucky and unlucky days and so on, which have played an important part in Chinese life right up to the most recent times. Although this philosophy has undergone many critical modifications, its basic principles, *yin, yang* and the five elements, have never seriously been called in question until the present-day.

Ts'ou Yen, also for the first time, extended the narrow view of world geography held by the Chinese and described China, doubtless on the basis of information from foreign lands reaching

Ch'i (Shantung) by the sea-route, as but a small part of the world at large. He probably advocated, perhaps for the first time, a view which assumed the existence of a mysterious central mountain of the gods (K'un lun), from which four rivers of four different colours flowed into the sea, while a fifth stretch of water, yellow in colour, surrounded the mountain. This image of the world appears frequently in early Chinese literature, especially whenever the origin of the Huang-ho is mentioned; and it is closely associated with a fabulous geography, based partly on fantasy and partly on hearsay and fact, which finds expression in works such as the *Shan-hai-ching* (*Classical Book of Mountains and Seas*) and others.

Soon, however, criticism began to be levelled against the imaginative extravagances and mystical features with which these theories were surrounded. The critic in question was Hsün-tzŭ (whose actual name was Hsün K'uang or Hsün Ch'ing), who lived *c.* 313–238 B.C.

Hsün-tzŭ's criticism was also directed against the unthinking veneration paid to the former sage-kings, since only unreliable information about their characters and behaviour was available. He recommended instead that the 'later kings', meaning the outstanding rulers of more recent and more familiar times, should be taken as models. His maxim was: 'If you wish to know a thousand years, then consider (first) today', and 'by the near you can understand the far'.[92]

Hsün-tzŭ was certainly the most enlightened man of his age and was unencumbered by most of the superstitious opinions which were then regarded as firm knowledge. He did not, for example, believe that large men of pleasing appearance were destined more often than small men to a happy fate and great deeds or that rain could be produced by prayers.

What he understood by *t'ien* (heaven) is much the same as what we call nature.

> The fixed stars make their round; the sun and moon alternately shine; the four seasons come in succession; the Yin and Yang go through their great mutations; the wind and rain widely affect things; all things acquire their germinating principle,

> and are brought into existence; each gets its nourishing principle and develops to its completed state. We do not see the cause of these occurrences, but we do see their effects — this is what is meant by the word *shên*, spiritual.[93]

Despite the fact that the miraculous and the mystical have been eliminated, this statement clearly represents no challenge to the real foundations of the philosophy described above which was based on *yin* and *yang* and their permutations and changes.

It is noteworthy, however, that Hsün-tzŭ denied any connection between nature and the moral situation of mankind. Natural catastrophes were in his view unconnected with the good or bad behaviour of rulers and if anyone desired to take heaven as an example, he should emulate only its regularity and constancy.

Hsün-tzŭ was best known for his contention that man was, in the depths of his being, evil, an assertion that was diametrically opposed to that of Mêng-tzŭ. This view derives from his different conception of 'heaven'. Since the motions of heaven are purely mechanical and possess no ethical values, so it is impossible for man, by his nature — which he receives from heaven — to be 'good'. He is naturally adjusted to what is useful to him and to the desires stimulated by the action of his senses. Good habits and correct behaviour are only the results of teaching and laws. He makes very little distinction between laws and ritual (*li*). 'In ancient times the sage-kings knew that man's nature was evil, selfish, vicious, unrighteous, rebellious. For this reason they created ritual and morality, precepts, laws and standards in order to improve human nature and make it upright.'[94]

To these discussions on human nature, a third was added by Kao-tzŭ, the best known of Mêng-tzŭ's debating opponents. He propounded the view that human nature was neutral and flowed, like moving water, into any space laid open to it. These arguments prove beyond doubt that the old aristocratic class, whose members had been noble and good from birth solely by virtue of their social position, had lost some of its power and reputation. In its place, other classes were emerging and those who belonged to them had to show that they possessed, or else they had to acquire, the qualities which made for social success.

The theme of human nature continued for many centuries to be one of the most frequent topics of the philosophical discussions indulged in by those whose education equipped them for administrative posts and by the officials themselves. In later times the chief problem was often whether a man of nobly formed character (Confucian) or one with a great range of expert knowledge (Legalist) made the better official.

They formed the theoretical basis on which officialdom, using in particular the examination system which was gradually coming into being, fought their centuries-long battle against the aristocracy and feudalism.

The final outcome of these debates on human nature was a resurgence in the Sung period (A.D. 960–1279), the golden age of Chinese bureaucracy, of interest in philosophical speculation, and the establishment of schools which dominated Chinese intellectual life until modern times. The new trends chiefly consisted of the basic opinions of the Chan-kuo period supplemented and modified by ideas borrowed from Buddhism and the later developments of Taoism.

One of Hsün-tzŭ's disciples gained a position of special importance. This was Han Fei-tzŭ, scion of an aristocratic family and chief representative of Legalism (*fa-chia*). He advocated the elimination of useless members of society, by which presumably he meant primarily the former feudal lords who were now living on their lands as property-owners; alteration of the laws which were to take the place of the education fostered by the Confucians; and the general application of punishments, by means of which petty rulers were finally to be liquidated and political power grounded and centralized in the king.

The first emperor of the new Ch'in dynasty, Shih-huang-ti, intended to employ him in building up his state. But before he could do so, Han Fei-tzŭ was removed by the intrigues of Li Ssŭ, another disciple of Hsün-tzŭ and a Legalist, and died by poison in prison in the year 233 B.C.

By this time the Legalists were also split into several schools which varied according to whether their teaching laid most stress on the authority of the state and statesmanship or on the development and application of the laws.

It would perhaps be interesting at this point to trace the development of the old Chinese book of laws, which begins with short notes on the nature of the punishments and the principal crimes. Under each dynasty, however, numerous regulations, enactments, directives and suchlike were added and were from time to time collected in vast compilations. Each successive dynasty took over these works from its predecessor, altering them as occasion required.

The original clear-cut opposition between Confucians and Legalists, which came to a head in the first Han period, soon vanished and at the end of the second Han period we find well-known Confucians compiling large collections of laws. In spite of this, the law in China has never, even to this day, gained the standing and importance it enjoys, at least in theory, in the west. Chinese society has always included groups to which the law did not apply or applied only to a limited extent. Another essential feature is that in the lower strata of society the enactment of laws, like every other governmental measure, depended largely on the activities of wide-reaching civil supervisory organizations with collective responsibility, compulsory denunciation and so on, as is the case today in Soviet Russia and its satellite states.

5. LANGUAGE AND POETRY

The great upheavals of the Ch'un-ch'iu and Chan-Kuo periods had repercussions in other spheres of Chinese civilization. Among other things, they caused a marked change in the literary language. It is possible that what was happening then is to some extent comparable with the development in this sphere which has taken place in recent times.

We may think of the ancient Chinese literary language more or less as follows: for groups of words — such as act, acts, to act, acting, active, acted, etc. — a single character was often used;

depending upon its position in the sequence of characters forming the sentence, this character represented a meaning of the root word which the reader had more or less to deduce from the sense. The ancient Chinese spoken language probably also comprised stems to which different shades of meaning and different functions in the sentence could be given by varying the pronunciation. Thus, for example, Karlgren believes that characters such as the ancient Chinese *ngịo* (modern Chinese *wo*) and *'ngâ* (modern Chinese *wu*), both of which represent the first person of the personal pronoun, stand for the different cases (I, to or for me, me (accusative)). There are other examples — such as *k'an* (modern Chinese *k'an*) = to see, *kian* (modern Chinese *chien*) = to see, to visit and *g'ian* (modern Chinese *hsien*) = to make its appearance — in which different characters for the various meanings of the same stem have survived to the present-day. We may conclude from this that in ancient times different characters were used to represent the different words of a group of this kind, if this seemed desirable for the sake of greater intelligibility and of precise definition of the thought. Thus today there are still different characters for the different aspects of negation, which is one of the most important of all linguistic phenomena; these include *pwöt* (modern Chinese *pu*) = not, *piwöt* (modern Chinese *fu*) = cannot, *b'iwöt* (modern Chinese *fu* or *fou*) = to say no, *piwör* (modern Chinese *fei*) = is not, and so on. But it also sometimes happened that no new character was created for a given concept but an existing one representing the same or a similar sound used. A well-known example is the character for wheat-ear, *lög* (*lai*), which was used for the phonetically identical word *lög* = to come and has survived in the latter sense only.

Whatever the exact situation may have been, we can be fairly certain that the ancient Chinese literary language represented only a selection of apposite words borrowed from the vocabulary of the spoken language. And although at first the reader probably used the root word in a phonetic variation which depended on the sense of the sentence, the character gradually came always to be reproduced with the same — and the simplest — sound. This amounts to much the same as if we were to reduce the sentence 'the boy eats a piece of bread' to the root syllables 'boy eat bread'.

We have already referred to the fact that writing in ancient times was in the hands of a small circle of professionals (priestly scribes), who passed on the use of the characters and their development from one generation to the next. By the first Chou period this had already produced a literary style which was so far removed from the spoken language that only experts could interpret it correctly.

The proliferation of studies initiated by Confucius and the emergence of the different schools of philosophy made considerably greater demands on the expressional powers of the literary language. This, of course, meant that the number of characters greatly increased. New characters were often created, now as in earlier times, by combining an element conveying a meaning with a phonetic element. The elements conveying meanings finally totalled five hundred and forty. It is true to say that they represent the main categories of the numerous objects of the human environment which were absorbed into the literary language, and it was thanks to them that it later became possible to arrange the characters in lexicographical order. In the course of time their number was reduced to two hundred and fourteen.

At the same time, changed circumstances caused efforts to be made to transform the literary language altogether in order to bring literary style into line with the language spoken in educated circles. And, indeed, even those who have read but little of the ancient literature can easily see that the language of the authentic old chapters of the *Shu Ching* (*Book of History*) is markedly different from that of the *Lun Yü* or of the work attributed to Mo Ti.

A feature of the new literary language was the introduction of an increasing number of 'empty characters' or particles which articulated and modified the thought-content of a sentence. This can be seen as a consequence of the fact that social groups who did not belong to the narrow circle of the old professional writers had adopted literary expression but not the traditional stylistic handling of the characters that went with it; and that the literary language had already imposed such uniformity on the sound that linguistic aids had to be interpolated to make the writing intelligible to the reader.

During the Chan-kuo period, the new literary language supplanted the old, which survived only here and there as a mannered official style and occasionally made its appearance in the literature of the time. The *Tso Chuan*, which is in all probability based upon earlier sources, presents historical events in the markedly livelier style of the Chan-Kuo literary manner and is thus certainly a rendering of the substance of earlier works and documents in the new expressional form.

If the literary language now took a turn towards what might be termed the 'popular', this applies equally to the art of poetry.

The leading poet of the time was Ch'ü Yüan (*c.* 343–277 B.C.) who held the position of minister in the powerful southern state of Ch'u. In this capacity he endeavoured, under the leadership of Ch'u, to organize the opposition of the provinces against the aspiring western state but was deposed as a result of intrigues. He was a fanatical patriot and, following the defeat of his state, is said to have ended his life by drowning himself in the River Milo.

The adoption of a popular style which marks his poetry has its parallel in the sphere of music. A clear indication of this is to be found in an anecdote in the work of Mêng-tzŭ. Mêng-tzŭ asked King Hsüan of Chi: 'I have heard that the king loves music. Is it so?' The king changed colour and said: 'I cannot appreciate the music of the former kings. I love only the ordinary music of our day.'[95]

The 'music of the former kings' is, of course, the classical music to which the songs and odes of the *Shih Ching* were recited on solemn state occasions. There are grounds for believing that it was largely based on percussion instruments and that it therefore consisted in the main of rhythmic tinkling sounds and drumbeats underlining the shrill voices of the singers.

But in the fifth century B.C. another form of music, derived from popular sources and using largely wind and stringed instruments, began to appear. We also learn, for example, that the same King Hsüan organized concerts in which three hundred musicians played in consort on bamboo flutes without any accompanying voices. In comparison with the ancient music which must, indeed, have been somewhat harsh and unmelodious, intended as it mainly was to build up and stiffen morale, this represented an unprecedented change.

Literary works, however, criticized the new music for being enervating, insipid, wistfully sentimental and decadent. And it may not be too fanciful to associate both the new verse rhythm,[96] with its irregular alternation of five-and eight-word lines, invented by Ch'ü Yüan, and the frequently sentimental substance of his principal poem — the celebrated *Li sao* (On Encountering Sorrow) — with the poignant, sentimental character of the new flute music.

> Hearing a long sigh, I brush away my tears.
> Grieving for man's life, so beset with hardships.

The main theme of the poem is an account of how the poet, who would 'rather quickly die and meet dissolution' than live as his contemporaries do, sets out to wander through 'all the world's quarters'. He circles the heavens until at last he alights and 'gazed on a jade tower's glittering splendour'. It was here that the Taoist goddess, Hsi-wang-mu ('Royal mother of the west') was wont to gather the immortals round her. And indeed he sees there a lovely maiden who has remained behind from the household of a legendary empress. He sends a bird to pay court to her. Finally the poet, riding in a chariot of jade and ivory, suddenly sees his former home in the distance. The chariot-driver's heart grows heavy and the horses refuse to go on. But the end is:

> *Envoi.*
> Enough! There are no true men in the state: no
> one to understand me.
> Why should I cleave to the city of my birth?

And with that the poet finally makes off to the abode of the genii.

It should be noted that the imaginary world of the poet's travels is similar to the image of the world described in connection with Ts'ou Yen; it must therefore by this time have become a general intellectual stock-in-trade and it undoubtedly served as background to numerous fantastic travellers' tales.

It is likely that, with the change in music, new types of dance also came into being. In the classical dances which formed part of the religious celebrations in the ancestral temples there were probably usually between two and eight rows of dancers, with eight dancers in each row (the number varied according to the rank of the court in question). The dancers took up different positions keeping time with the music and the whole effect must have been rather like that of modern gymnastic displays. The dancers waved pheasant feathers or whisks, and in some cases probably accompanied themselves on the flute. There were other, perhaps more popular, dances, in which two groups of masked dancers stood opposite one another; there were also exorcistic dances, performed by young men in black tunics and red shirts, which were intended to banish plagues and bring on the rains, and dances performed by men and women shamans to invoke spirits.

The dances of these women especially appear to have become more and more fashionable, with the result that clever female dancers, forgetting the magical purposes of their art, were now able to make careers for themselves at the courts.

The highly sentimental new music, combined with the erotic romanticism evoked by the female dancers and an imagination which loved to dally in the strange and colourful realms of fairies, genii and spirits, engendered a court culture which had little or nothing to do with the ideal of the old Confucians.

VI

The Chʻin and Han Dynasties

I. THE WESTERN STATE OF THE CHʻIN

The unification of the empire was finally and forcibly accomplished by the western state of Chʻin. Although the family tree of its ruling house connects it with the legendary emperors of China, Shun and Yü, from whom the forbears of the Chʻin are supposed to have acquired the clan name of Ying, this cannot disguise the fact that the Chʻin were outsiders and ruled over a population (Tibetans?) which showed marked ethnic differences from the population of the empire.

The legendary part of the pre-history of the Chʻin state contains clear suggestions that this was in the main a race of cattle and horse breeders and it is possible that its military successes were due in part to the use of cavalry. It also appears that the well-known story of the travels of the Chou king, Mu, originated in Chʻin, for the coach-driver, Tsao-fu, with his four famous horses, is also regarded as an ancestor of the ruling house. The main purpose of the story was probably to popularize the link with this foreign country in the west and to fix the earliest possible date for its beginning. It is also significant that Shih-huang-ti, the first Chʻin emperor, was well known as a horse-fancier and owned seven celebrated horses with names like 'Catcher of the Wind', 'White Hare', 'Tracker of Shadows' and so on.

Chronological historical recording is believed to have begun in Chʻin in about 753 B.C. From about 655 B.C. the western state gradually began to be drawn into the political sphere of the imperial states, doubtless because it was needed as a political counterweight to the up-and-coming hegemony of Chin (more or less corresponding to Shansi). But in about 360 B.C. Ch'in was still looked upon by the princes of the empire as a foreign and 'barbarian' country.

It was only the thoroughing social reforms instigated in about 356 B.C. by the Legalist, Wei Yang, who had moved there from the empire, which transformed Ch'in into a modern state. Thereafter it soon became a danger to the other states.

Wei Yang also raised the ritual and customs of Ch'in to the level of the Chinese states, which at that time were the ones which set the tone. Ch'in had no doubt always somewhat lagged behind in this respect, although its rulers certainly endeavoured to the best of their ability to emulate the central empire. Thus, for example, it was not until 384 B.C. that the custom was abandoned of burying many of his ministers, wives and servants — in one case these numbered nearly eighty — with a deceased prince; whereas following the rise of Confucius this custom appears gradually to have fallen into disuse in the empire. It seems also that the Ch'in were guided less by the ritual of the Chou than by the more ancient ritual of the Shang.

As a result of the reforms, Ch'in, originally the most backward of the states, gradually became the most advanced.

In particular, the social organization carried through by Wei Yang was superior to all the others. Most of the states of the time were weakened from within by conflict between the new landowners and the old feudal lords. It was, of course, the fiefs of the latter which were affected by the seizure of land and the lords themselves were increasingly forced into the position of ordinary landowners.

In the cities there was, moreover, a growing body of officials, as well as merchants and master-craftsmen. The rivalry between these social classes was a matter not only of the possession of property and land but also of labour. The old feudal lords, in other words, were being deprived not only of their fiefs but of their subjects as well. These now found employment as workers, particularly in the iron-foundries; they also became servants to the merchants (Lü Pu-wei is said to have had nearly ten thousand men in his employ), domestic servants to the officials and agricultural labourers to the new landowners. Labour markets were growing up in the cities and supplied anyone who could afford it with labour or with servants whose only duty was to see to their employer's comfort.

These social changes did not, of course, take place without opposition from those whose position they damaged. Thus a certain amount of unrest was to be found in most of the states, in addition to numerous elements who were discontented with the old conditions — a situation which in all probability aided the political aims of the Ch'in. Ch'in itself was enjoying a measure of social stability as a consequence of certain radical reforms, which Ssŭ-ma Ch'ien, the historian of the Han period summed up as follows: 'The high and low ranks were fixed, each according to its function (in the state), registered possessions, servants and clothing were graded according to family-groups (*chia*).'

This means that social positions, of which the two highest corresponded to the high nobility, were attained not on grounds of birth but as recompense for (military) achievements. And only those members of the clan of the ruling house who had distinguished themselves in army service were placed on the register of kinsfolk. From the second part it is evident that certain limits were set to the amassing of wealth. Both of these were familiar practices by which the Legalists sought to stabilize social conditions and secure the position of the monarch.

A hundred years later, at the time of Lü Pu-wei, Wei Yang's strict organization — to which opposition began with the death of those princes who had favoured his policy — had probably considerably weakened and could be evaded by those with power and resources. Several of the later rulers favoured their relatives without regard to the law, in the manner advocated by Confucius. Lü Pu-wei was not himself a Legalist but an Eclectic.

In the social conflict of the time, Ch'in came down firmly on the side of the innovators and, in particular, on the side of the rising landowners. It strengthened the 'root', as the expression was, of the life of the people, that is the rural economy. One of the measures which marked this policy was that the first action, when a city had been newly conquered, was to 'free' the 'convicts' — persons whose misdeeds had rendered them liable to forced labour without remuneration — and evacuate them from the city. Most of them were probably resettled and used as agricultural labourers. Scions of the nobility and the master-craftsmen, with their often numerous dependants, were also deported in these circumstances, though this was, of course, not in order to 'free' them but to clean up the unstable, rebelliously inclined elements of the newly conquered territory.

It appears that the new landowners, like the wholesale merchants, favoured the establishment of the unitary state. One of their main reasons was undoubtedly the fact that the irrigation systems which had been set up in the states along the Huang-ho were interconnected and it was possible for one state to drain off its neighbours' water or to set up dams to flood them. As the *Chan-kuo ts'ê (Intrigues of the Warring States)* says, 'when the fields in east Chou had been cultivated for harvest', the district of 'west Chou did not release the waters' or that 'as a result of the dams in the eastern state of Ch'i being blocked the waters rose in the western states of Chao and Wei.'[1] In order to safeguard the produce of the land, it was therefore desirable to bring the dyke and irrigation systems under a single administration.

Furthermore, the states whose northern boundaries marched with the lands of the nomadic peoples (Huns) had to withdraw a large section of their population from agricultural work and set them to defending the state against attack. This circumstance provided an additional reason for union and combined defence plans.

As a western state largely devoted to cattle-raising, Ch'in was far less involved in these difficulties and, indeed, profited from them in the conflicts over unification. Ch'in became the champion of the monarchist, anti-feudal unitary state. The *Lü-shih ch'un-ch'iu (Spring and Autumn Annals of Lü Pu-wei)* written by order of Lü Pu-wei by the wandering scholars gathered in Ch'in, says: 'The house of Chou has fallen and the Son of Heaven is deposed. Confusion is never greater than when there is no Son of Heaven.' 'When there is no Son of Heaven, the stronger overcomes the weaker, the mass oppresses the individual, with weapons, men inflict injuries upon one another and there is no peace.'[2] But the only possible new son of heaven was the king of Ch'in.

2. THE UNITED EMPIRE UNDER CH'IN SHIH-HUANG-TI

Shih-huang-ti, whose ordinary name was Chêng, was the first emperor of the united empire and the son of King Chuang-hsiang. Not originally destined to succeed to the throne, he was dwelling in the state of Chao as hostage for Ch'in. (It was part of the political usage of the time for members of the ruling house to be sent to other states as surety for good relations on both sides, and to guarantee that agreements were honoured.) It was only through the machinations of the merchant, Lü Pu-wei, who saw great business advantages in it, that Chuang-hsiang and later his son, a minor at the time, came to the throne.

Shih-huang-ti proved to be an extremely powerful personality. He has been described — not altogether flatteringly — as having large eyes, a prominent nose, the breast of a bird of prey, the voice of a jackal and the heart of a tiger.

His first action, after he was declared of age in the year 238 B.C., was to remove the dowager empress's powerful and rebellious lover. In the conflicts which developed within the palace, great assistance was afforded the young king by the eunuchs, who now made their first appearance as staunch supporters of the throne. Even the all-powerful minister, Lü Pu-wei, became involved and was forthwith dismissed by the young emperor. His numerous followers were deported after his death in the year 235 B.C.

This meant, in fact, the end of a state policy based on political eclecticism and large-scale trading interests. The emperor, who now had full power in his own hands, leant from then onwards on the Legalists, who found a celebrated champion in the minister, Li Ssŭ. By setting in motion large-scale espionage and sabotaging activities, Li Ssŭ hastened the break-up of the other provinces. In the year 221 B.C. Ch'i, the last asylum of the old aristocracy, was overthrown and the whole empire united under Ch'in Shih-huang-ti.

He at once set to work to implement the plans for more modern and far-reaching development put forward by his Legalist advisers. Most assistance was again given to 'the root', or agriculture. The inscription on a tablet set up by Shih-huang-ti in Shantung reads: 'It is the Emperor's merit . . . to have increased agriculture and to have deferred trade and commerce. The black-haired ones (the new designation for the common people) are happy.'[3] There are many passages recording how he resettled sections of the population and embarked upon the cultivation of new ground. When this happened, the new settlers were released from compulsory work for twelve years. The fiefs of the small feudal lords were finally abolished and the empire was divided into regions and districts subject to a central administration. 'Enfeoffments' persisted but they now meant only that a deserving man was given the benefit of a fixed, localized revenue.

On the initiative of the emperor, units of measurement, money, the gauge of vehicles and the laws were standardized for the empire at large. In the face of vigorous opposition from scholars, he also introduced a new and simplified script. A great, continuous wall, supplementing existing border defences, was built to secure the northern frontier, and great highways opened up the imperial lands.

Curiously enough, as it emerges from a few of his surviving inscriptions, he seems to have followed the Confucians in setting great store by the moral behaviour of his subjects and the strict segregation of men and women. He himself, however, had in his palaces close on a thousand ladies brought there by conscription and, as their titles show, graded into ranks. By this date there were already court entertainments given by actors, jugglers and singers. And from this time dates what must certainly be the earliest romance of its kind, the *Ch'in hui yao*. It is the story, told in a melodramatic manner, of the lives of young and beautiful maidens who had been wrested from their families and brought to court. It tells how the musician T'u Mên-Kao saw these court ladies at a wine-party in the palace, and seized his zither to serenade them. His playing grew so passionate that the instrument broke in his hands and he had to continue his recital on a fresh one. His song ended something like this:

With cloud-like dishevelled hair
They climb the high-stacked terraces.
Their eyes follow the paths winding far away.
Thus they walk tirelessly to and fro
And at last go down to the palace again.[4]

It is also recorded that the emperor had more than twenty off-spring and that at his burial all the court ladies who had remained childless were buried with him.

This shows that the emperor did not come within the jurisdiction of the laws or of his own edicts and commands. He stood in all respects above them. Shih-huang-ti also liked whenever possible to intervene in law-suits, so that it is only possible to speak with reservations of the impartial application of the law.

Just as he stood beyond the reach of the law, so Shih-huang-ti stood outside and above the rest of mankind. This is shown by the very fact that he adopted the designation *ti*, which, as we have already seen, was the title of the deified Shang rulers. His whole title means 'the first divine emperor'. The word *huang* (divine) was a predicate which it had previously been usual to ascribe only to three popular Taoist divinities of the land of Ch'i (north Shantung): 'the divine one of heaven', 'the divine one of earth' and the 'highest divine one' (*t'ai-huang*).

To have brought the empire together under a single ruler was an achievement surpassing all those of former kings, including the deified kings of legend; and a man who held the whole vast territory in such absolute thrall as did Shih-huang-ti was, in the opinion of the time, fully justified in considering himself closely associated with the gods and in naming himself accordingly. In the year of the unification of the empire (221 B.C.) Shih-huang-ti also granted his dead father the title of *T'ai-shang-huang* ('all-highest divine one'), which clearly recalls the *Shang-ti* of the Shang and may mean that he also had the idea of providing the dynasty with the religious roots of a divine ancestry.

The, undoubtedly serious, efforts he made to enter into personal relationship with the gods of his own time are highly significant. With this end in view, he surrounded himself with a host of expert counsellors whose mission was to help him to become an immortal. Among these learned men an important part was played by magicians from the former state of Ch'i, where belief in miracles was particularly deeply entrenched and received constant nourishment from rumours of the existence of lands beyond the sea.

The magicians declared that a certain herb growing on the Island of the Gods in the Eastern Sea would bring immortality. It happened in the time of Shih-huang-ti that a number of corpses were found on a track in a hunting-reserve. Suddenly a bird, like a crow, appeared bearing in its beak a plant which it laid upon the faces of the dead men. They stood up forthwith, having come to life again. The emperor ordered an enquiry to be made and a wise man, 'Sir Devil's Vale', was found, who declared that the plant was an antidote to death which grew on an island in the Northern Sea.

These tales of miracles concerning 'islands of the gods' made their appearance at about the beginning of the fourth century B.C. Shih-huang-ti immediately ordered a certain Hsü Shih (or Fu) to fit out an expedition to journey to this wonderland, where, it was said, all creatures, including beasts and birds, were pure white and where there were palaces and gates made of gold and silver.

After a time, Hsü Shih returned and reported that he had encountered a god in the sea who had asked him if he were an envoy of the king of Ch'in. Replying in the affirmative, he went on to explain to the god that he was searching for the herb that would prolong life. To this the god replied, 'The introductory offering of your king of Ch'in is very meagre. It will therefore be granted to you to see the herb but not to possess it.' The god then directed him south-eastwards to the island of P'êng-lai, where in front of a palace, he encountered an envoy with a face of copper and the body of a dragon, whose brilliance was reflected in the sky. The envoy informed him that in exchange for the herb of life he required a hundred youths and maidens of good family and a hundred artisans.

Shih-huang-ti immediately ordered another expedition to be fitted out. This one went to sea with a cargo of grain and never returned, for the sailors, it is said, found flat fertile land and settled there. (Some scholars believe that Japan was the site of these first Chinese overseas colonies.)

The emperor was later informed that a great fish barred the approaches to the Island of the Gods. Thereupon, so the story goes, Shih-huang-ti himself shot at the fish from a stone breakwater built thirty miles out to sea, 'so that the sea turned red with blood'. In spite of everything, he failed to obtain the herb of long life. In the year 212 B.C., however, a master-magician named Lu gave different advice. Lu declared that the emperor's efforts were being counteracted by evil influences; and that magical precepts stated that the evil influences could be avoided if the emperor would conceal his movements for a time. Then, perhaps, a 'real man' (i.e. a Taoist at the highest stage of perfection) would come to him.

> It is displeasing to the gods that everybody knows where the ruler is sojourning. A real man, however, is one who can go through water without getting wet, can walk through fire and remain unburnt, can ascend to the clouds and endure as long as heaven and earth . . . I should like no one to be permitted to know in which palace the ruler is sojourning. Then it might be possible to obtain the herb of immortality.[5]

To this Shih-huang-ti replied: 'I wish to be a real man.' In the neighbourhood of his capital Hsien-yang he had two hundred and seventy palaces built, all interconnected by underground or concealed passages and filled with gongs, drums, beautiful maidens and servants. These persons had always to remain in the same building. If anyone so much as hinted at the whereabouts of the emperor at a given moment he was punished by death.

In fact it once happened that the emperor saw from a palace window that one of his ministers possessed a suite of excessive size and he commented upon this to those around him. When, shortly afterwards, the minister cut down the number of his carriages and horsemen, the emperor had all those executed who were with him when he had spoken because they had given away his whereabouts.

The emperor's 'secret movements' also took him outside the palace precincts and he used to walk incognito among the people of his capital. Escapades of this kind persisted under later dynasties and became a favourite amusement of the Chinese emperors.

It is recorded that during an outing of this kind in the year 216 B.C. when, walking in the streets of Hsien-yang accompanied by only four men of his bodyguard, the emperor was molested by bandits. But his attackers were driven off and a police action against crime was subsequently carried through.

The great journeys undertaken by the emperor to all parts of his empire are probably also connected with his god-like nature. It has already been shown that to roam freely in all the countries of the world was a special privilege of those who had contrived to prolong their lives at will.

It came to such a point that it was forbidden to mention death and mortality in the presence of Shih-huang-ti, who emulated the gods even in his dress; also that on one of his travels he punished a local deity, whom he held responsible for an unfavourable wind, by felling all the trees on the mountain and having it painted red; just as, at that time, certain crimes were punished by castrating the criminal and marking him with red paint.

3. ARCHITECTURE AND CRAFTS

The building enterprises mentioned above were by no means the only ones undertaken by the emperor, who was extremely lavish in this respect also, and whose reign must have seen a great flowering of architecture. Not only in the neighbourhood of the capital, but throughout the territories he traversed, he had buildings of all kinds put up, including pavilions, terraces commanding fine views and so on. It is said that on his instructions nearly three hundred 'palaces' were built inside the passes (that is to say, surrounding the capital but at some distance from it) and in the rest of the empire about four hundred were built.

The buildings in the neighbourhood of Hsien-yang, for which the wood was brought from great distances, must have been on a very large scale. In their lay-out the emperor apparently sought to imitate the principal constellations, so that his dwelling-places also should as far as possible resemble those of the gods. All the palaces were interconnected by underground passages and roadways, and paths protected by walls led to points of vantage in the nearby hills. So, separated from his subjects and behind high walls, Shih-huang-ti dwelt like an emperor in a fairy-tale in the strange environment devised for him by the imagination of his time. It is also possible that his enterprises represented a grandiose attempt to translate into realistic terms the imaginative world of Ch'ü Yüan and the legends of the gods then current in popular religion. It is no wonder that his person came later to be surrounded by an aura of legend and marvellous anecdotes.

The emperor's burial-place on the Li mountain (Shensi), or more properly speaking, the permanent residence which he hoped to occupy when he departed from the general view, was naturally of especial magnificence. Seven hundred thousand convicts were engaged for ten years in building it. The chamber which was to house the sarcophagus was given a copper floor to protect it from rising damp and was faced with lacquer to prevent decay. A reproduction of the palaces and administrative buildings and a relief map of the empire, in which waterways and seas were represented by quicksilver, were also put into the tomb. The underground chambers were lit by pearls which shone in the dark and represented the sun and moon in an artificial heaven and by innumerable lamps fed by fish oil. All the entrances to the burial-place were defended by long-bows and cross-bows which were mechanically released and shot automatically at all intruders.

Despite these precautions, Shih-huang-ti's tomb, which might have conveyed to later ages an impression of ancient craftsmanship at its zenith, was broken into a few years after his death and completely plundered.

There were many other objects besides the burial-place which might have testified to the excellence of Ch'in art. Among such celebrated pieces were the twelve bronze figures after the model of a gigantic Tibetan (?), which the emperor had cast from weapons collected from the Chan-kuo states. They were set up as doorkeepers before the gates of palaces. Each of these figures weighed 240,000 Chinese pounds and bore the inscription, 'In the 26th year of his reign the divine emperor unified the empire, divided it into regions, set the laws to rights and standardized measurements . . . Written by Li Ssŭ.' The last of these figures was melted down during the political troubles at the end of the fifth century A.D.

There was also a group of musicians consisting of twelve metal figures grouped round a bamboo mat who were set in motion by cords and played different instruments, and other marvels as well.

4. RELIGIOUS CHANGES

The Ch'in dynasty was also the first to be run, in some degree, on 'scientific' principles. This means that the implications of the doctrine of the elements were applied.

It was established that the Chou had ruled in the sign of fire. The Ch'in, therefore, stood in the sign of the element which could not be overcome by fire. That element was water. The colour of water was black and so the official vestments, flags and ensigns of the Ch'in were black. The number of water was six. The officials' tablets used in public life, and the head-dresses of the officials were therefore six inches in length, the carriages were six paces in length, a team of horses numbered six animals and so on. The river Huang-ho was renamed 'Virtue water' (Tê-shui).

Later, as opposition to the emperor grew in consequence of his vast building enterprises and their excessive demands upon the labour potential of the people, the element of water also abandoned him. In the year 211 B.C., a commissar entered Shih-huang-ti's presence and handed him a jade ring which he said had been given him by an unknown man as he journeyed by night; the man had enjoined him to give the ring to the emperor and to tell him that the 'ancestor-dragon' would die that very year. The emperor recognized the ring at once. He had sacrificed it eight years before to the river-god of the Yangtze. This shows that the opposition to the Ch'in was strongest in the former southern states. When he saw the ring, Shih-huang-ti fell silent and sorrowful. He knew that the name 'ancestor-dragon' signified the pinnacle of mankind, or in other words Shih-huang-ti himself.

The adoption by the dynasty of a religious position governed by the doctrine of the elements, naturally represented a clear invasion of the privileges of the Confucian school of ritual, which, if assertions by its own members are to be believed, had monopolized official religion under the Chou. It is, however, not certain to what extent the situation recorded in the classics of the ritualist school corresponds with the true conditions of the period.

In my opinion, the official sacrifice, at any rate, which developed in the Ch'in united empire and in the first Han period, was at least as important an influence on the subsequent formation of the Chinese state-religion as were the classics of the ritualist school, however vigorous the attempts made in later times to establish these as the only model.

An indication of the rivalry existing between the doctrine of the elements and the ritualist school, and of the line victory which ensued, is to be found in the great encyclopaedia of the Sung period, the *T'ai-p'ing yü-lan*. This states: 'After they took power, the Ch'in did away with the ritualist teaching and the garments for all the state sacrifices were uniformly black'[6] (i.e., precisely in accordance with the precepts of the doctrine of the elements).

A fact which makes it a little difficult to place the emergence of the doctrine of the elements in its historical setting is that, according to records in the *Shih Chi*, sacrifices were being offered in the state of Ch'in as early as about 770 B.C. to a certain 'white emperor'. According to this doctrine, white was the colour of the west and this 'white emperor' could, therefore, have been one of the five emperors of the elements; if this were true it would push the origin and dissemination of the doctrine far back into antiquity.

In this instance, however, the colour white may have a different significance. Among the nomadic peoples of the north-west, to whom the Ch'in also originally belonged, white had been connected since ancient times with the beasts sacrificed to their god. It is therefore possible that white, the colour of the west, was later absorbed into the doctrine of the elements but that it was not the doctrine itself which attributed it to the west.

As far as the state religion established by the Ch'in is concerned, it appears that, in contrast to the Chou, ancestor-worship was replaced by sacrifices to non-ancestral gods. This was part and parcel of the change in policy by which, as explained above, the Ch'in sought not, as the Chou had done, an empire united under an ancestor-worship common to all princes and based on the ruling clan, but a military rule founded on modernized agrarian conditions. Ancestor-worship was in any case impracticable for the Ch'in kings, since they had only recently attained to that position and their forbears had been mere servants of the Chou ancestors.

It has already been shown that, in contrast to the Chou, who could trace their ancestors far back into antiquity, Shih-huang-ti had the idea of setting himself up as the divine forbear of future generations. This no doubt explains why one of his first measures in connection with ancestor-worship was to forbid the granting of temple-names to rulers, for these names were granted to the dead in the light of outstanding qualities which he considered implied undesirable criticism.

He also probably abolished the custom of 'appointing impersonators of the corpse', as practised in the imperial states. Shih-huang-ti, indeed, appears to have had no thought of maintaining the solidarity of the clan in the manner advocated by the Confucians. He was reproached with the fact that while he himself possessed the whole empire his descendents were mere subjects. In fact the security of the monarchy, which had in earlier times been assured by members of the clan occupying the most important fiefs, was now guaranteed by universal application of the laws and by the concentration of power that went with this.

But this new, previously untried, system lasted only for as long as the execution of the laws was controlled by a ruler with as powerful a personality as Shih-huang-ti. As soon as his successor came to the throne, power fell into the hands of the Legalist and eunuch, Chao Kao, who soon showed himself incapable of asserting the authority of the laws against the growing reaction of the feudalists.

The form of the ancestor-worship was also considerably altered by Shih-huang-ti's proscription of the classical Confucian works because they 'exalted the old and belittled the new'. Among these was the *Shih Ching* (*Book of Songs*), the verses of which, with their musical accompaniment, were indispensable to the celebration of ancestor-worship.

As befitted his opinions, the emperor commissioned the scholars around him to compose songs about gods and genii and about his journeys, which he then had set to music and performed by his court musicians. A new form of music had to be created for the new religious policy.

The state-religion in the Ch'in empire centred round the gods who influenced the yield of the harvests. One particular innovation seems to have been that a large number of star-gods came to be venerated. The official deities were collectively referred to as 'the eight gods'. Among them were a lord of heaven, a lord of earth, lords of *yin* and *yang*, as well as gods of the moon, the sun, the seasons and so on. In addition to these, spirits and gods of important mountains and rivers were venerated, as they had been in the old Chou states. And certain facts show that the Ch'in emperor was not in all and every case the fanatical opponent of the Confucians he is usually regarded as having been. For in the year 219 B.C., while travelling in the eastern regions, he took special counsel with the scholars of Lu, who were, of course, the chief representatives of Confucianism, as to how to set up such local sacrifices.

In order that agriculture should benefit, it was, of course, desirable to maintain the closest possible connections with all these nature-gods. To this end, a retinue of three hundred scholars was kept at the Ch'in court charged with making the most minute observations of the emanations of the stars and their influence on terrestrial events.

The overall impression of the Ch'in period is thus that an entirely new mentality was in the ascendant, one which had broken through the narrow framework of ancestor-worship based on the clan community and was endeavouring to apply the theory of the microcosm-macrocosm, derived from Taoist sources, to the practical organization and orientation of the people and the state.

5. THE HAN DYNASTY

The Han dynasty was founded by Liu Pang who bore seventy-two black marks on his left thigh — a lucky number. (72 = one-fifth of 360.) He started life as a small local functionary of the Ch'in civil surveillance system, in a hamlet in the neighbourhood of present-day Hsü-chou (north Kiangsu).

He came to the throne in the wake of a popular rebellion against the Ch'in which ended by becoming largely a reaction of the deposed nobility against the absolute monarchy of Shih-huang-ti.

Since Liu Pang owed his success to the intervention of the old aristocracy, he endeavoured to restore to them what they had lost under the Ch'in. The situation soon, therefore, came to resemble the feudal system which had existed in the Chan-kuo period. His successors also broke with the agrarian policy of the deposed dynasty and, flouting warnings from the Confucians, supported commerce and trade.

The first three Han emperors ruled in the spirit of the *laissez-faire* policy of the Huang-Lao school. The emperors took no part, or only a limited part, in the affairs of the feudal kings.

It was not until the accession of the emperor, Hsiao-wu-ti (141–87 B.C.), a strong and dynamic personality like Shih-huang-ti, that the united empire was re-established and the fiefs transformed into dependencies. The change this time, however, was neither instigated nor planned by the Legalists but was due to the influence of the Confucians.

One of its chief champions was Tung Chung-shu from Kuang-chou (176–104 B.C.), who had many discussions with the emperor and converted him to his views.

The form of Confucianism which now made its appearance in the political arena differed from that of the Chan-kuo period, although there can be no doubt that it developed from the teachings of Tzŭ-ssŭ and Mêng-tzŭ. The most remarkable thing about it was its fusion with the Yin-Yang and five elements doctrine, from which it derived an unequivocally mystical and religious character. It was now that Confucius came to be seen as the 'uncrowned king' (*su-wang*), who had been prevented only by unfavourable states of the elements from actually uniting the empire in his own hands. The *Ch'un-ch'iu* and its commentary the *Tso-chuan* was now studied, with particular attention to every feature which could be interpreted as a favourable or unfavourable sign for the course of politics. Observation and interpretation of these signs soon became one of the main concerns of the reign.

Yin and *yang* were now generally and officially recognized as the basic forces of the universe and their motions conceived as the cause of every change in heaven and on earth: they were guided in their interplay by the annual course of the sun. Each of the four seasons stands under the influence of an emperor of the elements. Each of these resides in one of the quarters of the globe: north, south, east or west. The Yellow Emperor (Huang-ti) occupies a special position, ruling over the centre. As long as government conforms to the march of the universe, all goes well with the people. The rains will come at the right time and agriculture will flourish. *Yin* and *yang* are therefore the chief concern of the emperor, whose business it is 'simply to take heaven and earth as model and carefully to observe how the former sage-kings behaved in this respect'.

The ideal condition to which the government aspired was described as *t'ai-p'ing*, meaning universal harmony or universal peace. *T'ai-p'ing* exists when all the forces and elements of the universe and all strata of society work in unison and contentment; its basic concept certainly does not suggest a Confucian origin.

The chief opponents of the Confucians at this time were the advocates of the Huang-Lao doctrine favoured by the empress Tou. The Confucians contemptuously called it the 'doctrine of the family circle (?)', which perhaps implies a reference to the restricted sphere of application and the sexual practices of this school. But even the Legalists who had been discredited since the fall of the Ch'in, seem, at any rate at the time of Hsiao-wên-ti (179–157 B.C.), the third Han emperor, to have had an extremely powerful influence. When the emperor without more ado ordered a man to be executed for having appeared without warning from under a bridge and caused the emperor's coach-horse to shy, a minister opposed this intervention in the judicial procedure in the following terms: 'It is the law which the Son of Heaven publicly has in common with the Empire. If punishments are made more severe over and above the law, which is already strict, the common people will lose faith in the law.'[7] It is therefore not surprising to find an attempt already being made by Chia I (201–169 B.C.), a well-known champion of Confucianism, then intriguing for power, to prepare the ground for some kind of compromise with the old opponent by delimiting the spheres of ritual and law in the following terms: 'Ritual applies to something which has not yet happened. Law, however, applies to something which has already happened.'[8]

As I understand them, these words show that the writer has recognized that one of the social functions of religion — or, in the Chinese version, of ritual — is to act as guardian of a moral system which does not permit crime and thus to render complicated systems of civil surveillance unnecessary. In contrast thereto, the law, with its threat of punishment, has only a negative, deterrent effect and requires for its implementation the assistance of a system of denunciation. An imperial edict of 124 B.C. also says: 'The people are led by ritual (*li*). Their mood is influenced by music.'[9] And a statement of the time of the emperor Hsiao-ch'êng-ti (37–3 B.C.) runs: 'The basic function of ritual is the protection of people. If in protecting people we commit the fault of excess, that excess is an excess of protection. But if we exceed in the matter of punishment, fatal injuries may ensue . . .'[10]

It was not until the reign of Hsiao-wu-ti that the great official sacrifices, the outstanding demonstration of the united empire, came to be performed in full panoply. An early view of the course of history in general runs:

Kao-tsŭ, the founder of the dynasty, ended the confusion and

> restored order. The emperors, Hsiao-wên and Hsiao-ching made it their business to protect the people, but finally they also began to seek out writings concerning the ritual of the past and much was seen to be lacking. Not until Hsiao-wu came to the throne did he firmly do away with all the other schools and commend the six classical books of the Confucians as the guiding principles of policy. He followed this up . . . by promoting study, organizing the state sacrifice . . . and inaugurating the Fêng-shan sacrifices.[11]

These sacrifices were an innovation which were later also absorbed into the official state religion.

The Fêng-shan sacrifices, which were celebrated on the peak of the T'ai-shan in Shantung and on Liang-fu, one of its foothills, were the emperor's announcement to the gods of the universe that the empire had reached the goal of good government, the state of *t'ai-p'ing*.

It seems very likely that these sacrifices were first enacted during the Han period. The statement that they were performed by Ch'in Shih-huang-ti when he climbed the T'ai-shan cannot be accepted. Their introduction was probably due in the main to the instigation of the Taoists from the province of Ch'i, who produced ancient writings which they quoted as saying that these ceremonies were first performed by the Yellow Emperor, Huang-ti, and that he afterwards went to heaven as a saint. In any case, 'Fêng-shan was only an expression for immortality'.

Although the Confucians declared that they knew nothing about the sacrifice, the emperor determined to perform it. He was influenced in this decision by a lengthy statement of the then well-known and celebrated court poet Ssŭ-ma Hsiang-ju (179–117 B.C.), which said that the virtue (*tê*) of the Han 'reached in all directions like water gushing from a spring,'[12] and that good omens in the form of strange beasts of all kinds, corn with six ears on one stem and suchlike had been seen. This, it was said, clearly indicated that heaven and earth desired the Fêng-shan sacrifice. The presence of a large number of old men had long been regarded as the most striking token of well-being in the empire and in later times these sacrifices were always heralded by mass demonstrations of old men.

When in the year 110 B.C. the emperor for the first time ascended the T'ai-shan to perform this ritual it seemed to him that he was greeted with *wan-sui* ('ten-thousand year') cries from an invisible audience. He repeated the ritual four more times in the course of his reign. Each time, after the enterprise had been happily concluded, great concessions were made to the people; these took the form of exemption from taxes, distribution of silk to all those aged over seventy as well as to widows and orphans, promotion of officials and so on, all of which, of course, contributed to the popularity of the sacrifice and the desirability of repeating it.

It is also significant that the ceremonial for the Fêng-shan sacrifice was prescribed in accordance with the sacrificial rites for the Supreme One (T'ai-i).

This god was also a new one which the Taoists of the time of Hsiao-wu-ti introduced into the state-religion. It is written of him: 'The most highly revered of the gods of heaven is T'ai-i. His helpers are the emperors of the five elements. In ancient times the Son of Heaven used to sacrifice to T'ai-i in spring and autumn on a site to the south of the capital.'[13] The name T'ai-i appeared for the first time in the literature of the Chan-kuo period and originally meant the same as Tao. We read in the *Lü-shih ch'un-ch'iu*: 'Tao is the finest essence. It cannot be given shape or name. When constrained to name it, we call it T'ai-i'.[14]

T'ai-i, however, also became associated with *li* (ritual). This undoubtedly occurred at a time when the Confucian ritualists were endeavouring to oust the Tao of the Huang-Lao school in favour of their principal concept, *li* (ritual). Thus it says in the *Li Chi*:

> Therefore *li* originates in *t'ai-i*. This separates and becomes heaven and earth. It revolves and forms *yin* and *yang*. It changes and becomes the four seasons. It is distributed and becomes the ancestral spirits and the gods. What it sends down is called the mandate (*ming*). It rules over heaven and earth.[15]

In the year 112 B.C., Hsiao-wu-ti set up an altar to T'ai-i and during the sacrifice placed the ancestral tablet of the founder of the dynasty, T'ai-tzu, opposite it.

Like that of the Ch'in, the lowly descent of the Han also appears to have caused them difficulties in establishing an imperial ancestor-worship, for it was evidently not their practice simply to grant the appropriate titles and ranks posthumously to the founder of the dynasty. The first ancestral temple was therefore set up to a certain T'ai-shang-huang, which, as has been shown above, was the courtesy title bestowed by Ch'in Shih-huang-ti upon his father who was anyhow a king. It was not until the reign of Hsiao-wu-ti that patterns were established which served as models for later dynasties.

6. PALACE LIFE

The refinement of the Ch'in court and the gulf separating it from the life of the people became further accentuated under the Han. The melodramatic harem atmosphere, which we have already fleetingly encountered was now greatly heightened.

This luxury did not really begin until the re-establishment of the united empire. We read that, in accordance with traditional moderation, the founder of the dynasty and the first two emperors had only ten court ladies. But for the first time under Hsiao-wu-ti more than a thousand young women of good family were taken to the palace.

As a result, the nobility, the high officials and the rich men of the people began to imitate the manners of the court and to keep concubines and singing-girls — the former some hundreds and the latter several score — so that 'in (the palaces and rich houses) there were a great number of unmarried girls and outside them many unmarried men'. It sometimes happened that in deference to public feeling some of the palace ladies were set free and allowed to marry.

It is significant that a class of women now existed who, like many film actresses in our own day, were able to make successful careers for themselves by skilfully exploiting their charms. Most remarkable was the fate of two sisters who were born into a family of musicians and rose to become empress and first concubine. They were Fei-yen ('Flying Swallow'), celebrated as a dancer, and her sister Ho-tê, the 'sex-bomb'.

They began their rise as night attendants to a princess and were at first so poor that they often went hungry; they possessed only one bed-cover between them and warmed themselves in winter 'by holding their breath and stopping the air'. But they used all their free time to practise singing and dancing and invested all their earnings in bath oils and powder. At last, Fei-yen managed to make her way into the emperor's presence (Hsiao-ch'êng-ti, 32–7 B.C.). He later described her in the following terms: 'She is so beautiful that she could give away some of her beauty to others, and so supple that she might have no bones; she is also reserved, modest and shy, so that she seems now to be near to one, now far away.' Nevertheless, after a short time she was supplanted in the emperor's favour by her sister. She entered the monarch's presence wearing a perfumed essence nine times distilled, her hair dressed in the latest style and her eyebrows shaped to a form known as 'distant hills'. She was powdered with 'maximum comfort' powder, wore a short over-garment, an embroidered short-sleeved under-garment and plum-patterned stockings. She was the product of what might be termed an industry conducted by experienced old ladies of the court for turning out sophisticated cosmetics and aids to beauty. It looks as though Ho-tê's triumph over her sister was therefore at least in part the victory of superior advice on beauty culture.

The rivalry of the two sisters for the emperor's favour produced scenes characteristic of the romanticizing tendency of the Han court.[16] One anecdote relates how the emperor was once dallying in a summer-house on an artificial hillock in the middle of a lake in the palace park. The empress (Fei-yen), whom the emperor had for some time neglected in favour of her sister, was wearing a glittering loose garment with wide drooping sleeves of light wild silk shot with green and red. She was singing before the emperor and dancing to the melody, 'Winds accompany those returning home from afar.' The emperor suddenly tapped a hair-slide made of rhinoceros horn against a jade cup and commanded the officer of the palace guard,* alleged to be a secret lover of Fei-yen, to accompany her on the flute. As the music went softly on a violent wind arose. The more it roared, the louder the empress sang and the more passionate did the music become. With her light garment fluttering about her, she cried, 'Look, look, do I not resemble one of the genii? I shall flee from you now and begin a new life. Do you desire that I should remember or forget you?' The emperor said, 'Wu-fang, hold the empress fast.' Wu-fang stopped playing, took her by the feet and bound her with green silk bands to a post so that she should not be blown into the water. Gradually the storm died down. Amid her tears the empress cried, 'I beg the emperor in his mercy to leave me to the genii, for my feet have been touched and I have been dishonoured.' The flute played sorrowful music and her tears fell like pearls. The emperor regretted the excessive favours he had shown to Ho-tê and, for a time at least, turned his affections towards Fei-yen once more.

If the stories circulated about the sisters can be believed, both seem periodically to have deceived the emperor on a large scale and quarrels flared up between them over lovers to whom both laid claim. These aberrations were no doubt caused by their desire for a child, which would have secured the mother's position once and for all. The emperor had in the end to be primed with artificial stimulants and died as the result of an overdose administered by Ho-tê when drunk.

The impression is thus one of a sophisticated and effeminate court atmosphere, full of amorous intrigues and desperate struggles for supremacy between the royal mistresses.

In a long prose-poem (*fu*) about life at court, by the court astronomer Chang Hêng (A.D. 78–139) there is a characteristic description of a scene from the 'Hall of Delights'. 'The Emperor likes only girls who are young and pretty and passes by those whose beauty is fading.' A carousal is arranged for each of his visits. The ladies display themselves in dances, virtuoso entertainments and song recitals. 'When they first enter, their steps are slow and their

* Fêng Wu-fang.

bearing weary, as though they could not stand even their light silk garments.' Legend recalls a court lady who was so sensitive that the seams of her clothes left marks on her skin.

> Then their attitude becomes more cheerful and they turn, thus showing their charms to greater advantage. When they have performed a sufficient number of dance-figures they suddenly run away like a flock of frightened cranes. Their red shoes trip in among plates and beakers and they wave their long sleeves.[17]

The court ladies were divided into fourteen grades according to their success in gaining the emperor's favour. Their arch-enemy was therefore old age, as it is of today's screen stars.

The same author describes performances by other artistes which were designed to amuse the court and which are important for the development of the entertaining arts in China at that time.

The emperor, he writes, goes to the palace of P'ing-lo ('Peaceful Pleasure'), where precious and curious objects are displayed to view. From a raised position he watches competitions and entertainments by magicians. Athletes lift heavy tripods; Turus (?) climb poles, twist their way through rings, plunge like diving swallows into vessels filled with water, and turn somersaults over mats bristling with lance-heads. Jugglers demonstrate their art with balls and swords. Rope-dancers perform together on a rope high up in the air. Mountain-ranges suddenly appear from nowhere; and on them sprout marvellous trees decked with red pendulous fruits, and all manner of other luck-bringing plants. Other artistes leap around like panthers or bears. A man disguised as a white tiger plays upon a zither, and another, made up as a blue dragon, blows a flute. Yet others, dressed as daughters of the sage-emperor Yao, sing long ballads with strange melodies. Or the legendary artist, Hung-yai, may appear in his costume of feathers. While the songs are being sung, clouds blow up and snow begins to fall thickly. The sound of thunder is imitated by rolling heavy stones across the upper galleries. 'The rumbling sounds like the angry majesty of heaven.' Or sometimes the snake-dragon Man-yen may appear and behind the monster a range of ghostly mountains rises. Bears and tigers fight one another on the stage.

All kinds of strange birds and beasts miraculously appear and disappear. There are sword-swallowers too, and men who spit fire and conjure up clouds and mist. Or a line may be drawn on the floor, which instantly turns into a stream. Others demonstrate how the magicians of Yüeh (roughly speaking, Fukien and Chekiang) cast spells upon wild beasts to tame them. Jugglers appear at the top of tall poles: suddenly they fall and hang by their feet in the air. There are skilled archers too who shoot with bows and arrows at figures of barbarians, and much else besides.

The Chinese theatre which developed out of these beginnings never entirely lost the character it had once derived from the performances of these acrobats and jugglers.

7. PALACE BUILDINGS

The Han took over certain palace buildings from the Ch'in but enlarged them according to their own plans. As under the previous dynasty, ladies of the harem and musicians were installed in each palace so that they did not need to be brought with the emperor when he moved from one to another. There were so many outlying residences and pleasure palaces that he could not visit all of them in his life-time.

Names of architects of important buildings and great parks are now heard of for the first time. One of them, indeed, was a member of the imperial family.

The following account has come down to us of the impression made on an onlooker by the palace buildings:

> The ridged and stepped roofs rise steeply into the air. We can make out the tips of the up-curved rims of the roofs and the floating galleries. The light of the sun and the moon finds its way into the building and is reflected there. The gate of the Bridge of Heaven Palace is so high that carriages with banners flying can pass under it and so wide that two coaches and four may pass through abreast. Long corridors, broad side-galleries and verandahs spread like clouds or luxuriant plants. There are

vast numbers of walls and courtyards, innumerable gates and doors, as well as hidden passage-ways and entrances, so that it is easy to get lost as though one were in a labyrinth.

The framework of some of the palaces was of cassia wood, so that: 'When a breeze blew softly over it, a most agreeable fragrance filled the air.'[18]

8. THE CAPITAL

During the Han period the imperial palaces in the metropolis, Ch'ang-an, were scattered throughout the city, but later, under the Sui and T'ang dynasties, they were all situated together in enclosed grounds to the north of the city.

Despite the numerous guards at the gates many secret exits to the city could be found. The city was surrounded by a high wall with three gates on either side. The great thoroughfares were broad enough to take twelve carts abreast while the side-streets were the width of four carriages.

From the point of view of appearance, the most striking of the city buildings were probably the residences of the high officials. These were built more solidly than the other houses and were painted red or purple, while their interiors were hung with precious stuffs.

There were nine large bazaars, the outer walls of which formed a circle. In the centre was a five-storey flag-tower from which all could be surveyed. As in the Chou period, marketing was now under official direction. Our information concerning the trade of the time is more or less as follows.

Valuable goods came in from all quarters, 'flocking together in one place like birds and fish'. Profits from the transactions were considerable. There were therefore many kinds of trader. Not all were honest: some mixed good wares with bad and so deceived the simple country-people. They worked on the basis implied by the question, 'What is the point of working when we can live off easy profits?' Some of the ladies of the mercantile world lived as luxuriously as empresses. There were merchants' houses in which the numerous servants were summoned by gongs to meals set out on great tripods. When they went visiting, many of the rich merchants were escorted by a large retinue of outriders and postilions.

During the first Han period there were no rules regarding clothing, the type of carriage to be used and so on. With the rise of the new social class comprising people who had grown rich through business, trade or other means, the circumscribed mode of life imposed on the lower classes by the feudal lords probably came to an end. It was not until the second Han period in about A.D. 58–77 that rules governing 'gowns and caps', such as had been prescribed in the classic works on ritual, were once again enforced. We learn that from then onwards merchants had to wear light yellow and light green materials. The lowest officials were permitted to dress in light blue, yellow, red and green. A choice of twelve colours was available to the highest ranks.

It is, perhaps, also interesting to note that the type of simple hat worn by the first Han emperor when he was an unknown village functionary later became the prerogative of the nobility. A special close-fitting cap became fashionable among the officials because a similar one had been worn by the emperor Hsiao-yüan-ti (49–33 B.C.) to cover the thick hair which grew low down on his forehead.

We also learn a few details about women's fashions in the capital in the later Han period: women liked to dress their hair high on their heads, favoured broad eyebrows and wore capacious sleeves.

The merchant class appears to have been extremely ostentatious and not to have been much liked by the officials. There is a revealing verse aphorism in the chapter on geography in the *History of the Former Han Dynasty*, which may be roughly paraphrased as follows: 'The man who uses cunning to amass profits, who values worldly goods and despises right, who fawns upon the rich and reviles the poor, such a man may well succeed in trade but never in office.' This is an obvious thumbnail sketch of a class of smart parvenus whose conduct was not above reproach — a type still not totally unfamiliar at the present time.

There were also, then as now, successful gang-leaders and crime kings, whose cowardly murders and furtive brutalities, like those of the American gangsters, were inordinately glamourized and attracted the morbid interest of sensation-seekers — especially, of course, the young.

Gangs were formed not only in the cities. In country districts also there were robber bands and individuals of rare physical strength and cunning who, with the assistance of hangers-on, terrorized and plundered the neighbourhood. They often also took advantage of anti-governmental feeling among the people and set themselves up as leaders of small popular uprisings and champions of the rightful demands of underprivileged groups, in short, as representatives of political opposition. One of their main sources of income appears to have been the pillaging of rich graves.

There must at times have been veritable crime-waves. It is recorded, for example, that between 96 and 16 B.C. a large number of criminal gangs were doing their worst in the capital, Ch'ang-an. Youths from the poor districts in the suburbs banded together and murdered functionaries and officials. For a consideration they would liquidate persons distasteful to their backers. They selected their victims by a kind of lottery in which coloured balls were used. 'Whoever drew a red ball had to liquidate an official or an officer of the punitive system, whoever drew a black ball had to dispatch a civil official.'[19] A white ball meant that whoever drew it had to arrange the burial of the person assassinated (?). After dark every night there were crimes of violence in the city and people who had been robbed were found dead or severely wounded in the streets. It was not until energetic and extremely tough measures were taken by one of the officials concerned with crime that this state of affairs was brought to an end. Official history contains repeated accounts of summary actions against the rising tide of crime.

9. CONDITION OF THE RURAL POPULATION

As these records show, the sophisticated civilization of the Han dynasty rested on extremely insecure social foundations. The principal cause of the growing incidence of crime was the highly unequal distribution of goods and the resultant social distress. The security of the government was based not on an increase in general prosperity but on the fact that it possessed the power brutally to crush the revolts of the discontented. There was also the fact that the upper stratum — and it was a fairly thin one — of rich and cultivated people looked down with sovereign lack of understanding and contempt upon the broad masses, who were composed mainly of backward, hard-working country-people.

A well-known author describes the peasant of the Han period as a semi-bestial creature. Practically naked, his skin caked with dirt, he dug in the earth with hands curved like claws. His food consisted of bran and vegetable remains. Texts expressing the view that the lower classes were on a level with domestic animals are many. Thus, for example, Tung Chung-shu describes the farm-workers: 'They dress like oxen and horses (which presumably means that they wore hardly any clothing), they eat the food of dogs and pigs.'

It is therefore scarcely surprising that gigantic uprisings of the lower classes prepared the way for the fall of both the first and second Han dynasties.

Statements in the chapter on economics in the *History of the Former Han Dynasty* enable us to calculate the annual budget of a small peasant's family of five persons during the reign of the emperor Hsiao-wên-ti (179–157 B.C.). The income from a cultivated area of 100 *mou* amounted to about 3,000 copper coins, while the outlay for maintenance worked out at about 2,000. In addition, however, the various taxes, such as land-tax, poll-tax, tax on children, on the house, tax to the provincial over-lord and so on, amounted to as much as 1,815 coins. This meant that the family needed about 815 coins over and above its regular income and this had in some way to be raised by extra work, trade or borrowing. These conditions condemned the small peasant to extinction.

The general economic situation took an even more unfavourable turn when, as a result of his military enterprises and extravagant building programme, the emperor Hsiao-wu-ti exhausted 'the resources and strength of the people'. 'The land was no longer cultivated and grew bare, the people left their homes. Output fell by half.'

We read in one of the biographies in the *History of the Former Han Dynasty* of the period of the emperor Hsiao-ai-ti (6–1 B.C.), about the seven misfortunes and the seven causes of death by which the people were threatened. Among the first are listed the natural catastrophes caused by the disharmony of *yin* and *yang*, the excessive burden of taxes, the corruption of the officials, the plundering of the gang-leaders and their tribes, inefficient distribution of labour, which prevented the farmers from doing what was needful at the right time, the disturbances of wars and the pillages of the robbers. The second comprised: thrashing to death by cruel judges, death in prison, death by unjust administration of the law, by the activities of bands of assassins, by blood-feuds, by hunger and disease. 'If there are seven misfortunes for the people and not a single point of assistance, how can we expect lasting peace for the country? If there are seven deaths and not a single point of life, how can we hope to make a mark with punishments?'[20] There were evidently a few who recognized the evil signs of the time and raised their voices in warning.

The people's distress found expression in songs which still survive and which very probably originated among the lower classes. One of the best known describes the consequences of long military service:

At fifteen I went with the army,
At fourscore I came home.
On the way I met a man from the village,
I asked him who there was at home.

'That over there is your house,
All covered with trees and bushes.'
Rabbits had run in at the dog-hole,
Pheasants flew down from the beams of the roof.
In the courtyard was growing some wild grain;
And by the well, some wild mallows.
I'll boil the grain and make porridge,
I'll pluck the mallows and make soup.
Soup and porridge are both cooked,
But there is no one to eat them with.
I went out and looked towards the east,
While tears fell and wetted my clothes.[21]

Another, which may date from the reign of the emperor Hsiao-wu-ti, describes the heavy losses of soldiers and workers:

They fought south of the Castle,
They died north of the wall.
They died in the moors and were not buried.
Their flesh was the food of crows.
'Tell the crows we are not afraid;
We have died in the moors and cannot be buried.
Crows, how can our bodies escape you?'
The waters flowed deep
And the rushes in the pool were dark.
The riders fought and were slain:
Their horses wander neighing.
By the bridge there was a house.
Was it south, was it north?
The harvest was never gathered.
How can we give you your offerings?
You served your Prince faithfully,
Though all in vain.
I think of you, faithful soldiers;
Your service shall not be forgotten
For in the morning you went out to battle
And at night you did not return.[22]

10. THE MUSIC DEPARTMENT

The songs quoted above come from the collection of the Music Department (*Yüeh-fu*), which was founded under the emperor Hsiao-wu-ti by his master of music, Li Yen-nien.

The foundation of this institution is connected with the fact that by the Han period most of the old music of the Chou had been lost or was no longer suited to the altered tastes of the time. New music had therefore to be created. The mission of the Music Department was twofold: in the first place it had to collect, edit and provide musical accompaniments for melodies, songs, rhythmically recited aphorisms and the like, so that they could be performed for the entertainment of the court; secondly it had to commission celebrated poets to write verses to fit the music played at state-sacrifices, religious and other court ceremonies.

The products of the latter operation comprised additions to the festival songs and odes of the *Shih Ching* while the former corresponded to the *kuo-fêng* (folk-songs of different lands) of this classic collection.

Among the 'folk-songs' there were 'songs to the shepherd's pipe and cymbal', which originated among the northern peoples, the 'antiphons', which were collected from the southern countries particularly from the former state of Ch'u, and songs of various kinds, in which all possible lyrical moods, such as laments of abandoned wives or orphaned children, were expressed. Although the few pieces which have survived are heavily interspersed with verses which are clearly later additions by literary writers, many of the *Yüeh-fu* songs are of undoubtedly popular character, like the following work song:

> South of the river we gather lotos
> How round, how round are the lotos leaves.
> Fishes sport among the lotos leaves.
> They sport to the east of the leaves,
> They sport to the west of the leaves,

They sport to the south of the leaves,
They sport to the north of the leaves.[23]

This is certainly also one of the earliest of the so-called five-word poems; these were lyrics in which each line consisted of five Chinese characters. The form, which probably originated through the *Yüeh-fu* songs of the Han period, dominated Chinese poetry until about A.D. 200.

Many songs express the humble position of the wife and her complete dependence on her husband's moods:

I went up the mountain to gather *mi-wu*,
The plant which brings many children.
On the way home I met my (former) husband.
Respectfully I knelt and asked him:
'How do you like your new wife?'
'They say she is pretty, to be sure, but not as pretty as you.
You are alike in build, but not in capability.'
'When the new one came in by the gate,
I stole out by the side door.'
'My new wife weaves me yellow silk.
You wove fine white stuff.
She only weaves one piece a day;
You wove five ells.
If I compare the silk,
The old wife is indeed better than the new.'[24]

The *Yüeh-fu* songs afford an extremely lively impression of the temper of the Han people. There is scarcely a single poet of repute in the later periods who was not influenced by them.

11. TRADE WITH THE WEST

It was during the Han period that a direct and historically verifiable link between China and the countries of the west first came into being. The link was created when the Chinese occupied the Tarim Basin, that is, East Turkestan. This in all probability meant freedom for the native population from the extortion and plundering of the Hsiung-nu (Huns), who had the disagreeable habit of summarily carrying off into slavery those whom they had captured in their raids.

It was to the credit of the Chinese that they safeguarded the country against these depredations. This they did by setting up a military colony and installing manufacturers of weapons, as well as by organizing the opposition of the natives. This resulted in a considerable increase in caravan traffic and exchange of goods between east and west. This explains the statement in the *History of the Former Han Dynasty* that, from the reign of Hsiao-wu-ti onwards, many strange new things poured into China.

We now know that both wine made from grapes and lucerne were introduced into China at this time. Chives, cucumbers, sesame, coriander and much else followed. In the opposite direction, oranges, peonies, azaleas and other plants found their way to the west. But China's principal export was silk. It was for this reason that the old trade route through Turkestan was often called the Silk Road, while the ancient Greek word for the Chinese, *seres*, is derived from *ssu*, the Chinese word for silk. Our word China, however, comes from Ch'in, the name of the first unitary state, by way of Sanskrit *cīnasthana*, Byzantine *tzinista* and Arabic *al-Sīn*.

Whatever may have been the true nature of this trade, it must in the main, at all events, have consisted in an exchange of gifts between the imperial court and the princes of the western states. Nevertheless a fair number of goods must have found their way into the hands of the prosperous officials of the people. And I can well imagine that there was a kind of expansionist mood afoot in business circles which formed a powerful incentive to people to give up working on the land and devote themselves to trade.

It was not only commercial wares but also cultural goods and ideas which passed to and fro with the caravans. Thus we find in China a new form of metal ornament exemplifying the so-called Scythian animal-style. This style employed radically simplified forms of tigers, oxen, horses and other animals, to which the

Chinese added the dragon and the phoenix. It probably originated in western Asia.

Of the greatest importance, however, for the spiritual history of China was the infiltration of Buddhism of which more will be said below.

12. CHINESE HISTORICAL WRITING

One of the principal achievements of Chinese civilization has been the writing of history. I know of no other people which possesses so vast a historical literature or one which extends consecutively over so long a period.

History for the Chinese was a great field of investigation which yielded an understanding of both the present and future of mankind. Truth, especially after the official class with its Confucian attitudes had prevailed, always signified that which had begun in antiquity and survived through the centuries. The Chinese people think — and this may still be true today — primarily in historical terms.

They have always, therefore, tended to regard the present as the direct extension of the past and to plan their political activities accordingly. The effect of this has been that the Chinese people and civilization are regarded, from the earliest times to the present-day, as an uninterrupted entity, with various incidental accretions.

The Chinese regard the *Shu Ching* (*Book of History*) and the *Ch'un-ch'iu* (*Spring and Autumn Annals*) as their earliest historical works. The first is generally held to contain records of important speeches, the second records of important historical events.

This probably led to the belief that two forms of historical writing had existed since the earliest times: records of speeches and records of actions. As a result, the later emperors were always provided with two historians, each of whom fulfilled one of these two functions.

The lengthy *Tso Chuan* commentary to the *Ch'un-ch'iu* — which in itself consists of little more than very short notes — represents the earliest chronological presentation of history in which individual events are broken down into day, month and year. The shortcomings of this method are said to have induced Tso-ch'iu Ming, disciple of Confucius and putative author of the *Tso Chuan*, to write the *Kuo-yü* or *Conversations from the States*, in which historical themes are treated in a connected manner. He regarded the separate countries of the Ch'un-ch'iu period as the historical units.

This may mean that scholars recognized that history was not simply a general progression in time but an interweaving of historical themes, events and so on which came into being through the interdependent action of cause and effect.

Whatever may be said about these early works, the writing of Chinese history, in the true sense of the word, began with the completion, in the year 91 B.C., of the *Shih Chi* (*Records of the Historian*) by Ssŭ-ma Ch'ien. With its hundred and thirty chapters and some 526,500 characters it was certainly the longest literary work of its time.

It has been said that 'the *Shih Chi* threads ancient and modern times on one thread' and 'embraces all phenomena'. In the genealogical Annals (*pên-chi*) of this work, history is for the first time divided into periods according to dynasties. And we may suppose that this was done under the influence of the doctrine of the elements.

The purely temporal course of history was represented by a series of chronological tables which probably again derived from earlier models. Of particular interest are the Treatises (*shu*) which deal with the interconnection between such themes as ritual, music, the calendar, heavenly phenomena, irrigation systems and other things as a whole, and which contain echoes of the different schools.

The 'file of traditions' (*lieh-chuan*) contains biographies of individuals of historical importance, accounts of sections of the population and of foreign peoples.

All this shows that the work in question is a universal history which attempts to do justice to every manifestation of the known universe.

The second great historical work is the *History of the Former Han*

Dynasty (206–24 B.C.) which was largely composed under the editorship of Pan Ku (A.D. 32–92) during the later Han dynasty.

Here, for the first time, is a work which takes a single epoch as its subject. It became the model for all subsequent dynastic histories, which came increasingly to be produced by official commissions.

But the Chinese mind scanned history in order to discover from it the underlying connections of the universe and such fragmentation left it unsatisfied. It craved for a survey of the total course of history which would clearly demonstrate the causes of the rise and fall of dynasties.

Thus there was always a desire for a 'continuous history', much in the style of the genealogical Annals of the *Shih Chi*. Such tendencies began to take tangible form at about the beginning of the sixth century A.D., but they did not reach maturity until the completion, in the year 1084, of Ssŭ-ma Kuang's *Tzŭ-chih t'ung-chien*.

This work, which was originally conceived as a continuation of the *Tso Chuan*, embraced the whole period from 403 B.C. to A.D. 959. The title chosen for the work by the emperor himself means, roughly, 'General mirror (of history) as an aid to government', and shows that the intention of the author of the history was a practical one.

Ssŭ-ma Kuang has this to say about his own work:

> Since the times of Ssŭ-ma Ch'ien and Pan Ku there have been so many new histories that scholars can no longer study them all and the Emperor even less, since he is overburdened with the business of government. It is certainly not true that, considering myself alone, I eliminated superfluous information and selected only the most important elements of that which set the whole in motion. In particular, I took in everything which has to do with the rise and fall of the dynasties and is linked with the well-being or misfortune of the people. The good will serve as an example, the bad as a warning.

After the *Shih Chi*, the *Tzŭ-chih t'ung-chien* is certainly the most read of all Chinese histories. It is therefore appropriate to quote an example to illustrate its nature and content. For the twelfth month of the year A.D. 220 we read:

> The Emperor (of Wei) wished to move a hundred thousand households of peasant-soldiers from (the province of) Chi-chou to (the prefecture of) Ho-nan . . . At this time, due to drought and a plague of locusts, the people were suffering from famine. Various officials of the Court disapproved of this measure, but the Emperor's mind was set on it. The Grand Chamberlain (*shih-chung*) Hsin P'i, together with other court officials, requested an audience with the Emperor. Knowing well that they intended to remonstrate with him on this score, the Emperor wore a vexed expression when he received them. No one else dared to speak; (Hsin) P'i, however, said, 'Your Majesty intends to move the households of the soldiers. What good would it do?'
>
> The Emperor asked him, 'Do you mean to say that you disapprove my moving them?' (Hsin) P'i affirmed, 'I definitely disapprove.' The Emperor said, 'I am not going to discuss the matter with you.'
>
> To this (Hsin) P'i said, 'Your majesty, not considering me unworthy, has made me one of your attendants and appointed me one of your counsellors. How can you now be unwilling to discuss the matter with me? It is not of a private nature, but concerns the dynasty itself. Why should you be vexed at me?'
>
> Without answering, the Emperor rose from his seat and went inside. (Hsin) P'i followed him, pulling him back by the lapel of his coat; the Emperor shook himself loose and would not return. After a long while he finally came out and said, 'Oh P'i . . . why is this affair so important to you?'
>
> (Hsin) P'i said, 'Should you move these households, you will lose their affection; and besides, you cannot feed them. That is why I could not help braving your vexation and contended as hard as I could.'
>
> In the end the Emperor moved half the original number.
>
> On another occasion, when the Emperor went out of his palace to shoot pheasants, he turned to his attendants and

> exclaimed, 'How delightful this pheasant shooting is!' (Hsin) P'i replied, 'Delightful indeed to Your Majesty, but very burdensome to all your subjects.' The Emperor did not utter a word, but thereafter did not go out so frequently, because of him (i.e. Hsin P'i).[25]

Finally, the sentences with which Ssŭ-ma Kuang introduces the work are most significant:

> I have heard that among the official obligations of the Son of Heaven, none is greater than the rites (*li*). In connection with these, nothing is greater than the apportionment of duties and in connection with these nothing is more important than the terms (*ming*). Ritual is, indeed, the basic, all-embracing law. The apportionment of duties is the difference between ruler and servant. The terms (i.e. mandates) are duke, earl, minister, official, etc.

This, expressed in the concisest form, is the basic concept underlying early Chinese historical writing.

It lies, unfortunately, beyond the scope of the present book to enumerate all the Chinese historical works which continue the *Tzŭ-chih t'ung-chien* or are in other respects connected with it. Nor is it possible to adduce the other important works which would show how the historical subject-matter contained in acts and documents was gradually transformed into history.

It should, however, be mentioned that Liu Chih-chi (A.D. 661–721), China's best-known critic of historical writings, who lived during the T'ang period, divided history as a whole into the same 'two bodies' or categories which have already been mentioned: history as a chronological sequence of events and history as a series of events each complete in itself.

The *Tzŭ-chih t'ung-chien* belongs to the first category, but in the Sung period Yüan Shu (A.D. 1131–1205) arranged the same material in the second manner. His work also led on to a number of continuations, the titles of most of which carry the designation, *Chi-shih pên-mo* ('Presentation of separate events from beginning to end').

An extensive historical literature also developed from the Treatises of the *Shih Chi*. It offers much material for a re-interpretation of Chinese history in the light of our own times. But this is not the place to pursue the matter.

I should like, however, in conclusion, to make one further observation, namely that I believe that historians such as Ssŭ-ma Ch'ien, Pan Ku and their imitators always remained to a greater or less degree conscious that history, however a writer may choose to regard it, remains, in the final analysis, a 'narrative'. Their works are, therefore, full of colourful details, anecdotes and so on, and differ — to their advantage — from many modern historical works, which have the distinct appearance of being products — some more, some less dry — of intelligent political speculation.

I should like to illustrate the point from two examples from the *Shih Chi*. The following passage occurs at the beginning of the chapter on the celebrated assassin-retainers:[26]

> Ts'ao Mo was a man from Lu. His boldness and bodily strength had made Duke Chuang of Lu, who liked strong men, take him into his service. He became general of Lu and fought in this capacity against the state of Ch'i; but he was defeated three times and fled.
>
> Duke Chuang of Lu grew fearful and sought to buy peace by ceding territory. But Ts'ao Mo kept his position as general.
>
> Duke Huan of Ch'i (the first ruler of the Ch'un-ch'iu period) met the Duke of Lu in order to conclude the peace treaty.
>
> As the two dukes, Huan and Chuang, were standing on the platform which had been erected for the signing of the peace, Ts'ao Mo grasped his sword and made towards Duke Huan. None of the followers dared to intervene.
>
> 'What would you, sir?' demanded Duke Huan.
>
> Ts'ao answered: 'Ch'i is strong, Lu is weak. It is too much that a great state should invade Lu. Lu has dismantled its defences and now Ch'i is pressing on its frontiers. Perhaps the Duke would consider this.'

When he heard these words, the Duke returned the territory he had occupied to Lu. As soon as this had been agreed, Ts'ao Mo dropped his sword, left the platform and mingled with the officials present at the ceremony, conversing with them as though nothing had happened.

Duke Huan grew angry and wished to cancel the agreement. But his minister Kuan Chung said, 'You cannot do this. If so slender an advantage causes a man to act according to his own pleasure there will be no more confidence in the princes of the Empire and the Empire will be weakened. You must yield.' Thus the territory which Ts'ao had lost in three battles, fell once more to Lu.

Another highly dramatic scene occurs in the same chapter and describes how Ch'in Shih-huang-ti was chased round a pillar in the audience hall by the notorious assassin Ching K'o and was unable in his haste to free his long sword from the scabbard until someone shouted to him to toss the scabbard over his back. Thereupon he extricated his sword and successfully beat off the assassin.

Some are not without a certain comic aspect. One of these occurs in the chapter about the 'cruel officials' (that is, the famous criminalists) of the Han period[27] and describes how the emperor Hsiao-wên-ti once went on an outing into a hunting park with his court ladies. During the day one of the ladies needed to disappear behind a screen that had been erected for this special purpose.

A wild pig suddenly broke into the emergency privy. The emperor glanced at the officer Chih Tu (commanding him to intervene). But Chih Tu did not stir. The Emperor then made as though to grasp a weapon to assist the lady. Thereupon Chih Tu flung himself down before the Emperor and said, 'If one concubine gets lost another will come. There is no lack of such ladies in the empire. But if your Majesty stoops so low how will he stand before the ancestors and the Empress?' The Emperor turned away. The wild pig also took himself off.

The Empress, however, saw that Chih Tu received a reward.

These examples reveal clearly enough that novelistic element which so often appears in Chinese historical writing and makes the reading of these texts a stimulating experience, not only from the purely informative point of view.

VII

Intellectual Life in the Period of the Three Kingdoms, the Chin Dynasties and the Period of Political Separation between North and South (A.D. 221-581)

1. THE BEGINNINGS OF BUDDHISM

In addition to the fall of the Shang dynasty and the emergence of the Yin-Yang philosophy, there were two events which had an overriding influence on the course of Chinese cultural and intellectual history. One was the infiltration of Buddhism and the other the impact of the civilization and economy of Europe.

Buddhism brought not only a new religious doctrine to China but also a new form of social life, the monastic community. In the form in which it occurred in China, Buddhism was a discipline of city-dwelling monks who lived apart from the lay community and were subject not to the political but to a special religious régime.

When a man entered a monastic community he ceased to belong to any of the social classes, which in China, as we have seen, were strongly defined. As 'every stream and river loses its name and identity when it flows into the sea, so does the monk when he treads the path of salvation'.

It would perhaps be true to say that in this respect Buddhism was a realization of the trends towards equality and withdrawal from the world which prevailed among some of the Taoists —

who prepared the way for the new religion in other ways as well.

It is extremely probable that the Chinese became acquainted with Buddhism as a result of their occupation of Turkestan towards the end of the second century B.C. But there is no historical account of the coming of Buddhism to China before the history of the Toba-Wei dynasty (A.D. 386–534).

There it is recorded that the general, Ho Ch'ü-ping brought back from his victorious campaign against the Hsiung-nu (Huns) in the years 122–117 B.C. a gold statue of a god, which the emperor had erected in the Kan-ch'üan palace. It was venerated not in the usual way with living sacrifices, but with ceremonial obeisances and the burning of incense. This is one of the principal external features which distinguished Buddhism from the other Chinese religions.

There is also a famous story of the Han emperor Hsiao-ming (A.D. 58–75). Hsiao-ming dreamed one night that a golden statue of a man, with bright light streaming from the crown of its head, flew into the hall of the palace. The emperor was told by those around him that this was a statue of the Buddha. Thereupon, he sent envoys to India who returned to Loyang with two Buddhist teachers, Shê-mo-t'êng (Kāśyapa Mātaṅga?) and Chu Fa-lan (Dharmaratna). They brought, on a white horse, a large number of Buddhist writings and this is said to have occasioned the founding of the 'White Horse Monastery' (Pai-ma-ssŭ) in Loyang (the capital of the later Han dynasty).

Close investigation, however, has shown that in their present form these anecdotes must be counted among Buddhist legend. Nor can it be established with certainty that the Pai-ma monastery in Loyang existed before the year A.D. 289, although monasteries of this name may have existed at an earlier date in Ch'ang-an and Ching-ch'êng (Hupei).

It is certain, however, that from about the middle of the second century A.D. onwards, small Buddhist communities — consisting mostly of foreigners — existed in the larger trading centres of North China.

More detailed information about one of these communities is available: it was situated in P'êng-ch'êng, the capital of the feudal prince Liu Ying in the south of present-day Shantung, and can be dated to the year A.D. 65. It is also recorded that this prince was a follower of Huang-Lao, a fact which underlines the close connection between Buddhism and Taoism which characterized the early phase.

The records show that this community consisted of *upāsakas* (lay followers of Buddhism) and *śramaṇas* (monks). It is probably safe to assume that there were already Chinese among the former.

Further information relating to this same community dating from the years A.D. 193–4 records that the ruler of the region, presumably from political motives, exempted believing Buddhists from statutory labour. This incentive is said to have brought the community five thousand members. 'When the celebration of the Bathing of the Buddha took place (i.e. the commemorative celebration on the Buddha's birthday, the eighth day of the fourth month) a great quantity of wine and food was provided and mats were spread out on the roadsides,'[1] so that the participants at this religious celebration could also have a free meal.

Buddhists, as is well known, are forbidden to drink wine and any other intoxicating liquor, and the fact that it was dispensed on these occasions shows that the new teaching was still at an extremely primitive stage and that the main concern probably was to give it publicity.

There were, moreover, at the time also Taoist communities which worked with similar means. In the state organized on religious principles by Chang Lu, founder of a celebrated Taoist sect in the upper reach of the Han river (roughly, southern Shensi), there were even hostels in which free board and lodging could be obtained. In the general poverty of that time of political warfare — as a result of which the united empire split again into three kingdoms — free nourishment was naturally an extremely attractive form of publicity.

It seems, however, that at about this time the Buddhists began vigorously to dissent from popular Taoism. This had been seriously discredited by the great uprising of the Yellow Turbans, the ideological background to which had been provided by a Huang-

Lao sect which appears to have venerated among others a medicine-god, the Yellow Ancient.

Another, larger, Buddhist community existed from the end of the first century onwards in Loyang. This was the source of the earliest surviving Buddhist work, the *Sūtra in Forty-two Sections*. Admittedly, we do not know whether this is a translation of one particular ancient Sanskrit text or a compilation of Buddhist maxims in the style of the *Hsiao-ching* (*Classic of filial piety*) — very popular at that time — and the *Tao-tê ching*. Furthermore, the text which has survived has been much revised in the light of later Buddhist opinion. Nevertheless, it can be said with certainty that the content of the work was greatly influenced by the Huang-Lao teaching. Phrases like: 'the way which can be expressed in words ends abruptly' may be taken as proof of this. The endeavour to eliminate human desires also corresponds to one of the fundamental tenets of Taoism: 'Just as someone who troubles the water with his hand can no longer see his reflection, so a man whose inner life is troubled by desires cannot see the way of salvation (in himself).'

A purely Buddhist idea, however, is, for example, the concept of the transitory and the evanescent which, as is well known, are the causes of the fear which constantly pervades all living creatures.

> Talking with some pupils, Buddha asked what they understood by transience. One said: 'A single day cannot be preserved.' The Buddha was not satisfied and he turned to another. This one said: 'The duration of a meal cannot be preserved.' The Buddha was still not satisfied. A third said: 'Even a single exhalation will not meet the case, for it belongs to the past even as it occurs — even so is transience.' Buddha said: 'Good! You are on the Way.'[2]

He who is on this way, however, is 'like a piece of wood which is carried down in mid-stream without striking against either bank'. Nothing can prevent it from reaching the sea. The sea, of course, is nirvāna. Nirvāna is changeless and deathless.

Nirvāna, the condition in which all individual impulses, all desires and sensations are extinguished, in which the constituents of the conscious individual existence are completely eliminated, may also be achieved, through meditation, in this present life, and strongly resembles the state the Taoists described as 'absolute self-forgetfulness' in which 'the heart becomes like dead ashes'. Moreover, the breathing technique (*ānāpāna*) associated with meditation (*dhyāna*) was the same for laymen as the breathing exercises practised by the Taoists for the purpose of lengthening life.

This explains the fact that Buddhism was at first regarded as merely a new sectarian variation of Taoist practices designed to achieve immortality. And it was, indeed, under the Taoist banner that Buddhism entered China.

A legend which grew up about the middle of the second century A.D. and tells how Lao-tzŭ emigrated to the west and there preached to the barbarians a doctrine which had by then found its way back to China in the guise of Buddhism, shows most clearly to what extent Buddhism and Taoism were regarded as one and the same. According to this doctrine, the Buddha was merely a reincarnation (*avatāra*) of Lao-tzŭ and both were essentially the same person. This theory at first brought advantage to both religions. The Taoists treated the new teaching as though it were part of their own, while the Buddhists could not be reproached for being propagandists for a foreign, barbarian religion. It was not until later, when the two were splitting apart, that this legend found literary expression in a work called *Hua-hu-ching* (*Classical Work of the Conversion of the Barbarians*), by Lao-tzŭ, which was vigorously attacked by the Buddhists.

2. BUDDHISM AND *HSÜAN-HSÜEH*

About the middle of the third century A.D. the victorious advance of Buddhism as a new and independent religion in China began to be increasingly noticeable. It is significant that a series of works dealing with monastic discipline (*vinaya*) now appeared in translation. The numbers of Chinese streaming into the monasteries had probably increased so greatly that it was possible to set about weeding out the undesirable elements, who, apart from the fact that they affected the tonsure, were indistinguishable from lay-people.

The first recorded journey to Turkestan made by a Chinese Buddhist for the purpose of securing texts falls in this period. The traveller was the monk Chu Shih-hsing. He reached Khotan, where at that time Mahāyāna Buddhism prevailed, in the year 260. There he obtained the principal work of this school, the *Prajñāpāramitā*, which was many times translated and became one of the most important texts of Chinese Buddhism.

The Buddhists of the territories on the western frontier of the empire now played an important part, for their knowledge of languages enabled them to interpret or translate the foreign texts. The greatest among them was the Indo-Scythian, Dharmaraksha (Fa-hu in Chinese; he was active between the years 266 and 308), to whom, probably incorrectly, the translation of a hundred and fifty-four works has been ascribed. It is likely that he was the son of a prosperous merchant and had in his youth studied the six Confucian classics and the philosophers.

Buddhism now began increasingly to find its way into educated circles. It is safe to say that the principal leaders of the monastic communities were chosen from prosperous circles. But there were also many monks who came from less well-to-do classes who joyfully seized upon life in the monasteries and the possibility of study undisturbed by financial worries as a means of following their academic inclinations.

With this there arose, at about the turn of the third and fourth century A.D., a new kind of intelligentsia, represented by scholars versed both in the new Buddhist writings and in the Confucian and Taoist literature of the Chinese world.

At this particular juncture Buddhism came into contact with an attitude of mind which was widespread in educated circles and which, under the title of *hsüan-hsüeh* (doctrine of the mystery), plays a part in Chinese philosophy. It was closely connected with the so-called *ch'ing-t'an* (*Discourses on pure* (*tradition*)).

The *ch'ing-t'an* were originally discussions on the qualities of personality required by officials; they originated towards the end of the Han period when the question arose of finding a yardstick for selection, the primitive method of examination originated under the Han having fallen into decay. They developed into discussions on the nature of the personality in general, and the *Jên-wu chih* (*Notes on personality*), which may be regarded as a kind of literary outcome of these conversations, says at the beginning: 'The root of the human personality springs from emotional reaction and natural disposition. But the principle of both is extremely subtle and a mystery into the bargain. Who but a saint could fathom it?'[3] In the sequel, mystery in general, in the sense in which it is to be understood in the expression 'mystery of mysteries' in the *Tao-tê ching* and the philosophy associated with this work and the *Chuang-tzŭ*, as well as in Buddhist teachings, came more and more to occupy the central position in these discussions. They finally provided the impulse towards the creation of a new literary form, in which these themes were treated in dialogue-form and were much favoured by Buddhists. The *ch'ing-t'an* themselves finally degenerated into epigrammatic judgments on personalities or into a fashionable cult of smart replies. Among those on whom its witticisms conferred fame was China's first great painter, Ku K'ai-chih, whose art was strongly influenced by Buddhism.

Among the most important concepts of *hsüan-hsüeh* were 'being empty' (*hsü*) and 'not being' (*wu*). Thus in the commentary on the *Tao-tê ching* by Wang Pi, one of the earliest of its famous exponents, for example, we read: 'The mysterious is the culmination of the subtle. All creatures have their beginning in the subtle and are then perfected, they begin in not-being and then they live. Thus a man who is constantly without desires can view the mystery of the beginning of creatures.'[4] Buddhist and Taoist meditation is in the main a process of 'emptying oneself'. The concept of not-being, absolute emptiness and Tao are so closely linked that it is almost impossible to distinguish between them. Wang Pi in fact expresses the view that Tao is simply another word for emptiness and not-being.

The extent to which *hsüan-hsüeh* coincides in this respect with

Buddhism emerges, for example, from the following passage in the *Hsin-ching* (= *Prajñāpāramitā*, a body of Mahāyāna literature):

> If we contemplate the five *skandhas* (that is, the components of human nature: visible form, joy and pain, thought and memory, life and death, and knowledge), they are all empty . . . Form is no different from emptiness, emptiness is no different from form . . . Neither to create nor to annihilate, neither to soil nor to clean, neither to increase nor to diminish is therefore the centre of emptiness . . .

Many of the great intellectual figures of the time — for example, Chu Tao-ch'ien (286–374) — represent a doctrine in which *hsüan-hsüeh* and Buddhism were fused. There are numerous cases in which the exponents of one doctrine wrote commentaries on the works of the other.

It is thus possible to speak, as I have already done, of a new type of Chinese intelligentsia. In many ways it resembles the type created later by the impact of the western world, except that the place of the exact sciences and the socialism of the west was occupied by Buddhism, its philosophy, dialectic and monastic life. Just as in modern times, this revolution in Chinese intellectual life appeared as a kind of liberation from authoritarianism and traditionalism, in this case from the strict rules of clan ethics and ritual (*li*). The following judgment from the opposing camp was later passed on Wang Pi and Ho Yen, the leading philosophers of the time:

> Wang and Ho disregarded the rules of custom and culture and did not observe the standards of ritual. They flooded young people with high-flown phrases and fantastic speech, they masked reality with fine, flowery words. They held mysterious emptiness and boundless freedom for quiet penetration (to the truth), they considered Confucian statecraft and orderly contentment inferior . . .
>
> In behaviour they thought it possible for everyone to abandon their dirty practices, but they permitted moderation and good faith only to a limited extent.

It is said, for example, that when Juan Chi, a well-known representative of *hsüan-hsüeh*, heard of his mother's death he did not rise from the game he was playing, and so on.

One of the commonest slogans of the time called for a 'return to the root'. The root stood for the unfettered, the free, that which is in and by itself 'just as it is'. People in consequence tended to live and act in accordance with their innate, individual nature. And this in turn caused them to seek to lay aside or divest themselves of all the trimmings of civilization by which human nature was 'falsified'. There was also a view stemming from the old debate about name (*ming*) and reality, that by nature every person was allocated a specific mission (*ming*) exclusively appropriate to his individual nature. It was only necessary to recognize this natural vocation and to give it free rein. This became identified with the old Taoist principle of non-action (*wu-wei*), which meant not opposing the course of one's own nature or that of great, universal nature.

Both attitudes produced extremely odd results. We read that people who were given to the study of the *hsüan-hsüeh* behaved in an absent-minded way, allowed their hair to grow wild, rose from their beds only in cases of dire necessity and so on. Some gave up speaking but liked to whistle and expressed what they wanted by gestures and sign-language. Very many of them dispensed with clothing and one is inclined to believe that there was a vogue for nudism. Many people also found the intoxication induced by alcohol a more convenient way of attaining to the state to which they aspired in meditation. In this the Buddhists were no exception, as is shown by the example of the celebrated translator, Chu-Shu-lan, son of an Indian family settled in Loyang. He drank an inordinate quantity of wine every day and usually slept off his drunkenness at the roadside.

Such behaviour certainly helped to give the members of the educated classes a sense of freedom and emancipation, which meant for them a release from the strict rules governing the smallest details of decorum of the previous period.

Supporters of the modern idea would often band together in friendly groups. The most widely popular of these was the 'Seven

Wise Men of the Bamboo Grove', an association of eccentric sons of rich landowners. One of the members was Hsi K'ang, whose attitude and opinions give him a place among the true Taoists of the time. These groups with their habit of protesting against every severe government edict began to have too strong an influence on public opinion and they were soon officially prohibited and persecuted.

3. TAOISM AND THE INTELLECTUAL MOVEMENTS OF THE SOUTH

However 'Taoistic' the behaviour of these eccentrics may have been, viewed in the perspective of the history of ideas, they belong to the peripheral areas of the Confucian philosophy. They honoured not Lao-tzŭ but Confucius as the saint of pure culture who was above Being (*yu*) and Not-Being (*wu*) and was precisely for this reason able to apply himself to Being. In contrast to Confucius, Lao-tzŭ, who had not yet reached this stage, wasted himself in dialectic argument over Not-Being and thus, they believed, was only a great man of the second degree.

In practice their efforts were directed towards penetrating to the mystic depths of human nature and exploring its full range by experimentation. But, in fact in the last analysis, this was all for the sake of solving the question of how the human personality could be used to the best purpose in the political community. They never severed the connection between ontological and metaphysical speculation and political thought. Their philosophy was in part based on the fact that they interpreted the character *tao* (way, road) — which frequently appears in classical Confucian works, such as the *Lun Yü*, and should probably be rendered 'correct behaviour' — in the sense of the Taoist Tao and altered their exposition of these passages accordingly. As early as the Han period, efforts of a similar kind had led to the emergence in Confucian scholarly circles of a rationalized form of Taoism and, indeed, if we view the situation as a whole, we can recognize the present trends as the historical development of those earlier ones.

It need not therefore surprise us to find that the exponents of true Taoism were opposed to *hsüan-hsüeh*.

Ko Hung, the leading Taoist of his time, describes the adherents of this doctrine in these words: 'They whistle and lounge about and give themselves over to idleness; this they call "embodying Tao".'[5]

In the meantime, of course, Taoism itself had changed. By the first Han period, Confucianism had already absorbed a number of Taoist ideas, such as the principle of non-activity (*wu-wei*), which were rationally acceptable to it. When the spiritual authority in the state was taken over by Confucianism, Taoism, as was to be expected, became largely restricted to the common people of the rural districts. But there the political trends of the Huang-Lao movement continued to be more active than any other and influenced the formation of numerous communities of varying sizes. These usually centred round some religious leader who had been successful in opening the way to special relationships with the gods and the spirits which determined the life of mankind.

At some time during the Han period, belief in the existence of a secret, superhuman system of accountancy, in which the fate of each individual was decided, probably took root. The sectarian leaders therefore frequently claimed to possess the ability to influence these entries in one way or another. They then evolved a series of prescriptions and rules of conduct for their followers which welded them into a kind of community. These communities, like the monastic bodies of the Buddhists, existed alongside the state: but, in contrast to the Buddhist communities, they often pursued political, subversive aims.

It has already been stated that one of these groups, enlarged by special conditions until it became a popular movement, brought about the uprising of the Yellow Turbans. The failure of this rising undoubtedly brought discredit upon Huang-Lao Taoism but by no means brought the existence of the Taoist sects to an end. On the contrary, it appears that they gained new life from a Taoist political system which had existed for several years in Han-chung.

Many of the practices which arose in these communities, such as washing in urine or rolling in ordure as a mark of penitence, were unacceptable to the Chinese educated class. And we may believe that in general they flourished only in the lowest strata of society and in the more inaccessible corners of the country.

These groups, therefore, at first offered no, or only minimal, competition to Buddhism.

But alongside this popular Taoism there was a current of Taoist thought which was taken seriously in educated circles and found not a few followers there. It even seems that, before Buddhism embarked upon its victorious progress, this movement had been on the point of becoming the dominant religion of the Chin dynasty (265–419), or at least of providing a religion acceptable to the upper reaches of society; and one that, like Buddhism, would have been able to fill the religious and emotional vacuum which ritual (*li*) was unable to satisfy.

The most important exponent of this new, speculative Taoism was Ko Hung (284–363), who has already been briefly mentioned. He came of a family of officials from the district of Wu (roughly corresponding to the western part of China south of the Yangtze), which in the year 280 was annexed by the Chin dynasty. In his youth he had studied the Confucian classics and held many official posts. His criticism cited above of the exponents of *hsüan-hsüeh*, in so far as it expresses a certain local patriotism, stems from a background which is extremely interesting from the socio-historical point of view. The criticism was aimed in fact against innovations which were spreading south from the capital, Loyang, and beginning to oust the ancient civilization of Wu.

In his work, *Pao-pʻu-tzŭ* (*Master who Embraces the Simple*) he criticized the new-fangled influences in the sphere of writing, language and mourning customs,[6] which the Chinese regard as the basic elements of what we might call national characteristics.

As far as writing is concerned, we may suppose that the somewhat ponderous style practised by scholars of the Han period had persisted in Wu, although there is no example available of the ancient calligraphy of this district.

In the north, however, a new, more flowing style had evolved from the cursive script used in official transactions, and this now also began to oust the old style in the south. It was in this same part of the empire about a hundred years later that Wang Hsi-chih (321–379), the greatest of Chinese calligraphers, evolved his style; this he developed on the basis of the new style, which the wave of immigration from the north — inspired by the political events of the time — had caused almost entirely to supplant the old southern style.

Calligraphy in China not only possessed aesthetic merit, but also, from time to time, served to fix the form of the characters, at least in certain basic features. Anyone who has had anything to do with Chinese manuscript texts recognizes the importance of this fact.

The style of writing in Wu had of course been hallowed by ancient popular tradition and the change to the new style was regarded as just such an unwelcome innovation and break with long usage as was the change from *Fraktur* to roman in Germany.

The district of Wu was distinct from the northern part of the empire in regard to speech too, and here again it is tempting to call it a separate southern nation. In a collection of witty sayings, perhaps dating from the first half of the fourth century A.D., there are instances of comical misunderstandings due to differences of speech. Ko Hung remarked of those who endeavoured to imitate the speech of the capital, Loyang, that they were like 'people whose inability to imitate the gait of Han-tan (in Hopei) made them take the most ridiculous tosses'. He found the new way of speaking both shameful and laughable.

In Yang-chou (a town on the lower Yangtze) there developed in official circles at this time a mixed dialect which was perhaps to some extent comparable with the mandarin Chinese ('official speech') of modern times. The common people, however, held fast to the ancient speech of Wu.

The customs of Wu, particularly those connected with mourning, also differed considerably from those of the north. In the south, for example, it was considered most important to express one's feelings of grief by loud, long drawn-out weeping. While in Shantung, mourners were apparently restricted to certain standardized cries and no weeping.

The mourning customs taken in conjunction with the differing modes of expression led to all sorts of misunderstandings. One example follows: a man from Wu brought a present to a friend in mourning who lived in the region of the mouths of the Huang-ho; the present was a contribution to the funeral-ceremony and consisted of a bushel of beans. The northerner expressed his feelings of grief with a cry which his friend took to mean, 'Oh, what shall I do now?' The southerner, to whom such mourning expressions were unknown, answered, 'You can make a meal of them.' Whereupon the northerner, following the custom of his country, cried out again, 'Oh, poor man that I am!' which caused the other to reply, 'In that case I will bring you another bushel.'[7] Even if these anecdotes exaggerate for the sake of comic effect they nevertheless show that marked differences existed.

Ko Hung spoke out loudest against the suppression of mourning laments. 'I prefer that people should show such violence of grief that they exceed the limits laid down by ritual . . . Harmonious sounds controlled by rhythm cannot be called "piercing grief".'

In general he advocated the preservation of the good old customs of Wu. This creates an apparent paradox in which a celebrated Taoist comes forward as a champion of ritual (*li*) in opposition to the frivolous antics of the basically Confucian exponents of *hsüan-hsüeh*. The paradox is, however, accounted for by the differences between the conservative and modern intelligentsia.

The situation was that the new teaching spread only gradually by means of the *ch'ing-t'an* from Honan, whereas north of the Huang-ho and even more in the state of Wu, the 'science' handed down from the Han period has been preserved.

Ko Hung saw this body of knowledge as divided into three main disciplines: the doctrine concerned with the prolongation of life and the art of prophecy, both linked with belief in the Taoist sages; knowledge of ritual and commentaries on the Confucian classics; and finally the Yin-Yang doctrine, astronomy and the science of the calendar.

The first was represented by Ko Hung himself who, as has been noted, began his career by studying the Confucian classics. The first part of his principal work is devoted to the science of prolonging life, alchemy, magical means of warding off evil and so on, while the second is devoted to all kinds of measures relating to the organization of society and the state. Since there can be virtually no question of Ko Hung having been influenced by the old Huang-Lao doctrine, it must be supposed that the Confucian tendencies of his youth left their mark in this second part of the work. It is also significant that he took his Taoist ideas from the Confucian classic, the *I-ching* (*Book of Changes*), which was much studied and was the subject of many commentaries at that period in Wu. He venerated Lao-tzŭ, however, as the progenitor of the doctrine of the preservation of life and did not regard him, as did the *hsüan-hsüeh*, merely as a sage of the second degree. His criticism of the lax habits of Loyang, however, stemmed from the conservative attitude to Confucian practice of those around him.

Ritual was now, as ever, the central point of Confucian studies. There were in Wu a number of learned families in which knowledge of ritual had been passed down from generation to generation. It was often they who provided the advisers who were called to the court over difficult questions concerning the imperial ancestor-worship and the state religion.

The third discipline is, however, of special interest for the series of cosmological theories which were evolved within its framework. Ko Hung gave credence to a theory which originated with the celebrated astronomer of the Han period, Chang Hêng (78–139). According to this theory, heaven was shaped like a hen's egg and the earth was like the yolk. 'Heaven is large and earth small. Inside the lower part of the heavens there is water. The heavens are supported by *ch'i* (vapour), the earth floats on the waters.'[8] Ko Hung overruled the objection that, if this were so, the sun in its course would have to plunge into water by pointing out that the dragons which embodied the *yang* element (= light) also lived in the water. According to this view, the earth remained stationary in the centre while heaven revolved round it. There was another and different theory, according to which both heaven and earth were at rest and only the stars moved. A third theory likened the earth to an inverted dish (with a rectangular rim) roofed by a hemispherical heaven. The rain ran down off the earth and formed the sea which encircled it. The vault of heaven rotated from right to left carrying with it the sun and moon, which also moved independently and very slowly from right to left.

Such were the three branches of knowledge passed down from the Han period and recognized by scholars in Wu. Although each one was represented by a celebrated specialist we must not think of these disciplines as irreconcilably hostile to one another. Many scholars concerned themselves successively with one or another or with all three simultaneously. They were all bound together by the old 'scientific spirit' of the Han period.

The common enemy was the new-fangled attitude of mind from Honan, which, as has already been briefly shown, was a kind of philosophical combination of Confucianism, Taoism and Buddhism on a Confucian basis. Ko Hung said of the innovators that 'they quoted without any proper understanding from the works of Lao-tzŭ and Chuang-tzŭ'. But when they were examined on the disciplines set out above, they became lost in confused and unintelligible talk.[9] They were, in other words, what we would describe today as 'unscientific'.

4. MASS MIGRATION FROM NORTH TO SOUTH

The development was accelerated and given a new turn by the political events of the years 307–316, which produced a mass invasion of northern peoples — Huns, Hsien-pi and others — and a corresponding migration of the Chinese towards the south. The Chin dynasty was re-founded in the year 317 with its capital at Chien-k'ang (Nanking) and the old governmental officials from Loyang.

From now until the year 589, when they were re-united, north and south went their separate ways. With the stream of refugees, the modern 'progressive' science from Honan reached Wu in growing volume, while the conservative knowledge of the Han was increasingly forced into the outlying regions.

The 'nationalistic sentiments' of the people of Wu, already

roused, flared up again at the end of the fourth century in a great uprising. Significantly enough, this was led by a Taoist miracle-man, Sun Ên, who seems to have represented the incarnation of a water-divinity.

The cause of this uprising was conflict over the cheap labour of the impoverished refugees from the north. They were taken in large numbers into the service of indigenous landowners, which led to a considerable increase in the power of the native clans, who, by ancient custom, also used their labourers as private troops.

The new Chin government endeavoured as far as possible to put a stop to this by wholesale impressment of the labour forces, who were then transferred to Chien-k'ang and enlisted in the state army.

As was usual in the south, the rebels fought chiefly on the water and the attacks of their easily manoeuvrable fleet greatly harassed the insecure Chin government. In the year 402, Sun Ên was beaten at last and, with many of his followers, both male and female, drowned himself in the sea. His brother-in-law, Lu Hsün, carried on the resistance in Kuangtung for some time afterwards. He is said to have been the progenitor of the people known as the Tangka. This is a particular ethnic group which still exists in southern China, the members of which live all their lives on boats.

5. THE TAOIST OPPOSITION TO BUDDHISM

Buddhism, which, by virtue of its skilful social policy, had during the fourth century A.D. become the dominant religion of China, represented not only a spiritual, but — to an almost greater degree — an economic force. In spite of the vows of poverty taken by the monks, the monasteries became extremely prosperous. By deed of gift they had often become owners of vast lands. This was, indeed, usually waste land unsuited to agriculture, but the inmates of the monasteries soon learned how to turn them to profit. Among other things, they erected many water-mills which were highly lucrative. Moreover, since the monastic lands were unproductive to lay eyes, they remained untaxed and therefore escaped the confiscations and re-distribution which sometimes affected agricultural land.

In times of political unrest, moreover, the monasteries maintained some degree of security and were much used for asylum and for the safe-keeping of objects of value.

The monks also knew how to circumvent the prohibition on their handling of gold and silver, by making every kind of use of loan and investment. In this way they created a source of credit which was extremely useful to the common people. Unions were also created among Buddhist laymen for mutual economic support and insurance.

Around the monasteries and Buddhist communities, therefore, there arose a strange economy with a religious slant which naturally led to antagonisms and clashes with the great landowners and other users of the purely secular economy.

As was only to be expected, the great success of Buddhism, which was beginning, indeed, to monopolize the whole of Chinese religious life, excited the jealousy of the two other spiritual forces of the country, the Taoists and Confucians. And countermeasures began to be taken.

Great importance attaches, in this connection, to the events of 386–550 in the state of Wei. This state had been founded by the family of Toba, the head of a league of northern tribes, especially Hsien-pi, and for some time embraced the whole of the northern region along the Huang-ho.

It appears that Buddhism in fact began to take possession of the north in about 379, when the celebrated Buddhist, Tao-an, appeared in Ch'ang-an, where he became extremely active as a translator and teacher. Under the Toba, Buddhism became the state-religion. Fa-kuo, the leading Buddhist, declared, indeed, that the emperor T'ai-tsu was a Tathāgata (Buddha) of his day. By this means the political problem of the relationship between church and state was cleverly circumvented, for the Buddhist clergy, who were properly speaking forbidden to bow before a worldly ruler, gave their veneration to the Buddha, not to the emperor. Since, however, the first Toba emperor also had leanings towards Taoism, petty jealousies and intrigues concerning religious primacy in the state were inevitable.

This rivalry extended to the lower classes, where shamanist doctors and predictors of periods of good fortune were deprived of their income by Buddhists versed in Indian calendar mathematics and methods of healing unknown in China.

Indian medicine, like Chinese, was based on the harmonious co-operation of the 'four great elements' (*mahābhūta*): earth, water, fire and wind; but it also brought with it a number of novel procedures such as washing with consecrated water against lameness, the use of fat mutton to expedite delivery and so on.

The Taoist opposition finally found a champion in the person of the religious reformer K'ou Ch'ien-chih (d. 448). He was the son of a rich and respected family, which, after the dissolution of the Taoist state in Han-chung briefly mentioned above, probably moved north to the environs of Ch'ang-an and had preserved its Taoist tradition. His brother was a provincial governor.

The intellectual background from which K'ou Ch'ien-chih staged his reforms is characteristic of the religious eclecticism which reigned among educated Chinese. He appears to have begun as a follower and student of the brand of Taoism expounded by Ko Hung in his *Pao-p'u-tzŭ*. Since, however, the observation of prescribed diets and the use of Taoist medicaments brought no success, he finally put himself to school with the 'saint' Ch'êng-kung Hsing, who was working as a servant in his aunt's household. The friendship began when Ch'êng-kung helped K'ou to solve a difficult problem of ancient Chinese mathematics by a novel arrangement of the numerical quantities. This shows that the 'saint' was in possession of modern 'scientific' methods. That these were imported from Buddhist teachings seems likely from the fact that after his apparent death, Ch'êng-kung Hsing wandered out into the unknown dressed in *dharma* attire, with *pātra* (begging bowl) and *khakkhara* (staff), in short as a Buddhist monk.

After his teacher had disappeared, K'ou Ch'ien-chih became a hermit on the Sung mountain and continued his studies without swerving. He reaped his reward. In the year 415, the T'ai-shang Lao-chün ('the all-highest ancient lord', that is to say, Lao-tzŭ) appeared to him in person, named him 'Master of Heaven' (*t'ien-shih*) and gave him a script in twenty sections containing the 'prohibitions of the nine articles to be recited in the Yün-chung accent' (a region in Shansi?) 'which had not been given to mankind since the beginning of heaven and earth'. He then charged him:

> You will make known my nine articles and purify and correct the Taoist teaching, eradicate the false doctrines of popular Taoism and sweep away the payments in rice and money and the sexual practices associated with it. Great Tao is pure and empty: what should it have to do with affairs of that sort? You will give greatest weight to ritual (!) and to calculations and will supplement these by diet and breathing exercises.[10]

In fact this represents a reform of popular Taoism modelled on the Buddhist *vinaya*, in an endeavour to render it acceptable to the educated classes again after the serious discredit it had suffered at the hands of the Yellow Turbans and Sun Ên. K'ou Ch'ien-chih probably thought of founding a church based on a community which he called 'the seed of the lord of truth', obviously meaning those followers of Lao-tzŭ whom he had selected and chastened by religious discipline. He probably hoped to make his followers a kind of spiritual élite.

K'ou Ch'ien-chih's writings were submitted to the government between 424 and 428 and at first had little success. In the end, however, they aroused the interest of the minister Ts'ui Hao, who thenceforth described the reformer as his teacher and energetically petitioned the emperor on his behalf. The petition shows, however, that at first Ts'ui Hao was not as greatly impressed by the content of the works as he was by the script in which they were written. This script derived directly from Lao-tzŭ and another, as yet unidentified, Taoist sage. They were probably the first examples he had seen of Taoist calligraphy, which at about this period was finding its way into the Toba state from the south. It acquired its virtue from the fact that a god or a sage 'allied himself with the writer, so that the brush in his hand became transfigured'. Ts'ui Hao was only secondarily impressed by the content of the writings.

He was a Confucian and a feudalist of the old stamp and it appears that he thought he recognized in K'ou the 'seed of the lord of truth', the old Confucian aristocracy rallying round the true king, for they, too, were disciplined and held together by the laws of ritual. He was also greatly interested in astrological calculations and here too derived much assistance from the up-to-date, modernized learning of K'ou.

As a result of his recommendation, K'ou Ch'ien-chih was officially recognized as 'master of heaven' and his teaching disseminated throughout the empire. This caused a falling-off among Buddhist sympathizers and Buddhism was described as an unnatural 'philosophy of renunciation and suffering'. 'Its adherents crop their hair, dye their garments and do not live a normal human life.'

As early as the year 438, all monks under fifty years of age were secularized and drafted into the army or the labour force. In the year 446, an arsenal was discovered in a monastery in Ch'ang-an which the emperor believed to have been destined to assist rebels. Among the implements seized in the monastery there was also a fermenting-plant; and an underground room was discovered where ritual deflowerings, such as were customary at the time among the rich families of the north-west, appear to have taken place.

As a result, Buddhists began to be persecuted and these persecutions continued until about the year 458. It is probable, however, that such radical action was not really intended by K'ou Ch'ien-chih, who may have felt himself to have been rather the protector of religious life in general, although with his particular brand of Taoism occupying a privileged position. But Ts'ui Hao encouraged every anti-Buddhist measure, for which he proclaimed the watchword, 'Away with the false, follow the truth.' The truth for him, however, was the old Confucian ideal of the ruler (*wang-tao*, 'the way of the king') which was, of course, irreconcilable with the rule of the Buddha.

But if this short period of persecution impeded the development of Buddhism under the Toba at all, it was only minimally. Only a few years later its position was such that the state of Wei, like certain other states of the period, could almost be called 'Buddhist'. It appears that those Buddhists who were versed in holy writ began to offer strong competition to the Confucian families who had by tradition long occupied the official positions. The hostile attitude of these people is fully understandable.

The most eloquent and enduring witness to the dominant position of Buddhism in the Toba state is afforded by the great cave-temples of Yün-kang, T'ien-lung shan, Lung-mên and elsewhere. The most striking feature of these temples is the gigantic figures hewn from the rock which are presumably an attempt to represent the Buddha in his true dimensions. They are moving examples of the close link that existed in China between Buddhism and sculpture. It should be noted in this connection that every temple, down to the smallest, had its statue of Buddha and the religious or magical efficacy of these depended, of course, upon the exactitude with which the Buddha's features were reproduced. In order to meet this need, the pilgrims to India brought back not only texts but a constant flow of new images of the Buddha which, to the eyes of believers, represented the features of the founder of their religion in ever greater truthfulness. In this way the art of India and of central Asia exerted a continuing influence on Chinese art.

6. THE CONFUCIAN OPPOSITION TO BUDDHISM

The Confucians also at first tended to incorporate Buddhism into their own teachings. The view of Sun Ch'o (320–377), also famous as a poet, who believed that Confucius and Buddha combined to represent respectively the outside and the inside, is typical. Each found its sphere of activity in different situations.

'Therefore Confucius rescued mankind from ultimate corruption and Buddha instructed them in the underlying truth. They are related to one another like the head and the tail, but their final goal is one.'[11]

But it soon became apparent that there were irreconcilable differences between the two doctrines. There was on the one hand the Buddhist commandment: 'The monk shall not venerate the (worldly) king.' While on the other, and irreconcilable with it, was the Confucian principle: 'All who dwell in the empire are servants of the king.'

No political conflict ensued at first as a result of these differences of opinion; but a clear-cut dialectical distinction was drawn between those who faced the world (*tsai-chia*, 'inside the family') or members of the *fang-nei* sphere (meaning 'inside the square' = worldly) and those who turned their backs on the world (*ch'u-chia*, 'outside the family') or members of the *fang-wai* sphere (meaning 'outside the square'). *Chu-chia* meant that all ties with the family and the civil community were severed.

In this respect also, Buddhism coincided in a remarkable way with the anti-ritualistic tendency of *hsüan-hsüeh*. A visitor who arrived to condole with one of the adherents of *hsüan-hsüeh* immediately after the death of his mother found him with his hair loose, drinking wine and playing a board-game. The visitor, however, threw himself to the ground and uttered the prescribed mourning lament. The difference in their behaviour is explained by the fact that one had broken away from worldly ritual (*fang-wai*) while the other was caught up in it (*fang-nei*).

Buddhists, however, came to believe that the spiritual sphere influenced the worldly one. We have already seen that the goal of good government was the state of *t'ai-p'ing* (universal harmony). In the opinion of Buddhists, this was attained in the following manner:

> When the registered population runs into millions, it can be assumed that there are a hundred thousand morally pure (people) among them . . . If one (of these) is able to do a good deed, one evil is eliminated thereby. One evil fewer means that

one punishment is abolished. If one punishment is thus abolished there are ten thousand fewer punishments for the empire . . . In this way a man attains to the condition of *t'ai-p'ing* by sitting (and meditating).

If I understand this somewhat remarkable piece of reckoning aright it must mean that the aim was that at least one person from each family should join the ranks of practising Buddhism by becoming a monk or a nun. The fact that one member of every family had trodden the path of salvation meant that the others would gradually be saved with him, and so on.

It is not difficult to detect behind such utterances the increasing economic independence and power of the Buddhist monasteries and the fact that they were gradually extending their power into the secular world as well.

The counterattack mounted by Confucian propaganda was directed principally against the doctrine of redemption, one of the key-stones of Buddhism. This doctrine was based on the notion that 'something' from one human life would be passed on to another, later, life and could be purified by the believer's conduct until it was finally freed of all dross — especially the will to exist — and attained to the condition of nirvāna. But the Chinese soon came to identify this 'something' which was transmitted from one existence to another with the concept current among them as *shên* ('God', 'spirit', probably in this connection best translated as 'soul'). In other words, the Indian doctrine of karma became a doctrine of the transmigration of souls.

For the Chinese, however, *shên*, or the soul, was in no sense a spiritual or eternal thing but, as we have already seen, something made of the finest substance, capable of surviving death and of living on for a long time, but certainly not for ever.

There had, however, long been scholars who expressed the view that no kind of survival after death was possible. This view was now used to cut the ground from under the feet of the Buddhists. The Confucian arguments have survived in a little work entitled *Shên-mieh lun* (*Discussion about the Transitoriness of shên*). It opens with the words: 'Body and soul are one. As long as one lives, the other lives. When one perishes the other perishes too . . .'

Attention has frequently been drawn to the paradox in which the believers in ancestor-worship appear as champions of a view which denies the existence of the spirits of the ancestors. But the above-named work also states that anything, such as 'plant, beast and man' which 'comes slowly into being also fades slowly'. As long, therefore, as the corpse has not decomposed or the dead man is remembered, he continues to represent a person to whom sacrifices can be offered with rational justification.

The *Shên-mieh lun* ends with a sharp criticism of Buddhism and the work was counterattacked by many Buddhist writers. The criticism runs: 'Buddhism harms the government, the *śramana* undermine morals . . . They dishearten soldiers in battle order and cause employees to sit around idle in the offices . . .' But against this, the writer had to admit that 'From family after family (monks) abandon their relations, man after man gives up (procreating) offspring.'

The new belief with its teaching of requital by damnation or by redemption — regarded, of course, as a kind of social compensation — proved stronger than the Confucian ideal: 'The small man loves his little piece of ground and the gentleman preserves his peaceful simplicity . . . There are subjects in plenty to see to the needs of the overlords.'

The controversies reached their climax under the emperor Wu (561-572) of the northern Chou dynasty (557–580). Wu endeavoured to strengthen the régime, by which he meant to bring it into line once more with the precepts of the sage-kings of classical Confucianism.

This in itself represented a rebuttal of the Buddhist tendency to withdraw from the world. The emperor's aversion was further strengthened by a prophecy current among the common people that the 'black habits' — meaning the monks in their dark garments — would at some time usurp the position of the Son of Heaven — which, indeed, in view of the great flow of men into the monasteries and their consequent escape from army service and civil labour, seemed not altogether improbable.

In the year 568, in the presence of the emperor, a discussion took place between officials trained in Confucian tradition, Taoists and Buddhists. The theme was the *Li Chi* (*Records of Rites*). The emperor sided overtly with the Confucians.

Similar discussions were later held on the subjects of Buddhism and Lao-tzŭ. Their purpose seems to have been to establish the relative position of each movement in the state. In the year 573, it was decided that Confucianism should take first place, Taoism second and Buddhism third. As regards second and third places, this order was changed from time to time in the course of later dynasties, but on the whole it remained constant. It should, however, be noted that, in practice, the circumstances of the 'churches' usually in no way corresponded to this official order.

Since, because of its association with the aristocracy, officialdom and the administration of revenue, the position of Confucianism became more and more firmly established until finally it was unshakeable, the 'church warfare' of the future affected in the main only Buddhism and Taoism.

In the year 574, the emperor again attended a discussion between the three movements. When he sought to intervene on behalf of the Taoists, he was subjected to personal criticism, with the result that an order was issued next day prohibiting both Buddhism and Taoism. All the sacred statues of these persuasions were destroyed, the monks and nuns were secularized and church property and religious buildings confiscated for the benefit of officialdom and the nobility.

When, in the year 577, the emperor annexed the northern state of Ch'i, he ordered the same secularization to be carried out there. Altogether forty thousand temples and monasteries and three million people are said to have been seized.

But even this persecution could not to any considerable extent halt the victorious progress of Buddhism. Under the successors of the emperor Wu it had already regained the position in the spiritual and economic life of the country which it had occupied previously.

It also benefited greatly from the circumstance that the empire was split into several states and that consequently it was always possible for religious refugees to find asylum in a neighbouring state. When they were persecuted in the north they fled south, and conversely. The Buddhists formed, so to speak, the international, or inter-state, element of the time.

Even after the restoration of the united empire under the Sui and T'ang (589–907), the position of Buddhism remained for a time unaffected. The economic power particularly of the Buddhist monasteries can scarcely be over-estimated. Indeed, for a short time it looked as though the empress Wu (690–705) was going to make the T'ang empire into a Buddhist state. It was not until the year 845, that, at the instigation of the Taoists and in order to restore the state finances, a wholesale operation of confiscation and secularization was carried out against the Buddhists and other 'alien religions'. This time 265,000 monks and nuns, together with 4,600 large monasteries and 40,000 smaller places of worship fell victim.[12] It was indicative of the economic situation in the monasteries that at this time 150,000 monastery-slaves were transferred back to the civil economy.

Although Buddhism recovered from this blow also, it never again reached the heights it had previously occupied.

7. DEVELOPMENTS WITHIN BUDDHISM

Buddhism in China assumed, from the beginning, a form which distinguishes it from its Indian prototype. The way in which it entered the country, fragmentarily, through the medium of foreign languages, forced its new followers to establish and develop it in their own way. It is therefore entirely justifiable to look upon and treat Chinese Buddhism as a special case within the Buddhist movement as a whole.

Its historical development can perhaps best be represented as a succession of three Buddhas which in turn occupied the central position in religious life. The first was the original Sākyamuni who has since become so well-known even in the west that it is unnecessary to say more about him. In about the sixth century he was forced into the background by Maitreya (Mi-lo-fo). From about the middle of the seventh century onwards Amitābha was in the ascendant.

Maitreya, the friendly or laughing Buddha, was the successor of Sākayamuni, who was reborn in the Tuṣhita heaven and is now waiting to begin his final reincarnation among men. This is supposed to take place five thousand years after the disappearance of his predecessor in nirvāna.

The emergence of the cult of Maitreya is bound up with the teaching activity of the great Buddhist, Tao-an (312–385). Tao-an gathered six of his disciples together before a standing image of Maitreya and made them take a vow that all their efforts would be directed towards rebirth in the Tuṣhita heaven. Legend has it that the *arhat* Piṇḍola (an *arhat* is one who has ceased to be reborn, having attained enlightenment — the ideal of Hīnayāna Buddhism) had once appeared to him in a dream and had told him that he would not pass into nirvāna but would remain in the western sphere (Tuṣhita) in order to help him, Tao-an, to spread the Buddhist teaching. Eleven days before Tao-an died a strange monk suddenly came to him and enjoined him to arrange a solemn ceremony at which food would be offered to the spirits of the *arhats*. Tao-an asked the saintly apparition where he would be reborn. In place of answer, the saint in a broad gesture pointed towards the north-west, whereupon the sky opened and revealed the Tuṣhita paradise in all its splendour.

The appearance of Mi-lo-fo, so it was believed, ushered in a new and in all respects better era for mankind. It is therefore not surprising that the old Chinese doctrines of world-renewal came to be linked with it and subsequently formed the spiritual background to innumerable disturbances of varying seriousness which run like a red thread through Chinese history.

Maitreya, a serene figure in earlier representations, is usually represented seated as a plump, laughing monk in later times. A wandering monk, Pu-tai (d. 916), who claimed to be the incarnation of the Future Buddha, is reputed to have been the original of this image.

Amitābha, whose name means 'infinite light', is probably the personification of eternal light. He came into fashion among Chinese Buddhists through the activity of the great translator, Kumārajīva, who, among other things, translated the classic work of this special teaching, the *Sukhāvatīvyūha*.

Amitābha is connected with the 'pure land' in the west, Sukhāvatī, which now replaced Tuṣhita as the abode of all those who had taken a vow to defer Buddhahood — that is, their disappearance in nirvāna — until all living creatures had been saved and gathered into Sukhāvatī. Other *bodhisattva* (the Mahāyāna ideal — one who is destined to be enlightened) emerged as well as Amitābha. The best known is Avalokiteśvara, Kuan-yin in Chinese, which means, perhaps, 'he who hears the complaints of mankind'. Although originally male, in about the eleventh century in China, Avalokiteśvara became a female divinity. She is the embodiment of beneficence and as such is often represented as having many arms and sometimes also several heads. She gives succour particularly at times of peril by fire and flood, in cases of sickness or of poisoning, when wild beats or demons threaten and other hazards of the kind.

Another *bodhisattva* also frequently encountered is Kshitigarbha (Ti-tsang — 'earth-granary' — in Chinese), whose main concern is rescuing souls from hell. He is the patron saint of convicts and dead children.

The rise of the cult of Amitābha was preceded, in 402, by a mass vow instigated and led by the Buddhist, Hui-yüan, taken before the statue of Amitābha. Unlike the vow before the Maitreya, however, this was not an internal monastic occasion. Most of those present at this gathering were members of the laity. Each man solemnly bound himself to do everything in his power to help others to reach Sukhāvatī. Those who arrived first were to do all they could to assist others to follow. In this way the mutual economic assistance practised in the lay-community was extended to the spiritual domain. At the same time it meant that the way of salvation, esoteric though it had been until now and confined to the narrow paths of monastic life, was now accessible to all who possessed the determination to follow it.

The success of the Amitābha cult was enormous. Indeed, during the following centuries, the whole of Chinese Buddhism was so powerfully coloured by it that one is almost tempted to assert that a new Buddhist religion had emerged. The idea of survival in paradise, together with some fitting compensation for sufferings endured in this life, was far more comprehensible and more attractive to the Chinese laity than the concept of nirvāna, which could only be grasped dialectically.

The most important exercise of Amitābha Buddhism was *nien-fo*, literally 'to have the Buddha in the mind'. *Nien-fo* was a simplified method whereby lay-people could attain to the state of *samādhi* (*san-mei*), that is, the union of the meditator with the object of his meditation — the Buddha. The person wishing to perform the exercise had to free his mind for a month from all thoughts of food, clothing and other everyday matters and to concentrate on the Amitābha. If, at the end of this period, he had attained to some kind of visionary state the *bodhisattva* would appear to him one day as a dream-figure or a mirage and proceed to instruct him. This explains the importance that was attached to having some image of the Amitābha always at hand, both as a stimulus and focus for meditation. Certain adepts became so proficient that they were able, by looking at any sacred object, to see a shining manifestation of the Amitābha before them in the air. It was, however, considered most essential that this visionary spectacle should appear in the last moments of life and that the dying person should expire with an expression on his face, 'as though he saw something in the void'. This was, of course, the surest sign that he would be reborn in Sukhāvatī.

Later, however, the *nien-fo* method was simplified to the point where the name A-mi-t'o-fo was repeated over and over again in either a loud or a quiet voice. In the T'ang period there was a group of Buddhists who made this their special duty. These belonged to the so-called Sukhāvatī sect, which received its definitive form in the seventh century from the patriarch Shan-tao.

Shan-tao made a distinction between 'the way of the saint', who attains to illumination by his own power, and the 'easy way', by which it is attained through the power of another; that is to say, a *bodhisattva*. As the time grew ever more distant when

Sākyamuni had walked among men, so the first way became increasingly difficult to follow, so that in the end it is almost true to say that only the second remained. By pronouncing the formula, 'Namo Amitafo' ('honour be to Amitābha'), a man declared his faith in the saving power of Amitābha and at the same time became a participant in it.

Another Buddhist group which was, in certain particulars related to the Sukhāvatī sect was the Dhyāna or Ch'an sect (Japanese, Zen) which stemmed from the patriarch, Bodhidharma. It occupied, and still occupies, a very important position. The founder is said to have come to Nanking from South India in about the year 520.

His conversation with the emperor, Wu-ti (502–549) of the Liang dynasty is significant. Wu had given orders that a number of Buddhist temples should be built and sutras be written down, and had put no obstacle in the way of his people's religious aspirations. He now wished Bodhidharma to confirm that he had earned great religious merit thereby.

But Bodhidharma replied, 'These actions carry no merit. They are actions which determine whether a man shall be reborn in heaven or on earth. They are like shadows which follow the body and they are not free from worldliness. But true merit is free of worldliness and lies beyond comprehension.'

The emperor then asked in what did true religious merit consist.

Bodhidharma answered, 'In absolute emptiness. Even the thing which you call holy does not exist.'

Whereupon the emperor asked, 'Who are you who answer me thus?'

Bodhidharma replied, 'I do not know.'

In general the doctrines of this school can be summarized in four principles.

1. Truth specially transmitted outside the recorded writings.
2. No recognition of the authority of the written word.
3. Direct path to the soul of man.
4. Becoming the Buddha by insight into one's own nature.

The principal exponent of Dhyāna Buddhism is the patriarch Hui-nêng (637–713), through whom this sect became widely disseminated. Although it acquired its name from Dhyāna or meditation, it is based, fundamentally, less on meditation than on sudden and violent insights into the 'truth' or, in other words, on illumination, although the way to illumination had to be prepared by a long period of attentive waiting.

Thus, for example, it is written,

> The more a man speaks, the more a man thinks, the less he recognizes the way. Give up speaking, give up thinking and you will penetrate all things.
>
> In emptiness things rise before us out of our empty imaginings. It is senseless to seek after the truth. Only bring your imagination to rest.

Another sect with a very wide following was the T'ien-t'ai school founded by Chih-i (538–597) and based on the *Saddharma-puṇḍarīka* (*Lotus Sutra*). This sect recommended a kind of meditative gymnastics in which correct deportment, correct breathing and concentration were essential. These exercises had to be accompanied by friendly and sympathetic thoughts.

The groups we have called sects cannot, certainly, be regarded as such in the western sense of groups which have splintered off from the church. They rather represent currents within the church. They often originated with a particular teacher, and persisted because his authority was perpetuated from generation to generation by his successors. They were often based simply on a preference for certain Buddhist texts. One example is the highly speculative Fa-hsiang (Dharmalakṣaṇa) sect, which was based on the translation of the Yogācārya made by the celebrated pilgrim, Hsüan-tsang (600–664), on his return from India. The concern of this school was to discover the final unity of cosmic existence by contemplation and examination of the characteristic features of existence. It had a particularly stimulating effect on the wave of philosophical activity in the Sung period.

The most important works of Chinese Buddhism are collected in the Tripiṭaka, or the 'Three Baskets'; they are the Sutra-,

Vinaya- and Abhidharma-pitaka, in which the writings are, in general, divided into the categories of doctrine, law, and discussions on these two subjects.

The first collection of Buddhist literature was made as early as the beginning of the sixth century, under the Liang emperor, Wu-ti. Another was made in about 600. The Buddhist canon appeared in print for the first time in the year 980. The edition most frequently used today is probably the Taīshō Tripiṭaka printed in Japan in 1924.

This canon, however, contains by no means every work of Chinese Buddhism. Other collections, some considerably more comprehensive, have also appeared. It still remains, however, our main source of information regarding the Buddhist religion in China.

8. OTHER FOREIGN RELIGIONS

Buddhism was not the only religion which came to China from abroad. In the great cities along the main trade routes were to be found in the T'ang period Zoroastrians, Jews, Nestorians, Mohammedans and Manicheans. But it was only the two last who played any considerable part in Chinese history.

Manicheism began to make itself felt in China at about the beginning of the eighth century. Like Buddhism and Christianity, it achieved recognition through the superior scientific learning of one of its followers; he intervened successfully in a dispute between the court astronomers with the result that his co-religionists were treated with great tolerance in the capital, Ch'ang-an. A further result was that, in about 762, one of their number converted the Uighur Khan to Manicheism.

The Uighurs, whose empire at that time bordered on China to the north-west, were for a short time one of the principal great powers of the period; through them Manicheism acquired a certain reputation based on political considerations and it appears from then onwards to have won a small following among the Chinese themselves.

When, in the period 840–843, the power of the Uighurs began

to wane, strong measures were immediately taken against the Manicheans, as a result of which some communities became extinct and some were exiled to different provinces of the empire. This process culminated, in the year 845, in wholesale persecution of all foreign religions in the T'ang empire.

This, however, did not mean the end of Manicheism in China. It reappeared in the Sung empire (960–1279), represented both by a few officially sanctioned temples in the capital and by illegal communities, who 'assembled in darkness and scattered in the morning' and were particularly numerous in the hilly districts of the south-eastern provinces.

A fusion took place in these communities between the Manicheans and certain rebelliously inclined underground Taoist sects. And indeed a number of uprisings, particularly that of Fang La (1120) possess an unmistakable Manichean character, as well as the familiar Taoist features. This was exemplified, on this occasion, by the fact that the female followers, whose lot was not to fall in battle like the men, lined up naked and committed suicide.

Chinese commentators regard as the principal features of Manichean communities the fact that their members ate only one meal (in the evening), observed a vegetarian diet, abstained from intoxicating liquor and from butter and milk, which, particularly in the pre-T'ang period, were among the staple sources of nourishment in North China, and were buried unclothed. Similar tendencies were apparent in many other Chinese religious communities. Moreover, the key-stone of Manicheism, the two principles of light and darkness and the 'five-fold division of the body of light' (that is, the elements), coincided so closely with the Chinese view of the world that one might say that this doctrine was predestined to be absorbed into Chinese thought.

It was also the Manicheans who first brought the planetary week of seven days to the knowledge of the Chinese; and their name for Sunday, *Mi* (Sogdian *mir*=sun), has survived until modern times in the local almanacks of the eastern provinces of China. It is also said that the name of the Ming (i.e., light) dynasty goes back to the Manicheans. Finally, another subspecies of the Kuan-yin — 'the white-robed Kuan-yin' — which gives souls to new-born children, appears to have been connected with this religion of light.

If the traces left by Manicheism on the spiritual life of China are few, Islam had even less influence, in spite of the fact that there are still a fair number of Muslims in Kansu, Shensi and Yunnan. The followers of Islam are mostly descended from non-Chinese whose children, however, by intermarrying with Chinese women, have in the course of time become Chinese in everything save their religious beliefs. This descent does not apply to Chinese orphans who were often bought up by Muslims from starvation areas and nurtured in Islam.

Like the Buddhists, the Mohammedans (*hui-hui* in Chinese) tried to use a legend of a certain dream of the T'ang emperor, in which a turbanned man had featured prominently, to establish an association between their own religion and Chinese influential circles. But in contrast to the Buddhist endeavour, none of their efforts to invade the upper classes achieved lasting success.

It is certain that, from the beginning of the T'ang period, a powerful Muslim colony existed in Kuang-chou, the main port for foreign trade. They differed from the natives in that they did not eat pork, drank no wine and touched the flesh of no animal which they had not slaughtered themselves. This colony suffered a severe setback as a result of religious persecution and political troubles at the end of the T'ang period.

Another wave of Mohammedans entered China by the overland route through Kansu, and Islamic battalions seem from time to time to have fought in the T'ang army.

But Mohammedanism as a religion in China always retained its alien character notwithstanding. It was never assimilated in the way that Buddhism and Manicheism were. One of the reasons for this may be that the Mohammedans, the great majority of whom were merchants and soldiers, were never in a position — to the same extent as the Buddhists and Manicheists and, later, the Catholic missionaries were — to make important contributions to the modernization and development of the calendar and of astronomy, both so important to the régime. Historically, however, they made themselves conspicuous by their violent uprisings in Yunnan and Kansu. The nationalist, separatist tendencies of the Mohammedans were particularly strong in Chinese Turkestan, and later, during the Manchu period, it sometimes looked almost as though an independent Islamic state would arise there.

VIII

The T'ang Dynasty

1. FOREIGN INFLUENCES

The T'ang dynasty (618–906), one of the most brilliant eras of Chinese history, was preceded by the Sui dynasty (581–617), which came to a premature end largely as a result of the extravagance of the second emperor's household. Like Ch'in Shih-huang-ti and Han Hsiao-wu-ti, this emperor appears to have taken advantage of the great economic activity precipitated by the unification of the empire to increase his power and magnificence to an immoderate degree. But he did — although apparently also for his own purposes — order the building of the important north–south waterway, the Grand Canal.

In spite of its short duration, the Sui dynasty forms the beginning of a socio-historical period which continued into the T'ang and is therefore usually called Sui-T'ang.

One of the first measures taken concerned the legal system, which at this date assumed the form and divisions which it retained until European legal ideas and formulae found their way into China. Two changes in the new code were generally regarded as important: the reduction in the number of death penalties to two — strangulation and decapitation — and the abolition of punishments by castration. Legal regulations under the T'ang were also divided into four groups: codified laws (*lü*), special laws (*ling*), decrees (*ko*) and promulgations (*shih*). This classification also lasted until very recent times. Whereas the first group remained a constant quantity, the others were from time to time altered according to circumstance and published in official compilations.

Great and important changes now also took place in the realm of music. In the previous period new instruments, such as the lute (*p'i-p'a*), a form of harp known as *k'ung hou*, the reed-pipe, the bamboo flute and others, had already reached China from the 'barbarian' countries, mainly from Turkestan. Music of a new type suited to these new instruments soon predominated in the north, while the old music of the Han persisted only in the southern states.

Since the Sui civilization followed the cultural line of the northern states in most things, it also adopted the prevailing trends in music. Among these music from Kucha, which enjoyed a rapidly increasing popularity among all classes, occupied a special position. The first Sui emperor endeavoured, indeed, to halt this development, but it was already too late. A veritable mania for music of all kinds — but especially foreign music — must have arisen under his successor and at the T'ang court. The statement that 'the ruler and his officials were drowned in music' is probably true.

In addition to the departments for classical ceremonial music and for Han music, others were set up for music from Korea, India, Kucha, Kashgar, Siam (Hsin-lo) and Burma, for the music, in short, of all the peoples with whom the T'ang court had cultural connections.

The number of native and foreign artistes gathered in the capital is said at one time to have amounted to ten thousand. The female singers and dancers were installed in two large quarters and could also be hired by prosperous private individuals for their own entertainment. The families of the court artistes lived in the same quarters and the daughters were permitted to visit their mothers or sisters only twice a month. Employment at court was of course much like a form of political appointment and was greatly sought after by these ladies.

The higher officials were also allowed to keep girl musicians and the like, although the numbers permitted were scaled according to rank. In the larger cities, vast places of entertainment sprang up in which travellers with money could meet singing girls. Famous poets wrote the words for popular songs.

A special feature of the new music seems to have been the replacement of the five-tone scale by a scale of seven tones. It also appears that ancient Chinese music had always been performed by a single instrument, and that it was not until the later Han period that, under the influence of Turkestan, several instruments began to be played together in harmony.[1] But this development did not reach its climax until the T'ang period. And it was at the same period that falsetto singing ('upside-down larynx' in Chinese) came into fashion and by degrees completely replaced the ancient Chinese style of singing. The music of the T'ang period survives to some extent in the Japanese music of today.

Music was not, however, the only cultural import. Many new dances, games and artistic performances came in at the same time. Stimulated by foreign innovations, the illusionist tricks of the Han period, already described, came to life again at all levels of society. 'Exciting customs', in the form of spectacles and competitions, were presented frequently in the cities and probably, though to a lesser extent, in rural districts as well.

One sport in particular, in which the onlookers stood round and sprinkled groups of naked youths with cold water,* enjoyed great popularity during the second half of the seventh century. The custom originated in Samarkand, where it had formed part of the celebrations to usher in the winter. Polo and football were introduced into China at the same period, women apparently sometimes taking part in the former.

Altogether it appears that great waves of pleasure-seeking periodically swept through the population. We have an account of the popular festivities which fell every year on the fifteenth day of the first month, at which competitions were a special attraction. Crowds so thronged the streets that it was impossible to force a way through.

> The din of drums filled the heavens, the glare of torches lit up the earth. Many people wore animal masks and men dressed up as women. Singing girls and jugglers went about in fantastic attire. Unseemly abuse (of the authorities) was received as rare

* P'o-han-hsü.

> fun and common obscenity as wit. The inmates of the inner and outer chambers (i.e., women and men) looked on together and did not remain separated from one another . . .[2]

Not unlike the riotous scenes at carnival time in the west!

It also seems clear that the new attitude of mind which was permeating China from the north and the west was bringing, to many sections of society, a change in the position of women. Women now often made public appearances outside the 'inner chambers' which ancient Chinese tradition forbade them to leave except on the rarest occasions. Fairly large numbers of women, presumably for the first time, now earned their own keep as singers, dancers and performers and, at any rate in the large cities, became a factor in public life. A note on the back of one of the roll-books found in a walled-up temple-grotto near Tun-huang (West Kansu) reveals that there were even women's societies at this time. Members were obliged to give mutual aid, to attend regular meetings and to make fixed contributions. It is true that most of these societies appear to have been inspired and directed by Buddhist monasteries, but they do nevertheless, show that the strict family spirit of the Confucians was no longer the criterion at every level of society, and that it was possible for women to have some life of their own outside the family circle.

2. ARISTOCRACY AND OFFICIALDOM

Taking this in conjunction with the spread of Buddhism into every sphere of Chinese life, we cannot but conclude that there is less truth in the theory of the unbroken continuity of Chinese civilization from the rise of Confucianism to the present-day than many writers appear to believe. And it is, perhaps, more correct to regard the end of the Han period as the conclusion not only of a historical but also of a cultural epoch.

How insecure the cultural situation still was during the T'ang period, can be seen from the fact that we now hear for the first time of measures which might be called 'race laws'. Their purpose was, as far as possible, to keep those foreigners entering the country — Uighurs, Arabs, Sogdians, Persians, Japanese, Koreans, Tongkingese and others — separate from the indigenous population. Men who had married Chinese women were no longer allowed to leave the country. The foreigners usually lived in separate districts under their own administration, or, one might say, in ghettoes or cultural quarantine establishments. Only persons who possessed useful knowledge or those nationalities, such as the Uighurs, who were recognized as being on a footing of equal political power with the Chinese, gained access to the cultivated classes. In the principal commercial cities, such as Ch'ang-an and Yang-chou on the lower Yangtze, there were colonies of five or six thousand foreigners or more.

It must, however, be recognized that Confucianism, although sometimes very much restricted and forced to accept all sorts of modifications, always came to the surface again and accommodated itself to new conditions. It runs like a thread, if sometimes a very tenuous one, from the Han period on through Chinese history and only in the present-day, since China has espoused Marx-Leninism, has it finally been broken.

The continuity of Confucianism throughout history is probably due less to any concept or ethical system than to the fact that as administrators the Confucians held a key-position in society.

Those who control the administrative system govern both politically and socially. And probably the worst aspect of the great catastrophe of the end of the second Han dynasty was the destruction of the huge ministerial records in the capital, which had, presumably, taken the previous two hundred years to build up.

In the circumstances, these records might easily have been reconstituted by scribes imbued with the Buddhist spirit. But however near certain states of the fifth and sixth centuries may have come to such a development, under the Sui dynasty the technique of administration was again largely in the hands of the traditional Confucian families.

The political centre of the T'ang empire was 'the land inside the passes', that is, the capital Ch'ang-an, in Shensi, and the surrounding country. But the rulers there were the aristocratic clans who had been taken over by the northern dynasties which preceded the T'ang, the Northern Chou and the Sui, whose tradition was military and whose origins were often non-Chinese. The imperial family of Li was one of these. The aristocrats enjoyed many privileges, one of which was exemption from taxes; and their livelihood was assured by the fact that, according to their rank, they were assigned a number of tax-payers responsible for supplying their households. Imperial princes, for example, enjoyed the income from the taxes from five to ten thousand families, and dukes, from one to two thousand. Marriages in these clans were usually subject to the consent of the emperor.

But, particularly in Shantung, the old families of officials and *shih* existed and these were the true representatives of the Chinese cultural tradition.

They enjoyed public respect on account of their 'fidelity and piety, classical studies and wide knowledge', qualities which distinguish not so much the brave warrior as the good state-official. They did not, however, occupy high and lucrative offices, for these were held by the nobility. In order to escape from poverty, they often sought marriages in which handsome dowries were the first consideration.

In fact, these families formed a coterie which stood in violent opposition to the T'ang military nobility, who they thought 'smelled of sheep and goats' — meaning that they lacked the culture appropriate to their position.

This problem was tackled under the second T'ang emperor by placing these families and the nobility on registers. Marriages were thereby made subject to official permission, a device designed gradually to break up these antagonistic clan cliques.

There were probably social and even economic advantages in being placed on the registers. At all events, quarrels soon broke out as to who should be so listed, with the result that this 'Almanac de Gotha' was constantly being revised. Presumably the question at stake was usually whether civil or military services should be given pride of place.

The conflict was, in fact, all part of the same opposition between the non-Chinese, nomadic military nobility and the true

Chinese or naturalized families of scholars which had earlier caused the Toba Wei state to split into two parts, an eastern and a western. This ancient antagonism was still unresolved when the T'ang period opened. The principal weapon of the scholars was now the examination, which required intensive work on Chinese classical culture.

The holding of examinations had already begun in about 589–618 under the Sui dynasty. The principal subjects for examination were literary style and thorough knowledge of the Confucian classics, but they also included law, knowledge of the characters used in writing and mathematics, although these last subjects were much less highly valued. Candidates had to have studied from two to five of the classics — which they selected themselves — with extreme thoroughness. According to the number of characters they contained, these works were divided into long (e.g. the *Li Chi*), medium (e.g. the *Shih Ching*) and short (e.g. the *Shu Ching*). In the examination itself, quotations had to be identified, texts explained and set themes developed in writing. The candidate also had to compose petitions, addresses to the emperor and poems. Elegance of style and a good memory were the main qualities required for success in these examinations.

Besides the ordinary examination, which usually took place annually, there were a number of special ones which were mostly decreed by the emperor for some particular purpose. The most remarkable were probably those held from time to time for boys of ten years of age and under. The little boys were required to master one of the classics, the *Hsiao-ching*, for example, or the *Lun Yü*. When one of them answered all the questions correctly he was given an appointment. Some of the official histories contain accounts of boys who were capable of reciting an entire classic by heart.

In the provinces the candidates usually prepared for the examination by studying at home and underwent a preparatory test by the regional or district board before being permitted to enter for the examination in the capital. There was a fixed quota of permissions for each region and district.

All this shows that the whole system depended upon the

families which possessed a tradition of literary activity and scholastic studies.

The candidates were described as 'provincial tribute' (*hsiang kung*), and at the great new year's reception at the imperial palace they stood next to the gifts brought from the various provinces. This practice stemmed, of course, from the old feudal idea that it was the duty of the people to place their best powers at the disposal of the ruler without thought of reward.

There was a special school in the capital open only to the sons of the high nobility and the superior officials. But from the year 631 onwards, the sons of foreign nobility — from Korea, Siam, Turkestan, Tibet and elsewhere — also studied there. Candidates for the examination were put forward by the masters of the school.

The examinations in law, knowledge of the characters and calligraphy, and mathematics (regarded as being inferior to the others) were usually taken by sons of the lower officials and sometimes even by common people. There were special schools in the capital for these subjects also.

Another form of examination was set up for serving officials trying for promotion. They were examined in four subjects: demeanour, speech, writing and stylistic expression.

In most respects, the examination system took on under the T'ang the form to which it adhered during successive dynasties.

It should be noted that at first the high nobility was but little affected by all this. In these spheres, sons obtained high positions in the state by virtue of their fathers' services. And even when they underwent the rigours of the examination they were tested far less thoroughly than the other candidates.

In the course of time, however, the political success of the examination system began to tell. Things had changed so greatly by the reign of the ninth emperor of the T'ang dynasty (712–756) that the most important offices were very largely filled by men who had reached their position through the examinations and mostly came of scholarly families from the east and south-east of the empire.

The empress Wu has already been briefly mentioned in connection with her sympathy with Buddhism, and her reign contributed much to this social revolution. In the year 684, Wu, a woman of great cunning and lack of scruple, deposed the weak emperor and reigned for a short period (705) over a new dynasty which she called Chou. She espoused the cause not only of Buddhism but also of the examination, which she used as an instrument to break the power of the high nobility. Her rule, in fact, marks the victory of the anti-aristocratic trends of the T'ang empire.

The spirit which arose with the new social group soon made itself felt in the capital and the central territories of the empire, where it took the form of a marked tendency towards pacifism. The emperor favoured art and science, and 'spear and arrowheads were melted down'. The registers of the nobility went to ruin and disappeared, which was another sign of the weakened position of the aristocracy. Contempt for the army and for military prowess dominated the public mind. 'The rich traded in silk and lived in luxury. The strong arranged competitions or indulged in sports such as weight-lifting and so on. But no one exercised himself in arms. And so, when troubles came, they were afraid and unable to defend themselves.'

The military strength of the T'ang shifted, however, to the frontiers, where military governors established and maintained strong armies. The result of the attempt by the minister and aristocrat, Li Lin-fu, to re-establish a strong central power in opposition to the frontier forces was a devastating uprising of the minor aristocracy in the northern provinces (especially Hopei). This rebellion took place under the leadership of An Lu-shan, a skilful courtier of Sogdian descent, in 755, soon after the death of Li Lin-fu. It caused a more decisive break in the continuity of the T'ang dynasty than the usurpation of the empress Wu. From then onwards the real power fell increasingly into the hands of the frontier governers, and as a result of their hostility both the central government and the T'ang dynasty finally came to an end.

3. FOOD-SUPPLIES, TEA AND PORCELAIN

One of the most important factors in the economic life of this period was the system of storage by which supplies were assured. There were several kinds of granaries which may be roughly classified as those in the capital, regular granaries in the provinces, equalizing granaries and 'voluntary' granaries.

This storage system was, however, primarily designed to provide for the official classes, the army and so on. In times of need, official provisions were handed out to the common people to alleviate or prevent famine, but this was always a special act of grace on the part of the government and often came much too late.

As early as about 583, therefore, the ministry of economics proposed that the common people should be required to help themselves by building 'voluntary granaries'. The proposal in question reads:

> I have heard that the state depends upon the common people but that the common people depend upon nourishment. It was therefore the special policy of the Former Kings to encourage agriculture. In ancient times men tilled the land for three years and could thus save provisions for one year. Thus, after nine years, they had provisions for three years. So that, even when flood and drought brought calamity, the common people had no semblance of hunger . . . Last year there was starvation in parts of Honan and south Shensi. Your Majesty, therefore, sent grain from Shantung and installed 'equalizing officials' who opened the public granaries. This may certainly be called great virtue and generous mercy. I therefore beg that the provincial and district authorities be urgently instructed to encourage agriculture and to store provisions.[3]

Although it appears from this that these emergency granaries were built at official instigation, they originated in the spontaneous initiative of the common people and were administered by them. They probably served not only as a temporary expedient in times of need but also as warehouses for seed-corn and were associated with the agricultural co-operatives, members of which were committed to assist one another in essential work on the land. We may well believe, therefore, that a far-reaching system of self-help had already been in existence and only now received official recognition and encouragement.

In the course of the T'ang period, however, these voluntary granaries were made subject to taxes and brought under state administration. In the end, the main purpose they served was that of supplementing the regular granaries. There was no further mention of voluntary action in connection with them and to stock them became only one more compulsory impost.

Equalizing granaries had already existed in the Han period. They were now seen primarily as a means of supporting the marketing system which was beginning to flourish vigorously but was also, of course, exposed to many shocks. The underlying idea was expressed in a petition of the year 764, in approximately these terms: '. . . to set up equalizing granaries and funds in every region, so as to buy corn on the spot when current prices are low in order to increase the prices, but to sell when prices are high in order to bring them down.'[4]

When this system was properly handled, it must often have brought some degree of stability into the prices of provisions and capital goods. Since, however, these granaries operated rather by granting credit than by actual transactions in capital goods, their function resembled that of credit banks. And so it came about that, in the hands of unconscientious officials, the granaries soon assumed the character of money-lending establishments charging usurious rates of interest. The main concern was skilfully to manipulate the basic capital so as to increase it as swiftly as possible. The original purpose of balancing the market was, however, often achieved solely by the fact that the merchants were tempted by the high prices into supplying corn and goods to needy areas. The state, in the persons of its officials, was also the principal buyer at the markets and was far from being neutral or disinterested. There was also the fact that the granaries were subject to strict controls and if only for this reason the managers lent or paid out only when they could be certain of obtaining an increased return. The incomes of the officials even depended in many cases upon the success of such financial manoeuvres.

In the end, the granary system sustained a severe blow from An Lu-shan's rebellion, mentioned above. An attempt was, indeed, afterwards made to balance the economy by increasing the taxes — these were even imposed, in 766, on 'germinating seed' since 'even by stretching effort to the utmost, the need of the country could not be met until the autumn' — but without lasting success. An attempt was made to meet the continually growing need of the army by official purchases – or requisitionings, as they soon became — from the rural population.

Special importance, naturally, attached to the granaries in the capital Ch'ang-an, for if they failed dangerous uprisings might easily ensue. During the Sui-T'ang period they came increasingly to be stocked from the south-eastern provinces. This meant that the Grand Canal, the waterway leading from Hang-chou (Chekiang) to Ho-yin (Honan) and from there up the Huang-ho and Wei rivers to Ch'ang-an, became the main artery of the empire. Since high or low water could cause the transport ships long delays in every section of the journey, a cargo took about a year to cover the whole distance. The final lap in particular, in which the San-mên rapids had to be bypassed by overland transport, caused great difficulties. The problem was at last partially solved by setting up intermediary granaries at the main depots. The boats then merely plied between these. Transport was later so much improved that large quantities of salt could be sent from Yang-chou (on the lower Yangtze) to Ch'ang-an by special consignment in forty days.

It is hardly necessary to add that this vital transport system was also catastrophically dislocated by An Lu-shan's rebellion.

The increase in transport from the south-eastern provinces is associated with marked changes in the eating habits of the population.

The northerners had until now lived chiefly on pulse and corn. Consumption of dairy products seems to have decreased as the nomadic element became more completely assimilated to the Chinese, although it had by no means ceased in the T'ang period.

A kind of round, flat bread-like cake was baked from wheatflour. These were enjoyed and eaten everywhere, and the northern peoples were glad to receive them in exchange for meat, koumiss and so on.

All the same, little meat was eaten, even by people who could afford to eat well, a circumstance which probably has something to do with the difficulty of keeping it and the fact that the price was relatively high as a result. An order of the second T'ang emperor (627–649) is worthy of note in this connection: 'I hereby forbid government commissars to eat meat, for I fear that this will too greatly increase the expenses of the regions and districts. There is no objection, however, to their eating poultry.'[5] That this was allowed is probably due to the fact that small animals could be eaten at once. Larger beasts or larger numbers of beasts were probably as a rule slaughtered only in the cities, where it was certain that they would be eaten quickly or where suitable arrangements for storage existed.

In the south, fish and rice replaced meat and wheat. Rice came to be eaten more and more in the north as well, although in the T'ang period it was still regarded in the capital as a form of luxury; this was presumably because the long and expensive journey kept the price so high that it was usually beyond the means of the mass of the people.

The primary reason for this growing change may have been that the harvests in the region of the mouth of the Yangtze were more constant and more plentiful, so that, in spite of its great distance, that area could furnish more regular provision than the northern territories, continually threatened as these were by bad harvests.

Tea also first became popular during the T'ang period. It had, of course, long been known in those parts of the empire where it grew wild. Originally, however, the leaves — which possessed refreshing properties despite their bitter taste — were probably only chewed. Towards the end of the third century, it came into fashion in the south in the form of an infusion made from the leaves, although at first it probably served as a substitute for wine.

From then on, however, it gradually became a universal beverage and one of the principal exports of the south-eastern provinces and of Szechuan. Its popularity was no doubt increased by the fact that a certain curative effect was attributed to it. In the year 793, tea-trading had become so widespread that the state introduced a tea-tax. In about 814, the tea-trade became a state monopoly, as the salt-trade had done many years before. Rest-houses were set up along the main trading-routes, at which tea could be bought. In about 841–846, the duty on tea was so high and need among the common people so pressing that tea-transports were sometimes plundered and an illegal tea-trade developed.

As early as the T'ang period, Lu Yü (d. 804), a strange character from Hupei, even wrote a book about tea. He describes the origin of tea, methods of preparing it and the utensils used. The work undoubtedly contributed to the popularity of tea-drinking in educated circles. Tea became, in the end, one of the principal exports of China; indeed, the country long held a monopoly, which ended only when India and other countries began to cultivate the plant.

Closely associated with tea is the porcelain which too has brought world-wide fame to China. Lu Yü's book on tea contains, for example, a classification of tea-cups according to their quality. He rates those from the kilns of the district of Yüeh-chou (Chao-hsing), Yü-yao and Hang-chou in Chekiang — highest. The cups from Ting-chou (Hunan?), Wu-chou (Chekiang), You-chou (Hunan), Shou-chou (Anhui) and Hung-chou (Kiangsi) came next. There was also a centre of production in the north, at Hsing-chou (Hopei), the wares of which were considered by many to equal those from the Yüeh kilns. Lu Yü, however, thought that the latter could be compared with jade or ice, whereas the former were comparable only with silver or snow.

It appears that the quality of porcelain was judged partly according to how well it showed up the colour of the tea. Thus we read:

> The porcelain cups from Yüeh-chou and You-chou are of a light bluish tinge and when they are filled with tea it appears reddish-white. The Hsing-chou porcelain is white and gives the tea a red colour. That of Shou-chou is yellow and makes the tea

> purple, that of Hung-chou is brown and the tea looks blackish. None of them shows the tea to full advantage.

But of the best porcelain cups from Yüeh-chou, he says that the tea in them took on a greenish colour, and this was apparently what he had valued most highly.

Great efforts had long been made, particularly in the south, to achieve a light colour, a glistening blue or greenish hue, for glazed pottery and porcelain. Part of a poem runs: 'Breaking open the kilns of Yüeh in the autumn, you see before you the colour of a thousand peaks and king-fishers.' And in another poem this porcelain is described as 'clear as autumn water'. Both aimed at light colours like the blue of distance and the green of the sea. But in the north, efforts were rather directed towards producing white porcelain.

After colour, hardness and lightness were the qualities looked for in assessing the merit of porcelain wares, also the ring of the porcelain when it was tapped with a chopstick.

All this shows that, during the T'ang period porcelain was by no means rare, but rather formed part, to some extent at least, of ordinary household equipment. The number of kilns shows that factories were already growing up in various places which, in order to satisfy the general demand, produced marked wares of different qualities. Porcelain was submitted annually as the official tribute from Yüeh-chou and Hsing-chou.

The fact that copper, and with it bronze vessels, had become scarce was a factor which, in conjunction with the growing popularity of tea-drinking, greatly contributed to the spread of porcelain. In consequence of the brisk foreign trade, a constant stream of copper money left the country. This caused such a scarcity of the metal, which was an essential means of payment, that, in the year 785, an order was promulgated whereby travellers were forbidden to export even one copper coin. This was not the first prohibition of its kind. As early as 713, it had been forbidden to use copper coinage in trading with the peoples of the south-west.

Porcelain vessels therefore took the place of those which had been made of bronze. Thus in a work of the Ming period, devoted to vases and flowers, we read: 'In ancient times there were no porcelain vases. They were all made of copper. It was not until the T'ang period that porcelain vessels came into use.'

Porcelain, in the true sense of the word, was not produced until the beginning of the Sui dynasty. Legend has it that Ho Chou, an official famed for his technical abilities, profited from the experience of artisans to produce a sufficiently high temperature in the kilns to make glass. In the process, the conditions for the manufacture of porcelain were also created. Thickly glazed pottery had, however, existed since the end of the Han period, when a kind of porcellanous celadon had been achieved, and this may be regarded as a first step towards porcelain.

For the rest, the history of Chinese porcelain and its periods of brilliance under the Ming and Ch'ing dynasties has been told so often in specialized monographs by European authorities, that it is unnecessary to go into it again here.

4. THE T'ANG SHORT STORY AND *PIEN-WÊN*

The outstanding features and achievements of the T'ang period in the cultural sphere are, however, neither economic nor technical, but literary. They are represented by the short story and by poetry.

The Chinese regard the short story as belonging to a category described as *hsiao-shuo* or 'short discourses'. This description accords with a saying of Confucius recorded in the *Lun Yü*: '. . . Even the minor walks (of knowledge) have an importance of their own. But if pursued too far they tend to prove a hindrance. . . .'[7] This means that those who govern should take heed of even the slight and apparently meaningless utterances of the common people, for they sometimes contain expressions of mood or opinion which may be of vital importance for the destiny of the country.

It is said that in ancient times there was even an official whose special duty it was to write down and collect the stories, sayings and songs current in the alleys and streets of the towns and in the villages.

In the form in which this literary genre appears today, it includes works of the most various content. There are collections of comments on and elucidations of other works, of anecdotes and short notes on historical events, personalities or political institutions, which often add valuable information to the historical works. Others are obviously popular in character, and record current rumours and witticisms or are reports of scandalous, strange or extraordinary events and marvels. They often constitute important sources of information on old legends, sagas, fairy-tales and folklore of all kinds.

While many of these works may thus be regarded as complementary to the historical works or as contributions to every branch of knowledge, just as many served primarily as entertainment.

Much space is taken up by accounts of the great variety of sensational miracles, for these appear to have been popular in many circles. The overwhelming majority of the population certainly firmly believed in the reality of these occurrences and even many educated people held that they probably did sometimes occur or at least that it was possible for them to do so. It is significant that a well-known author of commentaries on the Confucian classics brought out a collection of ghost-stories (*Sou-shên chi*) with the very purpose of demonstrating their credibility. This work gives the following rational explanation of miraculous transformations:

> Miraculous apparitions are caused by the subtle essence settling in things. When this essence is in confusion inwardly, things change outwardly. The outward form and the spirit, the essence and the substance — the two act like inside and outside.

This shows that in China, as in other civilizations, a small seed of rational enlightenment lay submerged in a vast sea of unknown, strange possibilities; in China, as elsewhere, the two existed side by side and fertilized one another.

In the period preceding the T'ang, these writings were usually no more than short anecdotes, such as:

> There was in the district of Yang-hsien (Kansu) an official of low rank named Wu K'an. A rich patron 'south of the stream' often invited him to his home. One day, as he was crossing the river in a high-sterned boat, he found a five-coloured stone in the water. He took it home with him and laid it at the head-end of his bed. During the night the stone changed into a maiden, who told him that she was the daughter of the river-god.[8]

The Taoist magicians, of course, played an important part and many of the tales about them, including this one, they probably circulated themselves for purposes of propaganda:

> There was a Taoist in East Pa (Szechuan). I have forgotten his name. But he had progressed far in the Taoist arts. He went into a room and burned incense. Suddenly a rain-storm broke. At that moment people saw a small white heron fly out of the room. The rain stopped but the Taoist had gone.

This also suggests that the reputation and position which Taoism enjoyed in the eyes of the common people rested largely upon the miracles performed by Taoist adepts.

As we can see from the following anecdote the Buddhists did not lag behind:

> A man from Wu lay bound in prison. Death was to be his lot. He charged his relatives to make an image of Kuanyin. He hoped thereby to escape death. At the execution the headsman made three times to strike him but each time the sword broke. When the headsman questioned him he replied that he believed this to be the effect of Kuanyin's mercy. They looked at the image. There on the neck were the marks of three sword-blows. The man was reprieved.

It is reasonable to regard these anecdotes as the point of departure for the short story of the T'ang period. Brief accounts like those just quoted were embellished with every kind of detail; events were explained and reasons given for them.

In the tiger stories of the pre-T'ang period, for example, the transformation of man into tiger was disposed of in a few words. Now, however, we read the following passages in the tale of an official who was turned into a tiger:

> At this inn he fell ill of a disease which took the form of outbursts of violent rage. When the fits were on he lashed his servants beyond endurance. The attacks lasted for more than ten days and became worse rather than better. In his crazed condition he often left his room at night and no one knew where he went . . . In the end, he left the inn and did not return.

Having thus prepared us for an exciting twist, the story jumps to another high official who is travelling through the neighbourhood on a tour of inspection. He is suddenly attacked by a tiger. But instead of leaping at the official after the usual manner of beasts of prey, the tiger crouches in the grass and is heard to say in a human voice: 'Alas! I had almost pounced on my old friend by mistake.' Then ensues the conversation between the official and his colleague in the guise of a tiger, which constitutes the true subject of the tale. The broken threads are resumed:

> In the inn on the borders of Honan I was again assailed by the attacks of rage from which I suffered in my youth. One night I heard my name being called outside the inn. Following the sound, I roamed about the hills. Without knowing it, I put my hands to the ground and was soon walking on all fours. At the same time I felt that I was becoming shy of human beings and that I was getting stronger. I soon noticed with surprise that I was growing thick hair on my arms and legs. On one occasion I saw my reflection in some water and discovered that I had become a tiger . . . At first I could not bring myself to eat living beasts. But when my hunger became too much for me I caught stags, wild pigs, deer and rabbits and ate them. Soon all the animals fled far from me and there was nothing more to catch. I grew very hungry again. One day a woman walked down the hillside. I could not resist it — I seized her and ate her.

She was very tasty. I left her head-dress under a steep rock-wall. Since then I have been pouncing on everything, be it official on horseback, traveller on foot, baggage-carrier, bird or beast. The habit has grown upon me. It is not that I have forgotten my family and friends, but I have turned my back on all high principles. Thus I have turned into this remarkable beast. When I meet men I feel ashamed and avoid being seen. Ah me! We sat the official examination together long ago and are friends. But heaven has destined you to an exalted position, while I hide in the thicket, withdrawn for ever from the world of men.

As the conversation proceeds it emerges that it was not without cause that the official came to this sorry pass, for 'at one time in the suburbs of Nan-yang (Honan) I had relations with a widow. Her family came after me meaning to murder me . . . But the wind was favourable, I made a fire and they all perished in the flames.' His metamorphosis is thus fit punishment for this murder, for which, normally, his high official position would have rendered him exempt from punishment. It may also be noted how this links up with the explanation quoted above, the 'cruel essence' here altering the outward appearance of the creature. The misfortune consisted in the fact that the inner and the outer realities were not in harmony in the person of this man-tiger. His outward form bore the impress of his inner cruelty.

But it is most amusing to discover that a studious man, who has passed the examination, cannot, even as a tiger, forget his high level of education. So, since he cannot, of course, write with his paws, he dictates a few literary sketches, first-class in style and moral quality, for his former colleague to write down. Finally, as a farewell to his family, he composes a poem in which he fluently describes his unhappy situation.

But at the last he cannot refrain from giving his former colleague a demonstration of his animal strength and wildness and in the distance the official makes out the shape of the tiger as every now and then it leaps high into the air.[9]

Comparison of this tale with short accounts in the pre-T'ang works immediately shows that here is an artist who is a master of the narrative effects of his period. It would, unfortunately, take too long to analyse the story in every detail. But expressions such as 'I have never possessed riches' from the lips of the metamorphosed official belong to a repertory of phrases which are to be taken no more seriously than similar protestations by politicians in our own day.

That he begs the successful colleague to look after his 'orphaned' son who is 'without a counsellor in the world' gives a glimpse of the clique system which existed among the officials.

By no means all the short stories of the T'ang period, however, draw upon the atmosphere of the miraculous. The motif of the gross and unexpected transformation, which was — in China as elsewhere — an important device for giving life and suspense to a story, does not necessarily involve metamorphosis of the outward form. It was just as exciting when the hero moved hither and thither between the various ranks of society, an activity which amounted in the end to a kind of metamorphosis.

These tales of wonder translated, as it were, into the social milieu, naturally afford many vivid impressions of the everyday life of the period. One such is the well-known tale — later dramatized — of the fair Li Wa, a lady of highly questionable social position, who seduces and financially ruins the son of a rich official, a promising candidate for the examination. The young man, thrown without resources into the street, at last finds a job as a mourning singer in an undertaker's establishment.

But the city of the story boasted two such establishments, one in the eastern quarter and one in the western, and they were locked in violent rivalry. The firm in the eastern quarter had better coaches and ceremonial coffins, but its mourning singers were less skilled. So, for a fabulous sum, the western firm secretly engaged the ex-examination candidate and then cunningly arranged a public competition with the rival firm, in which the loser was to pay five thousand pieces of gold.

Conditions were laid down with protocol-like formality and thousands of spectators assembled on the appointed day. The victory of the firm in the eastern quarter was assured, as was only to be expected, when the ex-candidate appeared and brought tears to the eyes of all who heard him with his burial-song, *Dew on the garlic leaf*.

Unfortunately, however, his promising career — as a singer now — was once more interrupted, this time by his father, who recognized his son and thrashed him nearly to death for having entered into an amorous association so little suited to his position. The unhappy young man, now completely down-and-out, a beggar forced to spend cold nights in dung-pits, came at last to the door of his faithless loved one. She recognized him by his voice, took him in, bathed him and made amends for everything. In her care, his health returned, he resumed his studies and in the end, having passed all his examinations with distinction, became a high official. In this capacity, he finally met his father again who now, of course, received his son with forgiveness and joy and even came to terms with his daughter-in-law, despite her social inferiority.

This short story expresses protest against the inflexible clan-system of T'ang society, for, as we have seen, even a girl of the common people was able to help the gifted and industrious candidate to attain his goal.

The T'ang short story *Ying-ying Chuan* became the classic love-story of China. Chang, the son of an official, and Ying-ying, a widow's daughter, meet in a Buddhist monastery. They fall in love and meet by night, without waiting for either their parents' consent or the customary marriage-ceremony. The association was broken off when Chang had to go to the capital to sit his examination. Although he sees Ying-ying again later, they are unable to resume the old relationship, for Ying-ying cannot a second time overcome her moral inhibitions. In the end both marry other partners. The verses and letters of farewell which they exchange are immortal and among the most touching in the whole of Chinese literature.

There are also, among T'ang short stories, some which might be claimed as early examples of the detective novel. A very well-known one is the tale of Hsiao-o, whose husband and father, a rich merchant, were murdered by robbers. The names of the murderers, in the form of puzzles based on writing characters, were revealed to her in two dreams. She at last met a scholar able to solve the puzzle and thus she learned the names of the criminals. Hsiao-o then took a job as domestic servant in the family of the murderers and, as both lay drunk in the courtyard, seized the opportunity to kill the one and to deliver up the other, bound, to justice. She became very popular for having avenged her father and husband and received many advantageous offers of marriage; but she preferred to spend the rest of her life in a convent as a nun.

The popularity of this short story was apparently due to the fact that Hsiao-o fulfilled her duty to exact revenge, as required by ritual, although this ran counter to the law.

Tales of strange adventures and travels were also popular. One of the earliest, dating from the beginning of the T'ang period, is the story of the white monkey. One night, during an expedition against the natives of Kuangsi, the wife of a general was stolen away, in spite of the fact that a sharp look-out had been kept. After days of searching, she was found safe and sound, in company with other women, in a hide-out in a bamboo forest. The prisoners were in the thrall of a spirit which had a weakness for dog-flesh and wine. With the help of alcohol, the demon was overcome and taken prisoner. It emerged that its shape was that of an enormous white monkey with a body so hard that no weapon could pierce it. Finally, however, a vulnerable spot was found below the navel. Before he died, the monkey told the general that his wife was pregnant and would bear a son who would become a famous scholar and establish the fame of the family. It is not very difficult to detect the pointed allusions to the military nobility in this story.

The authors of these short stories came from educated circles and were often scholars who had failed the examination. The writing of such tales must often have compensated them for lack of literary fame of another kind.

As we have seen, they often used this literary form to express their criticism of public actions and institutions. But they borrowed their themes from tales current among the common people, and the emergence of this literature has therefore, probably correctly, been associated with the life of the great city markets. Another reason why cultivated men turn to this form of writing may be found in the fact that, even under the Sui dynasty, private persons were forbidden to write histories and to gather documentary material relating to the dynasty. This was reserved for officials.

Not least important, finally, is the fact that this new literary fashion was connected with the so-called *ku-wên* (old-style) movement. At all events, celebrated members of this movement often also wrote short stories of this kind.

The *ku-wên* movement began shortly before the T'ang period, as a reaction against the artificial style of parallel phrases current in the previous era. The original background to the change was probably the antagonism described above between aristocracy and scholars.

The parallel style (*p'ien-wên*) consisted in placing sentences of a given length parallel to one another. The characters in each sentence had to correspond in sense. There were also certain phonetic rules. I offer the two following couplets as examples:

> The soft wind comes in uncertain eddies;
> The wild wind passes with rushing blast.
> (*Ch'i Chien* in *Ch'u Tz'ŭ* trsl. Hawkes)

> The stars drooping, the wild plain (is) vast;
> The moon rushing, the great river flows.
> (Tu Fu, quoted by Liu, *The Art of Chinese Poetry*, 1962)

Such a style may obviously degenerate into clever, empty phrases, in which the main preoccupation is with literary polish and not the relation of the words to reality. In contrast to this, the *ku-wên* style harked back to the brevity and lucidity of the *Lun Yü* and of Mêng-tzŭ. But this new movement also had a political aspect, as we shall see later.

The parallel style — which may perhaps be regarded as one of the products of the *hsüan-hsüeh* and the *ch'ing-t'an* — was described as 'divorced from reality, decadent and extravagant'. The ostentatious second emperor of the Sui dynasty was regarded as the representative of this spirit of 'modernity' and opposition to it arose in certain educated circles under the watchword 'back to the Old Style'. This movement spread under the T'ang and finally came to light in the *ku-wên* style. Its chief exponents were Han Yü (768–824) and Liu Tsung-yüan (773–819). They and their followers formulated the principle of *ku-wên*: 'This style abolishes the decadence of the previous eight dynasties (late Han to Sui), the way (Tao) saves the empire from foundering.' 'This style' was the form in which the Confucian classics were expressed, 'the way' was the sum of the traditional political principles of the sage-kings. Han Yü saw himself as carrying on in a line of tradition that had been broken after Mêng-tzŭ. He was therefore also a convinced opponent of Buddhism, not on account of its religious doctrines but because of its influence on the social, economic and cultural life of the empire.

It appears from all this, however, that the *ku-wên* movement was not only a 'return to the Old Style' but equally an approach to real, everyday life, in contrast to the court atmosphere I have tried to describe, which was so far removed from the common people. We could also characterize the novel attitude of this movement by saying that it demanded that literature should serve present reality and not indulge in stylistic beauties unconnected with life.

Both, however, contain elements of the popular *hsiao-shuo* literature. Even among the works of Han Yü there are some, such as the *Mao-ying chuan* (that is, 'biography of master brush', whose ancestor is the hare) which are certainly to be placed in this category.

The literary trends briefly outlined above can also be taken to mean that the Chinese cultured classes were, so to speak, opposing from above downwards an intellectual movement which was threatening to gain mastery of the Chinese world from below — that is, from the common people — upwards.

This movement was Buddhism. The means it used were the *pien-wên* or 'tales in changing style', an expression which may derive from the fact that they are made up of alternating verse and prose. They originated in the Buddhist monasteries and temples and expressed basic Buddhist doctrines and opinions in a form easily understood by lay-people. Their principal themes were stories and legends about well-known Buddhist saints. The verse passages were sung to popular melodies and served sometimes merely as a kind of advance announcement or a device to attract listeners.

In order to give an idea of the *pien-wên* and the way in which they drew the mass of the people, I should like to tell briefly the story of one of them; it is entitled *Mu-lien seeks his mother* and is based on an Indian tale. Since the death of his parents, Mu-lien (Maudgalyāyana) has become a monk and has therefore given up his lay name of Lo-pu. Thanks to his good religious life he has attained to the grade of *arhat* and, 'supported by the power of the Buddha', he comes at last to the hall of heaven. From here he begins to look round for his parents but finds only his father; of his mother there is no sign. In tears, he asks the Buddha after her and learns that, as a result of unpardonable misdeeds (which she need not necessarily have committed herself) she has been condemned to hell. He at once prepares to seek her there. But he cannot find her in any of the more supportable purgatories. Finally, however, Mu-lien learns from a guardian of the lowest and most terrible hell that she may well be there and he induces him to call out her name through the various tiers. At this very moment the mother is having eighteen iron nails driven through her body and dares not open her mouth lest yet more unpleasant treatment befall her. But a servant of hell recognizes her and asks why she does not announce her presence, since her son, the monk, Mu-lien, is asking for her. She answers that she has no son of this name or calling. Thereupon Mu-lien explains that during her life-time, when he was a layman, his name was Lo-pu. At this she recognizes her son and he leads her out of the lowest hell. But they advance no further than the region of the hunger-spirits (*preta*). There the mother is plagued by a terrible hunger which cannot be satisfied, for all food is changed to flames and all liquor to pus before her eyes. So Mu-lien asks the Buddha for advice and learns that on the fifteenth day of the seventh month on the occasion of the Ullambana festival arranged for the hunger-spirits his mother will receive a meal. Shortly after this the mother is re-born as a black dog. Mu-lien then also returns to the human world and at last finds his mother by a pagoda in the capital. He now recites Buddhist sutras without intermission for seven days and seven nights and accumulates such great merit thereby that his mother is restored to human form. The dog's coat is hung as a memento on a tree near the pagoda. At last Mu-lien brings his mother into the presence of the Buddha, who absolves her of all the sins of previous existences. And here the story ends. It is not difficult to imagine what a touching and morally edifying effect is has.

The *pien-wên* were a form of public story-telling which may not have been known before and they quickly achieved the greatest popularity. For this reason, they soon found their way beyond the confines of the monasteries and came to be recounted in the market-places. By about the middle of the T'ang period they had become part of the permanent repertory of public entertainment.

At the same time, their themes became wider-ranging and began to include subjects other than Buddhist ones. This does not merely mean that they were taken up by Taoist rivals, but rather that they now began to draw their material from the Chinese classics and from history. Of these, the *pien-wên* about Wu Tzŭ-hsü was particularly popular.

Wu Tzŭ-hsü was the son of a minister of the state of Ch'u during the Chan-kuo period (*c.* 520 B.C.). Since his father and elder brother had been unjustly put to death by the king of Ch'u, he fled and, after many adventures, came at last to the ruler of the state of Wu. On his advice, this monarch undertook a victorious campaign against the state of Ch'u and took its king prisoner. In the meantime King P'ing, by whom Wu Tzŭ-hsü's father and brother had been executed, had died and Wu Tzŭ-hsü now had his body exhumed and stabbed it through. Blood miraculously poured from the dead man, whose wrongdoing was thus avowed. The captured king was beheaded as a sacrifice for the dead. But later Wu Tzŭ-hsü fell into disfavour with the king of Wu for having expressed his opinion too freely and was forced to end his life. His last words were, 'When I am dead cut my head off and hang it over the eastern gate so that I may see the entry of the warriors of Yüeh.' In the year 474 B.C. the state of Wu was destroyed by Yüeh. There was clearly no lack of bloodthirsty heroism in China.

These *pien-wên* soon came to be used as a means of clothing criticism of current conditions in historical garb. Its hearers probably rightly interpreted the one about Wu Tzŭ-hsü as a challenge not to remain silent in the face of government wrongs. The piece contains rhythmic passages which cannot have failed in their inflammatory effect. One of these describes Wu Tzŭ-hsü's wanderings through mountain and valley, across torrents and rivers; his way was frequently barred by dragons and serpents, he shot wolves and tigers and lived on plants and spring-water; so consumed did he become by the thirst for revenge that death seemed to him a blessed release.

It is hardly necessary to mention that the market-police regarded such inflammatory utterances with mistrust and distaste; the *pien-wên* were looked upon with concern in high places, especially since little could be done about them as they only followed good Confucian doctrine in setting up the past as an example to the present.

There were, of course, *pien-wên* on sentimental and erotic subjects also. Probably the best known of these was the story of Chao-chün who was married by mistake, so to speak, to the prince of the Huns and who, distracted by grief, 'climbed a thousand times to the mountain-top and, weeping a thousand tears of homesickness, called upon her mother and upon her lover, that he should come and set her free'. There were also frivolous pieces with seductions and illicit love-affairs as their themes.

As has already been said, the *pien-wên* were performed in bazaars up and down the country as though a great wave of literary creativity was welling up out of the common people. We shall perhaps find an opportunity later to demonstrate in detail the great influence which the *pien-wên* exerted on Chinese literature. Their influence on the short stories of the T'ang period, briefly mentioned above, scarcely needs further elaboration.

5. T'ANG POETRY

Versifying was the intellectual sport, so to speak, of all educated people in China. When it was made part of the examination too, it gained, in addition, a practical significance. The great flowering of poetry which is characteristic of the T'ang period, is at least in part explained by this circumstance. Another incentive was the emperor's liking for verse, for, as Yü Shih-nan (558–638), a celebrated man of letters, said: 'What those in high places praise as being good soon comes to exist in quantity below.'[10]

In spite of this, it had become possible, as early as the period of separation between the northern and southern states, for good poets whose work was widely valued to live fairly comfortably on the gifts of their admirers, despite the fact that they held no position.

A passage in the work of a literary critic of the pre-T'ang period states that, as had already been established in the classics, 'the poem should give words to the drift of the mood, the song should immortalize the words.' In ancient times, accordingly, a special official had been entrusted with collecting all the poems and songs that could be found, since they could provide the ruler with an indication of the measure of his success or failure.

There had since ancient times been poems in which each line contained three, four, five, six, seven or nine characters. But in the earliest poems a line of four characters was usual. Later, as has already been said, the five-character line and, later again, the seven-character line came into vogue.

Another formal element was introduced into poetry by Shên Yo (441–513), when he classified the tones in Chinese speech. This resulted in much stricter rules of rhyme than had previously been in use. They were principally applied in a new verse-form, called 'rule-bound' or regulated verse (*lü-shih*), which came into being in the fifth century. These verses are governed by strict rules regarding the parallelism of ideas, poetical images and the sequence of tones. The basic tonal rule was that 'floating' or 'swimming' tones were to be alternated with a 'short, abruptly cut off echo'.

Another poetical form, which also had its beginning in the pre-T'ang period, is the 'cut short line' (*chüeh-chü*), which consisted of verses of four lines, each of five or seven characters. Originally combined with music, it became during the T'ang period an independent form. It was, in fact, the most concentrated form of all and it was said that the twenty characters of a *chüeh-chü* contained as much meaning as a *lü-shih* of double the length, despite the fact that it was merely a special short form of the *lü-shih*. The following is an example:

For ten years this sword has been whetted,
But its frost-white blade has not been tried.
Today I grasp it to show it to you —
Who has any wrongs to requite?[11]

(Chia Tao, *Knight-errant*)

The virtue of the *chüeh-chü* consists in the fact that they give the impression of being extracts from longer poems or songs, the next lines of which the reader is supposed to supply from his own imagination.

Of the celebrated poets of the period immediately preceding the T'ang, I will mention only one here: this is T'ao Yüan-ming (later T'ao Ch'ien, 365–427), who, after a short period of activity as an official, withdrew to his country estate to devote himself entirely to writing poetry. He is one of the classic writers of the bucolic lyric:

At the foot of the mountain I sow beans,
The weeds tangle them, the bean-shoots are weak;
I rise early and scratch in the wilderness.
Under the moonlight I return with my hoe on my shoulder.
The footpath between the furrows so narrow, the grasses so long
That my clothes are moistened with dew.
Why should I care when my clothes are wet?
I only hope to make myself a hermit.[12]

With the exception of a few outstanding writers like T'ao

Yüan-ming and the no less famous Pao Chao (d. 466), the verse-writing of the pre-T'ang period seems to a large extent to have been dominated by an extremely artificial mannerism and traditionalism, whose main characteristic was the parallel style briefly described above.

Although these tendencies persisted throughout the T'ang period, it is still distinguished as a new era in verse-writing by the fact that its poets turned towards all that was natural and real. Poets now wanted to express their own moods and feelings, and they laid less store by stylistically perfect renderings of conventional themes. This links them primarily with the *yüeh-fu* songs mentioned above, and they evolved a poetic form which was known as *ku-shih* (old verse). Just as the *ku-wên* style was a liberation from the strict rules of the *pien-wên*, so the *ku-shih* represented a break with the rigid formulae and rules of the *lü-shih*, and now came to be known as 'New Style' (*chin-t'i*).

The output of poetical works of all kinds during the T'ang period must have been enormous. The pieces which have survived in anthologies and collections represent a mere fraction of what originally existed.

Pretty well everyone who could read and write tried his hand at versifying. Thus the authors of the time include not only emperors, courtiers, aristocrats, officials and scholars who had retired to the country, but also Buddhist and Taoist monks, and even woodworkers and shepherds. There were also a fair number of poetesses.

Verse-writing was the favourite occupation of scholars when they foregathered over their wine-cups. A kind of competition would then be held in which one of the company would write a line or two of a poem which the others had to continue, keeping to the same subject and using the same form. A notched candle was often lit and the man whose turn it was had to finish his lines before the flame reached the next notch.

Many poems of this kind have survived and the name of the writer appears at the end of each section. Thus a series of these 'joined sentences' (*lien-chü*) begins in something like the following manner:

'Parting words with no reunion arranged;
To think of meeting and seeing one another again becomes all the harder.' (Chang Chi)

The continuation runs:

'When a man falls ill his children's affection grows;
Age grieves for the valour of manhood'. (Han Yü)
'Taste for the sword has not yet faded from (my) consciousness;
Lonely as an orphan child the thought of poetry arises.' (Mêng Chiao)
'Sorrow vanishes as the arrow flies;
Joy comes like water bubbling up from a spring.' (Chang Chê)

Whatever the complicated rules governing such lines, they obviously belong to the parallel style and it thus emerges that the best writers of the *ku-wên* also handled the *pien-wên* with mastery. As with us, what literary style and forms were used depended entirely upon contingent circumstances and the poet's attitude of the moment. But in the case of the *lien-chü* what mattered was clearly quick-wittedness and formal skill, not emotional content.

The variety of form in T'ang poetry is matched by the wide range of content. There were lyrics of every kind — heroic, idyllic, humorous and so on — as well as descriptive poems, especially descriptions of landscape, also satires, ballads, narrative and didactic poems. The period was, in a word, the golden age of Chinese verse.

The great importance attached to poetry in the T'ang period may be demonstrated by an anecdote: In the street one day, an absent-mindedly gesticulating monk got in the way of the famous Han Yü, at the time supreme civil official of Loyang. When Han Yü took the monk to task, the latter explained that he had at that moment been preoccupied by the problem of whether the word 'knock' or 'tap' would be better in a certain verse about a monk at a door in the moonlight and that he was now going through the motions of knocking and tapping in order to make up his mind. Han Yü unhesitatingly settled the matter in favour of 'knock' and took the monk into his protection. The monk was the poet Chia Tao (777–841), who later became extremely well-known. He had the habit of laying out his poetical output on a table at the end of each year and offering it a sacrifice of wine and food. He also addressed a prayer to his inventive energy which he said he had worn out, but now hoped to replenish with his offering.

Under the Sui dynasty — a period characterized by a gradual fusing of the cultures of the ruling courts of the preceding dynasties — the themes of poetry were already slowly changing. Once again oppressed by military service and civil labour, the common people now began to express their misery and incipient opposition in an outburst of short songs and aphorisms. These were soon echoed, to some extent, in the verse of the upper classes. Certain well-known poets, such as Yang Su (d. 606), were also generals and therefore in close touch with actual events. In his poem 'Departure from the pass fortification (to the north)', Yang Su describes the atmosphere of the Mongolian winter:

> Through the fog, dim, uncoloured, the signals flare.
> In the frost, unmoving, the flags stiffen.
> Oh, fame and glory now rest upon the sword's length!
> The sun is setting and dust blows into the night.

This is essentially different from the charmingly beautiful images devised by the court poets and conveys something of the atmosphere that really surrounded the campaigning soldiers.

The new movement had not yet achieved its real break-through by the first T'ang period, and court poets such as Shang-kuan I (616–664) dominated the field. Verses from this quarter run something like this:

> Pleasant breezes envelope the emperor's chair,
> Cheerful songs accompany it to the palace lake.
> Golden orioles crowd the lakeside trees
> And bright grasses deck the happy shores.
> Sun and wind have dried the pearls of dew.
> Snow-white blossoms pierce the azure space.
> The flower butterflies have not ceased their coming,
> Yet light from the mountain masks the dusk.

Some of the artificiality of these parallel lines may come over even in translation. We can see by comparing them with the previous quotations that no genuine feeling informs them. This is a poem which was produced at the emperor's behest, and was paid for by him.

There is not space to show every step in the transition from this formalism to the realism of the T'ang period. The new movement finally came to a head in the verses of such poets as Ch'ên Tzŭ-ang (661–702). Ch'ên Tzŭ-ang came of a prosperous family in Szechuan and for some years lived a rather restless, vagrant life. At the age of twenty-four, however, he took the literary examination and thereafter held various offices, some with the frontier guard.

He consciously departed from the dominant poetic movement, which had 'wandered off the road and degenerated into empty words'. As he himself maintained, he took up the thread of a tradition which had been broken after the glorious era of verse-writing (196–219) during the late Han period (not discussed in the present book). He felt himself to be carrying on the 'mood and content' (*fêng-ku,* literally 'wind and bones') of that period.

This, in fact, means that he took the subjects of his poems from his own time and surroundings, a procedure for which the same slogan 'back to the old' was used, as for the *ku-wên* movement. He required that, as regards content, a poem should be 'truthful and ascending' and, as regards sound, bold and clear, with sudden pauses 'like the sound of metal and ringing stone'.

These are the words he uses to describe himself:

> I am the sprig of a noble family,
> I have spent a life-time fostering my talents.
> I ceaselessly strive to serve my country,
> To go into the wilds with my shining sword drawn . . .

T'ang patriotism, a reaction to the foreign elements streaming into the empire from all sides, finds expression in these lines. The poem, 'The Ancients', one of the best-known of Ch'ên Tzŭ-ang's works, shows him in a melancholy mood:

> I look before, and do not see the ancients.
> Looking after I do not see the coming ages.
> Only Heaven and Earth will last for ever.
> Alone I lament, and my tears fall down.[13]

That Ch'ên Tzŭ-ang's verses inaugurated a new phase of Chinese poetry is confirmed by a sentence in his biography in the T'ang history: 'Tzŭ-ang changed the polished, correct style of writing.' In other words, he finally broke through the formalism of the court verse.

Members of his circle included the celebrated Chang Chiu-ling (673–740) and the little-known Chang Jo-hsü, whose poem, 'Stream in spring and flowers in moon-light', was judged by his contemporaries the best of all T'ang verse.

The subject of this poem was not new. It was based on an old folk-song which the last emperor of the state of Ch'ên (583–589), a man of artistic talent, had re-written and introduced into court circles. His version was lost, but the theme was later revived by other poets, among them Chang Jo-hsü. Since the poem is long, I will quote only extracts from it, in the hope that they will give the reader some idea of the work as a whole:

> Mingling with the waters of the sea, flood-tide and spring
> river become as mirrors.
> Partner of the tide, the bright moon climbs over the sea.
> Wave follows wave for a thousand miles and more.
> Where over the spring river would there be no moonlight?
> The tide curls round the scented shores.
> The moon's touch is like hoar-frost on the forest in flower.
> In the moonlit space frost flies unnoticed
> And the white shore-sand cannot be seen.

The world of nature is now brought into relationship with man:

> Age follows age in human life
> But year in year out river and moon stay the same.
> Perhaps they are waiting for us men?
> But we see the endless flow of the waters.

The poem then shifts to the subject of separation and solitude, which all peoples in every age have seen as having some kind of emotional connection with the moon:

> Far, far away the white cloudlet travels.
> But the maple on the shore cannot curb my parting grief.
> Who is that alone there in the boat?
> Where does longing look out from the moonlit tower?

The poem finally ends with an allusion to the inevitable transitoriness of all things:

> Steeply the moon drops down into the sea's dew.
> Memorial tablets stand in endless rows by the road.
> So many find their way home in the full light of the moon!
> Yet its waning moves every sea-shore tree to sorrow.

Whatever our impression of this moonlight lyric, it shows one thing: that the new idiom which characterizes the poetry of the T'ang period was often, at first, merely the court idiom transferred to verse designed to be popular.

The best example of this in the 'Stream in spring . . .' occurs in two lines not quoted above which refer to the 'jade door curtain half rolled up' and the 'linen beaten on the washing stone'. Sometimes, as in the present instance, the theme of an old folk-song was transposed from the court circle back to a romantic environment not far removed from its original one.

It is this combination of romanticism and realism which modern literary historians like to regard as the distinctive feature of T'ang poetry.

It would take too much space to follow the details of T'ang poetry through every phase of its development. We must therefore limit ourselves to saying something about the greatest of the poets.

One of these was Wang Wei (699–759).[14] After a career as an official, in which he was continually changing situations, he retired into private life and finally became a Buddhist. He left an *œuvre* comprising over four hundred poems, which reflect all the vicissitudes of his life. He is noteworthy primarily, however, as the master of the *chüeh-chü* form, and represents a movement which sought to combine painting and poetry.

Indeed, Wang Wei is known equally well as both painter and poet; and it was said that his painting resembled poetry while his poetry was like painting. Although a political or patriotic note dominated his earlier verse, he became, in the end, one of those poets who, like T'ao Yüan-ming, having retired to the country, lived solely for his art.

Two short poems typical of his later period follow:

> Lying alone in this dark bamboo grove,
> Playing on my flute, continually whistling,
> In this dark wood where no one comes,
> The bright moon comes to shine on me.[15]

This is an evocation of the atmosphere of his country property near Lan-t'ien in Shensi. The second example comes from his 'mixed songs':

> You who come from the old village —
> Tell me what is happening there?
> When you left, were the chill plum-blossoms
> Flowering beneath the white window?[16]

The 'white' window is an allusion to the custom of sticking thin silk or paper over the windows in winter as a protection against dust and cold. The wild plum is one of the first heralds of spring.

The best-known poet of the T'ang period is, however, Li Po (701–762). So many translations of his works have been made, that they may be regarded as part of world literature.

As the son of a rich aristocratic family, Li Po was not obliged to take serious steps — in other words, to sit the examination — to secure office. He spent his youth in Szechuan. His education embraced not only the classics and philosophers, but also sword-play and the military arts. He was tall and strong, his eyes gleamed like the eyes of tigers and he loved — in the manner of sons of the military nobility — to roam the countryside, 'wandering like a hero and seeing that right was done'. These travels, which cost a great deal of money, soon took him beyond the confines of his native province. In the year 732 in An-lu (Hopei), he married his first wife, the granddaughter of a minister, but she seems not to have been able to endure life with him for long. He was probably married three times altogether. A few years later we find him in company with five others of his own kind who had settled down together in the Tsu-lai hills in Shantung, calling themselves, the 'Six idlers of the bamboo stream'. The spirit which reigned in this small group of young noblemen is expressed in lines like:

> My sword invites resistance from the masses.
> But I steal rhymes from the whole world of songs.

His fame as a poet had meanwhile spread, and in the year 742, Li Po was summoned to the court in the capital Ch'ang-an. This, as for every nobleman, was the great opportunity of his life. He set out full of joyful expectation:

> Looking up at the sky, I laugh aloud and go.
> Am I one to decay in the depths of an old jungle?

He hoped to return an official, with the golden seal hanging from his belt. Although his art brought him great honour, it soon became clear that his unfettered, extremely vital artistic nature was quite unsuited to court life and its intrigues. Like all the courtiers of the time, he sang the praises of the imperial favourite, Yang Kuei-fei, whose successes he compared with those of Fei-yen, who has already been mentioned. Nevertheless, this celebrated beauty, who was apparently inclined to stoutness, took a dislike to him, and in the year 744, at her instigation, he was dismissed from court service. His reckless drinking and life of idle amusement fully justified her action. Resigned and disappointed, he left the capital.

He went to Honan, where he met and made friends with Tu Fu, the other great poet of the T'ang period. Many of the poems are the literary expression of this relationship.

Li Po was fifty-five years old when the An Lu-shan rebellion broke out: 'In the heart of the country a wild tiger roars. Raging fire consumes the ancestral temple.' 'White bones are piled up in mounds. What wrong have the people done?'

But political events do not on the whole appear to have made much impact upon the poet; his unsettled life kept him remote from them. Later, however, he became involved in the subversive plans of a certain prince, was condemned to death and thrown into prison. An influential friend spoke on his behalf and he escaped from this predicament.

He died at last in the house of a relative in Anhui. The story that he fell out of a boat and was drowned while trying to grasp the moon's reflection in the water is no more than poetic legend.

It is quite possible, however, to see from his poems how the heroic mood was gradually replaced by a longing for the Elysium of the Taoist sages. Sometimes, perhaps, — especially when under the influence of wine — Li Po felt himself to be what an admirer had once called him, 'a celestial being banished to the world of men'. He probably believed in the existence of the supernatural world of the Taoists, and his action when he threw the verses he had just written into the water and let the current bear them away may indicate that he wished to communicate not only with the human public but also with the world of spirits. He was certainly one of the great romantics of all ages and of all countries. Poetry came as naturally to him as plain speech does to ordinary people.

The works which have survived represent a mere fraction of all that Li Po wrote. Since translations have appeared in all languages, I will quote just one poem here:

> The rain was over, green covered the land.
> One last cloudlet melted away in the clear sky.
> The east wind came home with the spring
> Bringing blossoms to sprout on the branches.
> Flowers are fading now and time will end.
> All mortal men perceive it and their sighs are deep.
> But I will turn to the sacred hills
> And learn from Tao and from magic how to fly.[17]

The other great poet of China is Tu Fu (712–770). He came from a family of Confucian scholars and knew how to write poetry by the tender age of six. But it was not until after his thirty-fifth year that he wrote the works on which his true fame rests. Like Li Po, he spent the greater part of his life journeying and roaming the country. He sat the examination and failed. Nevertheless, probably because of his fame as a poet, he held a succession of humble offices and, later, a few higher ones. His life and work passed in the shadow of the An Lu-shan rebellion. Poverty and privation were the constant companions of his journeys. One of his children died as a consequence of these unhappy conditions.

Whereas Li Po's poems are largely a reflection of his personality, Tu Fu's work rather holds up a mirror to his times. Two things appear to have impressed him more than others: on the one hand the brilliance and high civilization of the court, and on the other the terrible distress of the common people. The poem in which he describes how, inside the palace, wine flowed and a superabundance of fine victuals were served, while outside, before the gates, bodies lay frozen to death, can be said to epitomize his whole work. Wealth and poverty, as he expressed it, are separated by nothing but a flimsy wall.

In contrast to the lightness of Li Po's verses, which he simply, as it were, shook out of his sleeve, those of Tu Fu are weighty and often bear the marks of the pains the author took in composing them. They therefore present considerably greater difficulties to the translator than the work of Li Po.

I will content myself with quoting a rendering of one only of Tu Fu's poems, though one which seems to me particularly characteristic of his style. It is called 'The Emaciated Horse' and was probably composed in the year 758, when Tu Fu was assistant official for ritual and administration in the district of Hua-chou in Shensi;

The emaciated horse in the Eastern suburb causes me distress;
He is a bony skeleton, a waste of sand and rubble surrounds
him like a wall.

Attempt to lead him: he tries to move, but weakly lurches to
the side;
Can this be his intention, who was wont to gallop and curvet?

Look carefully: a brand of the sixth grade bears official seal;
People say the Three Armies in their passing left him by the road.

His hide is dry, is caked with mud and filth, peals off and falls in flakes to the ground;
He is left here like a withered branch in frost and snow, his coat dull, lifeless.

Last year he advanced like a rolling wave to expel remaining rebels,
It is not the habit of Hua Liu not to carry Generals.

Men at arms all rode horses from Imperial stables;
Although dreary, depressed, perhaps this is an ailing spirit horse capable of covering ten thousand *li*,

Which, on a time, passing a clod, made a mis-step — stumbled once;
You, who could not provide a perfect mount were rejected, cast away.

In misery and distress, on seeing people, you seem anxious to tell your woes;
Through a mistaken action you lost your master, your intelligence did not shine.

Now let loose to pasture, far away under cold skies, wild geese of autumn keep you company;
At sunset none stable you, crows peck your sores.

What household will now take pity and give you nourishment,
That when the bright year comes you may again savour the long Spring grass?[18]

The horse is, of course, simply a metaphor for the poet's own unhappy fate in having just been transferred to a provincial post. But it also expresses in a grandiose image the way in which the common people were milked by taxation, war and hunger. The poet's statement is clear: people in our time are treated like animals.

Finally, I should like briefly to mention Po Chü-i (772–846), the best-known poet of the mid-T'ang period. He passed the examination and spent the greater part of his life as an official. His fame as a poet was earned primarily by a style of poem called 'new *yüeh-fu*'. These poems are characterized by their free verse-form, but in other respects have little or nothing to do with the *yüeh-fu* we have encountered. Their popularity was due to the fact that, like Tu Fu's poem about the horse, they contained allusions to the evil conditions of the day. It appears that Po Chü-i felt almost greater pity even than Tu Fu for the privations of the common people. He often clothes his feeling in metaphors, like the one of the stone-surfaced road that was laid so that the minister's horses should not get their hooves muddy; but nobody gives a thought to the oxen who have to drag the stones into place, their necks rubbed sore with toil.

He makes abundant use of popular idiom, with the result that, in recent times, he has sometimes been considered a kind of forerunner of the movement towards colloquial language (*pai-hua*). Tradition has it that he used to read his poems to an old country-woman. Not until he saw that they were intelligible to her did he write down the final version. He himself told a friend that he regarded poetry as a form of instruction, and some of his poems may be called moral tales in verse. He was one of the most widely known and most popular of the poets of the T'ang period. His verses were recited by high and low and were often to be seen written on walls.

Po Chü-i's charitable nature brought him at last to Buddhism. In a poem written shortly before his death, and which is probably intended to be taken as a joke, he sees himself as a *bodhisattva* in the Tushita heaven:

> A traveller came from across the seas
> Telling of strange sights.
> 'In a deep fold of the sea-hills
> I saw a terrace and tower.
> In the midst there stood a Fairy Temple
> [i.e. the Taoist paradise]

With one niche empty.
They all told me this was waiting
For Lo-t'ien to come.'

Traveller, I have studied the Empty Gate
[i.e. Buddhism]
I am no disciple of Fairies
The story you have just told
Is nothing but an idle tale.
The hills of ocean shall never be
Lo-t'ien's home.
When I leave the earth it will be to go
To the Heaven of Bliss Fulfilled
[i.e. the Tuṣhita heaven].

(*Taoism and Buddhism*, trans. Waley)

Towards the end of the T'ang dynasty, as a result of the excessively high value set on verbal effects, Chinese poetry again degenerated into mannerism. In the following period — that of the Sung — a new style of verse writing, known as *tz'ŭ* (words), arose out of this. It was this form which was primarily cultivated by the great poets of that period, among them Su Tung-p'o. The *tz'ŭ* is made up of lines of unequal length and is usually set to music. But Su Tung-p'o divorced it from music and used it as a purely literary form. It has, nevertheless, certain connections with the airs from the opera, a form then gradually coming into being.

Viewed, however, as a whole, by the end of the T'ang period Chinese poetry had seen its greatest days. I do not, therefore, propose to deal here with its later development.

6. WRITING AND PRINTING

After the T'ang period, China again split into several states and was not reunited into one empire until the year 960, under the Sung dynasty. A popular account of the history of the time, as it figures in one of the professional story-tellers' notebooks, tells how 'tiger fought dragon for year after year, like Liang and T'ang, Chin, Han and Chou, light upon light flared up, soon to be blown out by the wind, while prince followed prince like the post-courier's relay'.

From the point of view of cultural history, however, this period is of great importance for having seen the beginnings of book printing. This is a suitable juncture at which briefly to review an important aspect of Chinese civilization, namely, the materials used for writing.

Leaving out of account special cases such as inscriptions on oracle-bones and on bronze and stone, bamboo, wood and silk were the materials most commonly used for writing until paper was invented towards the end of the first century A.D. The small bamboo slips used were prepared by splitting the smooth section between two knots into thin strips which were then dried over a fire and smoothed off. After this they were laid together from left to right and joined by four cross-wise threads. The writing ran from the top right to the bottom left. Whereas the characters on the oracle-bones had been placed in whatever order was possible, the narrowness of the bamboo slips necessitated their being arranged in vertical lines running from top to bottom. The arrangement persisted and they appear in the same order, still running from right to left, to this day. Only in most recent times have works appeared in which the vertical lines of the Chinese text follow the European practice and run from left to right. As a rule, these bamboo slips carried one line containing, on an average, between twenty-two and twenty-five characters. Not until the Han period did pieces come to be written in several lines. Then, when a certain stopping-place had been reached, they were rolled up from left to right and the title of the work, details of the section and so on, written on the outside.

This will give the reader an idea of how unmanageable and heavy a long work, such as that of Mo-tzŭ, in this form must have been. Another factor has to be taken into account by modern scholars studying ancient works which were originally written on bamboo: naturally enough, the joining threads often rotted and broke, with the result that the order of the slips was lost and could only be re-established by a careful reading of the text. Anyone who has been concerned with ancient Chinese knows that this task is fraught with difficulties, also that there is always the danger that a text may make sense — though not that of the original — even when the order is wrong. It was also easy to make good an imperfect text simply by inserting passages. The spotting of such interpolations and faulty sequences in ancient bamboo texts is among the most difficult tasks facing the modern sinologue — although how important a one will be recognized when we recall that the problem arises in a work of such universal interest as the *Tao-tê ching*.

Large numbers of writings on bamboo slips have been found on the sites of the old frontier garrisons of the Han empire in present-day Kansu. The news has recently also been received that a coherent bamboo text comprising a large part of one of the works on ritual (*I li*) has come to light in this very province. As may be imagined, specialists are eagerly waiting for this find to be described and published.*

For letter-writing, as opposed to the transcription of texts, specially prepared wood tablets were largely used. An ancient Chinese letter consisted of two wooden boards, with the sides which had been written upon lying against one another, held together by a cord sealed on the upper side of the letter. Much more could be written on wooden boards, as we read in an old text: 'A hundred characters and more fit on to a wooden tablet but as many as a hundred characters cannot be written on a little bamboo tablet.' Wooden tablets were also used in early times for pictures and plans.

If now we recall how great is the volume of ancient Chinese literature, we must assume that in the pre-Christian era there existed a large industry producing these important writing materials. We know little or nothing about it, however, although from time to time we read that, for example, a whole bamboo grove had to be felled when a great literary work was in course of preparation.

* The following work has now appeared in Kansu: *Wu-wei Han-chien* (*Han Bamboo Slips Found near Wu-wei in Kansu*), Kansu Provincial Museum, 1964.

Another material used at that time for writing was silk. It came into use presumably because the bamboo books were too heavy and cumbersome. A strip of silk was cut to the length required by the extent of the text in question and rolled up. There seem, however, also to have been books in which the silk was folded layer upon layer and this has an important bearing on the later development of the make-up of books. Fragments of old texts on silk have been found in burial-places. Unfortunately, however, they are in such poor condition that it is impossible to draw any firm conclusions as to their original form. It seems that silk began to be used as a writing material at about the beginning of the Chan-kuo period. But it was much too expensive to be used in large quantities.

Although we sometimes read of attempts being made to write on all kinds of leaves — particularly, perhaps, on reeds, since these were most like bamboo slips — all that is meant, no doubt, is that the cheapest possible materials were selected for learning and practising upon.

We may, however, conclude from all this that, because of the very nature of the materials described, the art of writing in ancient China was in the main the prerogative of a minority who could afford both materials and time for study. Ts'ai Lun's discovery of paper and its use as a writing material therefore in many respects represents the beginning of a new phase of Chinese writing.

Ts'ai Lun was chief eunuch at the court of the Han emperor, Ho-ti. In this capacity he was, from about 97 A.D. onwards, overseer of the imperial factories. The paper which, in the year 105, he presented to the emperor was made of bark, hemp, shreds of cloth and old fishing nets. This invention did not, of course happen without preparation but was the culmination of earlier experience. Certain remarks occur in literature which show that paper made of left-over pieces of silk was known as early as the first Han period, in the last century B.C. The earliest known piece of paper was found in 1931 on the Edsin-gol in Mongolia, among some Han period ruins; basing their opinions on other dated finds, Chinese scholars have placed it in the period between 98 and 105.

Ts'ai Lun's paper, therefore, was a development of earlier fabrics of a similar kind and his innovation perhaps consisted primarily in having simplified the processes of production. Paper was at first regarded as merely a cheaper substitute for bamboo and silk, as indeed it was. Since lower costs now enabled the less well-to-do to participate in the art of writing, the use of paper spread very quickly throughout the empire and beyond its frontiers. Paper is encountered in Turfan in about the year 200, in Egypt in about 900 and in Spain around 1150.

Tso Po, a younger contemporary of Ts'ai Lun and well-known as a calligrapher, further improved manufacturing processes. Accounts of the period 246–285 inform us that the paper made by him, as well as his ink and brushes, surpassed in fineness all other similar products. This shows that by then several kinds of the new writing material were already being produced.

It is impossible to discuss here the formal changes that took place in literature as a result of the transition from bamboo to paper. The sequence and the roll form of the books remained, however, unchanged. Just as the texts on bamboo and silk had previously been unrolled from left to right, so it was now with those on paper; the left-hand end was fastened to a short rod, while a piece of paper was stuck to the right-hand end, lengthening it and thus protecting the opening lines of the text. The rod on which the book was rolled as on an axis was made, according to the value of the work, of wood, metal or jade. In the larger libraries these rollers were made of different colours in order to differentiate the various sections. Certain libraries contained between sixty and eighty thousand such rolls, of which several often went to form one work.

In the year 1900 a Taoist, who had settled in a Buddhist cave-temple near Tun-huang in Western Kansu, discovered a library which had been immured there in the year 1035. It consisted largely of texts on rolls and most of it is preserved today in London and Paris.

In addition to these rolls, there were also folding books which were a development of the works on folded silk mentioned earlier. This was the form preferred for books of reference, such as the encyclopaedias which began to appear during the T'ang period, for rolls were unsuitable when specific passages in the middle or at the end of the text had to be consulted. It was this form that was later taken as the model for printed works. But the work which may be the earliest surviving printed book, a *Diamond Sutra* (*Chin-kang ching*) dated 868, consists of strips of paper pasted together in the form of the rolls.

The invention of block-printing, like that of paper, is attributed to a named individual, Fêng Tao (882–954), who served during the Wu-tai period as a minister in the powerful northern states of T'ang and Chin. But this invention was not, any more than the earlier one had been, the work of one man; indeed, Fêng Tao clearly had even less to do with the invention of printing than Ts'ai Lun with that of paper.

Fêng Tao in fact discovered the technique of printing from blocks in the year 932 in Szechuan, then the state of Shu, where it had already been perfected; and his whole merit consisted in instigating the first engraving on wood-blocks and printing of the classical texts. This enterprise lasted from 932 to 953 and resulted in a complete edition of the classics with commentaries in a hundred and thirty volumes, of which nothing remains except an extremely doubtful fragment in Japan.

All that mattered to Fêng Tao was that the revised text should be permanently established. That this was achieved by printing for the first time from wood-blocks appears to have interested him only in so far as this process was considerably cheaper than it would have been to chisel the texts on stone, as had been done under the Han and T'ang dynasties. The new edition of the classics was undertaken by the state of T'ang, which wished, for purposes of prestige, to continue the legal traditionalist policy of the dynasties.

The technique of printing from blocks had, however, already been developed by the Buddhists and Taoists. They probably began by forming characters on small blocks of clay, hardening them and printing from them, in order to be able to meet the needs of the numerous faithful for effective magic formulae and religious maxims. In the course of time these formulae, and later the short popular works which were demanded by large sections of the common people, came to be cut on wood, the text being written on thin transparent paper and transferred to the wood-block in mirror writing.

Printing was thus in the first place — and for a time largely remained — the concern of the religious bodies and was confined to the works used by them. But it appears that other works in frequent demand, such as encyclopaedias and others, gradually came to be printed too.

It was Fêng Tao, at all events, who introduced block-printing to the higher and influential levels of Chinese society. As has already been said, his purpose was in no sense to use printing to disseminate works of literature more widely but only to establish the readings of the classical texts on a firm basis. Until the year 1064, the printing of these and other politically important texts was restricted to authorized official quarters. But after that the new technique spread swiftly and inevitably. The age of the copyists was at an end. They were ousted by the printers from the dominating position they had held hitherto. Nevertheless Chinese texts have continued to be copied, often as a means of completing imperfect printings, until the present day, although copyists have been fewer.

The Sung dynasty may justly be regarded as the great period of printing from wood-blocks and the surviving pieces are highly valued, not only on account of their rarity but also for their quality. The form of the characters used at that time was much imitated later on. Their effect is one of great vitality and strength, which makes them attractive by comparison with later rigidly correct forms. The earliest important centre of printing was Szechuan, but other large private centres were soon set up in Hang-chou and Fukien. There were in addition presses in all the larger administrative departments.

We know that a little later works were being printed in colours. There is in existence a *Diamond Sutra*, with commentary, printed in red and black, dating from about the year 1340, under the Yüan dynasty.

Also in the Sung period, between about 1041 and 1048, Pi

Shêng, of whom nothing more is known, invented printing from movable type. We possess an extremely detailed description of this technique, which records how the individual characters were made of clay, baked in a straw-fire and then composed in an iron chase. Unfortunately no piece of printing of this nature has survived. The technique was much improved during the Yüan period. This is the period of, for example, the movable type for printing Uighur characters, which was found on the floor of a grotto-temple in Tun-huang. This form of printing had by that time already penetrated to central Asia. The earliest surviving Chinese works printed with movable type date from the Ming period and it appears that the technique reached a culmination at that time.

Having reached the end of this brief account, there is surely no need for me to stress the enormous importance for the whole of world civilization of the twin inventions of paper and printing, both of which spread from China to all literate peoples.

IX

The Sung Dynasty

1. GENERAL POLITICAL POLICIES

The Sung dynasty came into being as a result of a successful generals' putsch. The following conversation between the first Sung emperor and his dying mother is indicative: she asked him: 'Do you know whom you really have to thank for this success (i.e. the founding of the new dynasty)?' And he answered: 'The immense blessing which streams down upon me from my ancestors.' But the old lady's words as she corrected him were dry and down to earth: 'Nonsense! You owe it to the simple fact that the emperor (of the previous dynasty) was too young to have sufficient following in the army and the country.'[1] Indeed, the revolt proceeded so fast that the soldiers who supported the old dynasty had no time to organize resistance. It also appears that the behaviour of the middle and lower classes in the capital contributed much to the success of the enterprise.

The foregoing conversation is in a certain sense symptomatic of the basic currents of the intellectual situation under the Sung. On the one hand there was the swift and intensive expansion of the religious institutions pertaining to the imperial ancestor-worship and state sacrifice, together with strong religious faith among the vast majority of the people; and, on the other, an extremely realistic economic system and a small group of intellectuals so far enlightened as to be unbelievers. These attitudes sometimes combined to produce a pacifist prestige policy which strikes us as in many ways strange.

Thus we read that the emperor Chên-tsung, forced in 1004 to conclude what he considered to be a dishonourable treaty with the aggressive northern state of the Kitan, planned 'to wash away this shame' and addressed his counsellors accordingly. On this occasion the minister Wang Ch'in-jo pronounced as follows:

> It is impossible under present conditions to subdue the Kitan by force of arms. But it is in the nature of these barbarians to fear Heaven and to believe in ghosts and demons. It will therefore be best for us to fabricate miraculous signs to show that Heaven has appointed the Sung dynasty controller of mankind and thus to increase our prestige in the eyes of the barbarians. They will then certainly no longer dare to regard our power as insignificant.

The Emperor, however, was still unresolved and consulted a scholar from the state archives: 'You, who are familiar with ancient literature, will be able to tell me whether the gods really communicate with men in writing, as, for example, in the "Chart from the Huang-ho" and the "Script from the River Lo". The scholar replied: 'These are most probably works by holy men designed to instruct us in the way of the gods.' Thereupon the Emperor acted upon the advice of Wang Ch'in-jo and commanded letters from Heaven to be secretly fabricated.[2]

These letters were documents wrapped in yellow silk, which appeared to have been thrown down from Heaven and were solemnly retrieved from where they were found hanging on the pinnacle of a tower in the palace quarter. Using ancient characters and turns of phrase, the gods affirmed that all the measures taken by the emperor found their full favour and virtually repeated the divine mandate made when the dynasty was founded. The effect of these letters was similar to that achieved today by 'voluntary demonstrations of the will of the people', that is, moral reinforcement of the régime in both foreign and domestic spheres.

It was not only the state, however, but also hostile elements which exploited the religious faith and superstitition of the time. During the Fang La rebellion of 1120, unarmed troops of rebels, using primitive magical means of intimidation, succeeded in putting the provincial troops to flight and in over-running the greater part of the south-east. It is interesting to note that the same has occurred at other periods of Chinese history, even in the rebellions and risings of very recent times.

This pacifist policy which exploited the temper of the age was, however, the result not merely of ideological, but, even more, of economic considerations. It was, in fact, dictated largely by the deficit in the government finances. This, in turn, was due mainly to army expenditure. Having learnt from the bad experiences of the T'ang, the Sung adopted the policy of distributing the military power in the state in such a way that different groups held one another in check, or, as it was expressed at the time, 'Inside and outside must balance one another.' The military outcome of this policy was apparent even under the first Sung emperor who divided the troops equally between the capital and the provinces, so that in an emergency the one group could be played off against the other. In addition to this, the generals were forbidden to maintain private bodyguards.

One of the pronouncements of the second Sung emperor is symptomatic of their policy:

> If no danger threatens the state from without, there will surely be unrest within. External danger, however, applies only to the frontiers and precautions can be taken against it. But what is to be feared is that rebellious elements within will join forces and take concerted action.[3]

This point of view, however, committed the Sung to a policy of passivity *vis-à-vis* the neighbouring states of the Kitan, Hsi-hsia and others.

One of the ways of ridding the state of unruly elements in its midst was to conscript them into the army. Thus, for example, the male population from disaster areas was usually enrolled in the army. The result of this, however, was that, while the numerical strength of the army was continually increasing, its fighting power diminished. In the period 960–1068 the army grew from 200,000 to 1,162,000 men. Of these, however, a great many of the soldiers were weakened to such an extent by deficient training, idle living and old age 'that riders in full armour were unable to mount their horses and when they shot an arrow it fell to the ground ten or twenty paces away'.[4] The discipline in the garrisons was so lax 'that the soldiers wandered round the bazaars all day long and spent their time peddling embroidered materials'.[5] Even soldiers of the guard did not stand watch themselves, but paid wretched hirelings to do it in their stead and also to carry their weapons on marches. Campaigns, for which they received special allowances into the bargain, were for the soldiers largely an opportunity to plunder friend and foe alike.

This army, however, absorbed more than 60% of government revenue; indeed it appears that the tax on textiles, for example, was levied solely to meet the army's needs. The Sung régime was obviously anxious not to engage in costly campaigns which would cause this difficult situation to develop into a disaster. They therefore, as we have already seen, preferred to use inexpensive means to increase their religious and political prestige abroad. They soon also adopted the expedient of paying appeasement money to the aggressive northern peoples, which was, presumably, less of a charge on state finances than an effective reform of the army would have been.

Similarly, the Sung régime endeavoured, from the beginning, to thwart any concentration of power within the ranks of officialdom. They pursued this aim by breaking down the departments into many small units which held one another in check, and also by a law whereby all officials had to be replaced after three years' service. This resulted, however, in an excessive increase in the size of the official corps and, in the longer term, in the fact that, despite all precautions, the real power ended up in the hands of the bureaucracy — which was no longer balanced to the same extent as it had been under the T'ang by the restraining influence of a privileged aristocracy.

The old antagonism between nobility and officialdom now gave place to a conflict of interests between large factions — mainly at first the higher officials on the one hand and lower on the other — within the official corps.

2. ATTEMPTS AT REFORM

Some idea of the increase in governmental expenditure can be gained from the statement that disbursements to the official corps, for example, doubled between the reigns of the third and fourth emperors, as did those for the state sacrifice during the period 1004 to 1053. The government found delightfully simple means of alleviating this evil: they increased the taxes. Thus we have to record that, in the period 1004–1048, taxes rose about three and a half times. The history of the collection of taxes during this period resembles a duel between two intellectuals: one, the official one, is constantly concerned to find new stratagems for increasing the taxes, while the other is equally skilful in finding fresh ways of dodging them. The minister of finance, triumphant as a victorious general, then informed the emperor of the sums which, by force and cunning, he had managed to extort from the people.

There was no question of social justice in collecting the taxes. All those who were able to use their position of power to evade them or shift them on to other, weaker persons, did so. It appears that it was even possible to force poor peasants to sell their land but to keep the taxes and services which encumbered it. Su Tung-p'o observed, for example, that the rich were constantly acquiring more land although their tax liabilities did not increase correspondingly and that the landed property of the poor continued to shrink, though their liability did not diminish.

Accelerated, perhaps, by costly campaigns against the Hsi-hsia on the north-west frontier of the Sung empire, events appear to have reached a crisis in the period 1038–1045; and the kind of mood which commonly presages an uprising was apparent among much of the population. Something had to be done to secure the régime and plans to reform existing conditions began to be put forward. The first were proposed by the minister Fan Chung-yen. Between 1041 and 1048 he brought about certain changes in the government. The principles of his reform have been expressed approximately as follows: 'Whoso wishes to correct the stem and the branches must begin with the root, whoso wishes to clarify the river must begin with the source.'[6] But it appears that in his view the root and the source were the official corps and that reform consisted in practice of limiting its authority. His criticism was also aimed at the nature of the examinations, by means of which it was possible for a man to attain to a high official position simply by virtue of poetic or stylistic proficiency. He called for knowledge of economics and administration instead.

These attempts at reform, furthermore, had no effect, since it proved impossible to carry them through in the face of opposition from the officials involved and from the imperial clan. They also overlooked what may be called the fundamental ills: voracious land-grabbing by the high officials, rigging of the prices in the markets by the rich and the evil machinations of small-time terrorists among the common people.

The proposed reforms of Li Kou were rather more closely related to economic conditions and an essay of his, characteristically entitled 'The ritual of the Chou brings universal harmony' (*t'ai-p'ing*), has survived. It discusses such themes as 'the enrichment of the land', 'the strengthening of the army' and 'appeasement of the people'. Its point of departure is: 'The ground is the origin, fields and harvests are only consequences.'[7] If there were no soil, the peasants and their tools would be useless. The basis of his plans is that the peasants should once more be securely tied to the soil, as they had been under the feudal system at the beginning of the Chou dynasty, since then 'no work potential and no strip of ground would remain unused', and thus the land would be certain to flourish. The first necessity, therefore, was to encourage the numerous dispossessed peasants, the numbers of whom were probably growing to menacing proportions, to return to the soil. Although Li Kou mentions a 'law of land compensation', this does not at all mean that dispossessed peasants should be restored to ownership of their land.

> Keeping the common people in good order meant in ancient times that those in power wished to enrich the masses. But nowadays this slogan betokens great animosity towards the powerful local clans. These local clans, however, have in many

> cases risen above the masses by virtue of their cleverness and strength and their possessions enable them to give employment to others. Why should not they be the people to surmount the economic difficulties (of the present-day)?[7]

The conclusion to be drawn from this was that the returning workers were to find employment with the landowners as cheap labour. Similarly, Li Kou's plan for strengthening the army amounts to the suggestion that the powerful clans should once more be permitted to maintain private troops. But the acquisition of land by successful merchants was to be restricted. This shows that all that Li Kou ultimately proposed to do was to restore the age-old governmental principle of giving preference to agricultural economy over trade and commerce. He also shows himself to be a champion of the interests of the large-scale landowner, a class, which, including as it did all the high officials, ruled the country both politically and economically.

One of these reformers who produced proposals which were in fact intended to do nothing to alter existing conditions, but, on the contrary, to anchor them more securely than ever, was Su Tung-p'o, equally celebrated as a poet and writer. Whereas the opinion was widely held at the time that conditions must be improved by 'changing the laws (or methods)', he proposed that 'it is not the laws and institutions but the people who are to blame for the Empire being in poor shape'. He was chiefly concerned with reforming the army, which, as he said, 'is able neither to hold the bandits in check nor to prevent the depredations of the barbarians'.[9] He again advocated general conscription, by which the common people could be employed as fighting men or as land-workers as occasion demanded.

In contrast to these purely academic reformers, there arose a man of another mettle, who may fairly be described as China's greatest reformer. This was Wang An-shih (1021–1086). 'His purpose,' (according to his biographer), 'was to reform his contemporaries and to change their morals.' In the year 1058, he presented his proposed reforms in a document known as the 'Ten Thousand-Word Memorial'. He wrote:

> At the present time the economic strength of the Empire is diminishing from day to day and morality is worsening from day to day. (The present age) suffers from having no principle and no standard. The reason for this is that the policy of the Former Kings is not taken as the principle. As regards the policy of the Former Kings, their intention should be accepted as principle and that is all. The power of the Empire must be used to create the economic means for the Empire. These means must be used to meet the expenditure of the Empire. In regard to good government, inadequate means have never since ancient times been regarded as a public misfortune. The misfortune, however, lies in the fact that the methods of the Former Kings have not been used in handling these means . . .

Wang An-shih came of a rising family of officials and was, indeed, born at an official post in Kiangsi. He learnt in his youth to understand the difficult conditions of the rural population in the provinces and the various localized attempts to alleviate them. He gained further experience during his term of office as district magistrate in the year 1047.

Wang An-shih also clothed his proposals in the form of an interpretation of the classics — that is to say, of a return to the methods prescribed in the classical works — since in any other form they would have been displeasing to the educated people of the time. They differ, however, from the proposed reforms outlined above, in being to a large extent based on measures which he had tested practically, having become familiar with them during the life-time of his father, who had occupied official positions in various provinces, and during his own term of office.

Wang An-shih was by no means the unworldly theoretician many authors have represented him as being. Above all, he saw quite clearly that the execution of his reforms would be in the hands of the officials, who would first have to be made able and willing to co-operate. With this purpose in mind, he not only sent out forty commissars whose mission was to make the new regulations or laws (*fa*) known throughout the empire but also for the first time paid fixed salaries to the lower officials and employees, in whose hands the execution of his reforms ultimately rested. Furthermore, numerous officials from the lower levels were promoted, often so that they should be available to carry through the reforms.

Wang An-shih clearly set great store by creating from below a circle of devoted and trustworthy collaborators. Frequently, however, these newly promoted men were unused to the manners of the court and their unpolished ways made them laughing-stocks. It also appears that there were many ruthless and cunning careerists among them. At all events, a breach opened within the official corps, which lasted throughout the Sung period.

In connection, of course, with these attempts to reform the official corps, the educational system was also reformed. Under the Sung, as there had been under the T'ang, there was a special high school in the capital. It was, however, poorly attended and run-down. In about 1068 a beginning was made in reorganizing it. The teaching staff was increased. Two professors were engaged for each of the classics. The pupils were selected by provincial examinations and, when they reached the high school, were formed into study-groups (*chai*) of thirty. They could choose one of the classics as their main subject and were divided into three classes, passing from one to the next above it by examination. The number of pupils was at first unlimited; in about 1078–1085 it was fixed at two thousand. Of these, some three hundred reached the second and some hundred the third class.

The provincial schools were reformed at the same time. In about 1071, there were outcries for suitable teaching staff. The schools received field allowances, out of which they could cover their expenses. In the year 1078, there were fifty-three of these schools under official administration. They enabled the sons of less prosperous families also to rise to the higher official positions. Now, as before, the classics formed the focal point of the examinations since they were thought to contain all the knowledge required by those who governed. Scholars from among the ranks of the reformers now wrote new commentaries to the classics. One of them, that of the *Chou-kuan* (or *Chou-li*, 'Chou officialdom'), is the work of Wang An-shih himself. In the foreword he praises the classics as the most important instrument of statecraft and states that a student who had absorbed their principles (*fa*) 'was fit to hold an official position and, in his capacity as an official, to translate them into action'. He was in fact expressing his own ideas of reform under the cloak of a commentary on one of the classics.

In addition to the high school, which was devoted to classical studies, schools were founded during the years 1072–1076 for military, legal and medical instruction. In the first, pupils were taught from the ancient works on the art of war, and military exercises were held. The purpose of the school was to provide a better, more thoroughly trained body of officers for the army. Students in the law school were instructed in the general character of the laws and regulations as well as in practical verdicts on every kind of legal case.

The founding of the medical high school may be regarded as an innovation which set the Sung apart from the earlier dynasties. Healing was, indeed, placed under state supervision during the Sung period and only officially approved doctors were permitted to practise. Those who evaded this ruling were suspected of belonging to a secret, illegal religious community, in which the sick were treated by faith-healing and similar practices. Three hundred pupils were at first admitted to the school; they were instructed by specialists in the subjects of pulse-reading and the treatment of abscesses. During their training the students treated the sick from the other high schools and the officers from the barracks in the capital. They were judged annually by the successes they achieved in this treatment. The successful doctors were paid monthly, in varying amounts. This high school did much to raise the social standing of a professional group which until then had been on an equal footing with soothsayers and magicians.

It is unfortunately impossible to show in detail here how the stimulus behind all these reforms can be attributed to the conflict of interests between the large-scale landowners and the medium and small landowners. Wang An-shih was unequivocally on the side of the last. Even when examined superficially, most of his proposed reforms, therefore, reveal his efforts to stand out for the interests of the broader sections of the population and to base the régime on them.

His 'Law relating to germinating seed' seems to show this particularly clearly; it was designed to help farmers over the economically difficult period between 'green and yellow', that is to say, between sowing and harvesting, and to save them from accepting loans at usurious rates of interest. As we have seen, this aim had been followed in the so-called equalizing granaries, though these, as we have already noted, soon degenerated into undesirable money-lending establishments. In the end they aggravated rather than alleviated the mounting debts of the medium-sized and small farmers.

The law introduced by Wang An-Shih provided that the stocks of the equalizing granaries should be converted into money and this, under certain conditions, placed at the disposal of the rural population in the form of loans. The loans were paid on the thirtieth day of the first month in advance and on the thirtieth day of the fifth month in advance. Repayment, in either money or goods, was correspondingly made in the fifth or the tenth month. Interest was at the rate of 20%. Dispossessed persons, that is to say, the rural proletariat, were excluded from the loans and, apart from this, the size of the sums loaned was scaled according to the resources of the borrower. In order to prevent people absconding with borrowed money and other abuses of the loan capital, groups of five families were constituted to keep one another under observation. Tenants required a landlord's guarantee before they could receive a loan.

All these reforms show clearly that this was a measure to protect the rural middle class, assuming that this expression is applicable to conditions in China. It enabled the independent peasants to hold their possessions during periods of want, whereas until then, they had generally been forced to sell their land when harvests were bad. The rates of interest, which, of course, seem to us excessively high, were still far below the demands of the land-grabbers and usurers, whose loans were quite brutally designed gradually to expropriate the debtor and force him into a kind of bondage.

These parties, who, to a great extent dominated the agricultural situation, lost no time in expressing their violent opposition. In so doing they used such characteristic catch-phrases as 'squandering the state capital', 'collecting loans by the use of force and cruelty'.

Another reform introduced by Wang An-shih brought a further alleviation to the medium-sized and small landowners: they could now buy remission from compulsory labour. With the money thus received, the authorities engaged labour for the work to be done. The amount of the payment was reckoned according to local conditions and also according to whether the substitute labour was paid by the day or the month and whether heavy or light work was needed. Smaller payments were exacted from those social groups — such as persons living alone, widows or monks — exempt from compulsory labour, but whose property justified their being placed in higher financial categories. Obviously the classes mentioned above profited from this equalized distribution of labour.

A new form of land-registration was also introduced at this time. According to a newly created standard, the ground was divided into five grades according to its situation and productiveness and correspondingly registered and taxed, a measure which naturally incurred violent opposition from the powers in the land, the wholesale buyers and the great land-owners, who had benefited from the old system.

Wang An-shih's army reforms are also typically 'middle-class' in character. They provided that every member of the rural population capable of bearing arms should be registered, and that every second man should be instructed in archery and fighting discipline. Units of ten families were also formed. Compulsory breeding of horses was another element in the system. These military organizations were obviously less useful for attack or defence against a foreign enemy than for maintaining law and order, that is, for putting down armed popular rebellions within the country.

It is, however, impossible within the framework of this general history to go into every detail of this great attempt by medieval China to bring in social reform, which, had it been successfully carried through, might have given history a different turn.

The main cause of its failure was doubless the fact that although he befriended the lower grades of officialdom, Wang An-shih failed to create a devoted and trustworthy official corps. In addition, the interests of the great landowners and the higher officials proved to be too closely interwoven for him to overcome them with the means at his command. The conflict between reform and anti-reform did, nevertheless, continue for a long time, though it became increasingly marked by personal and petty jealousies rather than by planned opposition.

3. SHIFT IN THE ECONOMIC CENTRE OF GRAVITY

Mention must at this point be made of another phenomenon of the Sung period, namely the fact that the economic centre of gravity of the empire now finally shifted to the south-eastern provinces, that is, to the region of the mouth of the Yangtze. This move began in the T'ang period when the administration of the government salt monopoly was transferred to Yang-chou on the lower Yangtze. The monopoly meant that the producers were bound to sell their salt to the government, who then passed it on to dealers at a profit. It soon became one of the main sources of governmental revenue. As a result, Yang-chou gradually developed into a kind of southern financial capital until, particularly after the devastations of the An Lu-chan rebellion, it became the economic centre of the empire. From the first the Sung pursued an economic policy expressed in the slogan, 'The south first, then the north'.

Looking back to an earlier period, we see that in the later Chou dynasty the supply centre had been, roughly, North Anhui. Now it had clearly shifted to the provinces south of the Yangtze.

The Sung government developed these provinces as a basis for defence against the north and north-west. A comment made by the first Sung emperor about his very active brother is indicative of the new political line which did not allow for any active expansion in the north: 'Since the time of Wu-tai there has been no let-up in the evil of warfare and the state coffers are empty. We must therefore now occupy first the south-west and then the south-east of the Empire. In this way the needs of the country will be satisfied.'[10]

As soon as they had annexed the region of the mouth of the Yangtze, the Sung began to enlarge the arable areas to the south and south-east of the river. Special attention was paid to improving and developing the irrigation system of the province of Liang-Chê (Chekiang and part of Kiangsu). At the same time, great dykes were constructed against the sea and the T'ai-hu, a great lake in Kiangsu, providing large areas of reclaimed land, on which nearly 26,000 families could be settled. It is noteworthy that of all the arable land in the Sung empire — it was given as 4,616,500 *ch'ing* (1 *ch'ing*=approx. 13 acres) — 2,953,578 *ch'ing* fell to the south-east.

From the point of view of population also, the centre of gravity of the empire lay in the south. Because there was so much political unrest in the north, a constant stream of northern Chinese continued throughout the history of the country to migrate southwards. Whereas in the first Han period the figures for the population of north and south China stood in the proportion of ten to one, in the Sung period, in about 1085, more than half the whole population of the empire was in the south. This meant that, since the T'ang period, southerners had increased in number by 10%. In the Sung period, in about 1080, the figure for the total population was about 40,072,606; of these there were 3,223,700 persons in the province of Liang-Chê alone and in Chiang-nan-hsi (roughly the later Kiangsi, including the region of the Po-yang lake) about 3,075,847; in the second Sung period, that is, in about 1162, these figures increased to 4,327,322 and 3,221,538. The latter figures provide a clue to the extent of the influx of population to the south after the break-up of the northern Sung dynasty in 1126.

The greater part of the imperial revenue from taxes also came from the south. In the period about 1068–1077, the total revenue from the trading-tax was about 7,803,727 monetary units, of which 4,415,170 came from the south. The tea-tax came exclusively from the southern — principally the south-eastern — provinces. Historical sources repeatedly state that, from the time of the second Sung emperor onwards, the total needs of the army were met from the south-eastern provinces of the empire.

The increasing importance of the south-eastern provinces in providing agricultural supplies can also be seen from the growing quantity of produce despatched to the north by the Grand Canal. Whereas for the T'ang period there are figures of about 3,000,000 *shih* (1 *shih* = 120 *catties*) this rose under the Sung to 7,000,000 *shih*.

Fang La's uprising, briefly mentioned above, was therefore a direct threat to the supply centre of the empire. And it is thus easy to see why, in order to combat it, the troops which had been stationed ready to attack in the north were withdrawn and moved to the south. This move, however, revealed the weakness of the Sung empire to the Chin (Tartars) and determined them to attack. The conflict ended with the fall of the northern Sung dynasty.

On the whole, the significance of the re-establishment of the dynasty in the south with its capital at Lin-an (Hang-chou) is simply that of a withdrawal to the supply base of the empire. The move does not represent a break with the first Sung period.

It is hardly necessary to state that as the economic centre of gravity shifted, it by degrees carried cultural life with it, a fact which became obvious in the second Sung period when the northern part of the empire was cut off.

4. CITY LIFE IN THE SUNG PERIOD

The reader will, perhaps, have gathered from what has already been said, that the Sung period derived a special character from the social regroupings which were then taking place. This is not to say that new social classes came into being, but merely that some now became more prominent and acquired greater consequence than they had enjoyed in previous epochs.

This shows most clearly in the city life of the period, of which we possess a number of lively and extremely interesting accounts. The residential and business districts of a medieval Chinese capital lay outside and to the south of the imperial palace and the government quarter, where the most important state departments were located. They extended to the east and west of a main thoroughfare and were divided into rectangular blocks.

These quarters were separated from one another by walls or broad streets. This was to prevent fire, the worst of all hazards. Since most of the houses were built of wood the effect of fire was clearly devastating. In every quarter, at intervals of about three hundred paces, there were fire-alarm posts manned by fire-fighting soldiers. These soldiers had to patrol their beat continuously throughout the night and watch out for fires. Fire watch-towers several storeys high were also erected at suitable points and look-out men stationed in them night and day. There were fire-brigades over a hundred men strong, equipped with large and small buckets, hoses, axes, saws, iron grappling-hooks, forks, ladders, ropes and other implements. The fire-service was entirely in the hands of the administration and the citizens did not have to trouble about it.

In other ways also urban life was extremely well-organized. At the street crossings there were small towers with drums on which the hours of the day and night were sounded. At the beginning of the fifth hour (seven o'clock in the morning) the populace was woken. The great gongs were beaten in the temples. Monks and novices went through the streets drumming on their wooden instruments to see that no one overslept. At the same time they called out the state of the weather, indicating whether it were raining or the sun shining.

Then the gates between the different quarters, the bridges and the great outer gates were opened. Lamps and lanterns were hung up in the shops and the life of the city began. Men selling water for washing, tea or soup were soon in the streets loudly crying their wares. The officials and ushers betook themselves to their places of work. As the morning wore on, vehicles of all kinds, horses and donkeys, carrying people from the countryside and the suburbs began to stream into the city.

Business activity in a city like this was extremely vigorous and took place in the bazaars. Each trade was confined to one row of streets (*hang*) and formed a guild with its own divinity, which was worshipped in a small temple. Thus there was the butchers' alley where supplies of beasts for slaughter arrived early in the morning. Just as today, the customer could pick the part he liked and have it cut for him. Slaughtering was usually forbidden on religious feast-days. The fishmongers sold live fish from flat tubs, putting willow-leaves in the water to keep the fish fresh. Fish were delivered to the city fresh every day, even in winter. There were also bazaars selling fruit of all kinds, as well as flowers and sweetmeats.

There were many cook-shops and eating-houses offering a copious choice of dishes. Many of these eating-houses already specialized in the local dishes of other provinces, such as Szechuan or the south. Most of these houses consisted of a central hall in which festivities of all kinds could take place, with smaller side-rooms for other customers. As soon as the customer had seated himself he was given chopsticks and a paper napkin and numerous servants saw to his every wish. Some customers liked their dishes hot, some luke-warm and others cold, one wanted his meat boiled, another grilled and yet another roast. It is clear that the clientele of these establishments were scarcely less demanding than we are today and gave the people serving them just as much work. A waiter sometimes carried nearly twenty dishes of food on his right arm up to his shoulder and yet never failed to give the appropriate dish to the man who had ordered it.

For people who were on the road late or had business during the night, there were a few places selling noodles, as well as small tea-stalls at the gates which were permitted by the police to stay open all night.

There was also many establishments which sold a large selection of alcoholic drinks. The better ones were in buildings of several storeys. The premises opened not on to the street but on to an inner courtyard. These courtyards were surrounded by brightly painted galleries and balustrades hung with lampions and mirrors and full of all kinds of decorations, including dwarf trees. A house of this type would employ a hundred singing-girls and courtesans to entertain the customers. They were often managed by the state and, particularly in the second Sung period in Hang-chou, they accounted for a large proportion of the revenue which paid for defence in the north. There was, at this time, a great flood of all kinds of sentimental love-stories centring round the courtesans of these houses, which can, to some extent, be regarded as propaganda designed to increase state revenue.

The less well-to-do, however, had to be content with booths constructed of bamboo-cane and hangings where, at the most, soya-bean soup or edible shell-fish were served with the drinks.

The many tea-houses did not only sell tea. They were frequently a kind of employment agency, where servants, domestic staff, as well as persons with all kinds of manual skills, could be hired. In all such cases a guild elder acted as intermediary: he took a guarantee from both parties and was called in if trouble arose.

Finally, we must not omit street-cleaning and refuse removal. The men concerned received payment from the inhabitants of the street in which they worked. There were also other men who removed ordure. In the poorer quarters, where the houses had no pits, buckets were much used and these had to be emptied daily. Each bucket-emptier had his appointed district. Any encroachment into a colleague's district led to violent quarrels. Even at that time, human dung was considered highly desirable as a fertilizer and presumably represented a good source of income. Later on, the removal of ordure in the big cities was concentrated in the hands of contractors who amassed great wealth from their business and whose children rose to the upper classes of society.

The big cities also had an extensive system of public assistance, such as homes for the aged, orphanages and, from 1102 onwards, hospitals and graveyards, which came into existence largely through Buddhist initiative. The following account describes one aspect of this social welfare:

In the Sung period every regional town had an official house for looking after children. If parents were poor and unable to bring up a child they could hand it over to one of these institutions. Its birth-date was registered there and a nurse cared for it. If a childless family wanted children, it could obtain them from such a house. Many children were handed in during starvation-years instead of simply being left on the streets.[11]

The social structure of an urban community of this kind is naturally of great interest from the point of view of the history of civilization and an attempt to present it in the briefest outline therefore follows.

The position of the imperial court is obviously distinct from all other social classes. One might say that it forms a society on its own, with its own divisions. In relation to the other classes, the court society occupies something of a spectator's position, looking down from its elevated seat.

Even the officials were considerably closer than the court to the common people, for their well-built and well-appointed houses were situated in the residential quarters outside the palace. The officials were not infrequently financial speculators with interests in many different kinds of business, such as pawnbrokers and wine-shops. These groups were nevertheless expected to remain at a great distance from the other classes, as is demonstrated by, for example, the fact that officials were forbidden to visit the courtesans' quarter. This, however, did not prevent their having singing and dancing girls and girl acrobats to their houses for all manner of private entertainment. The chief off-duty amusement of those with a literary education was versifying. As we have already seen, people often met simply in order to try out their poetic skills over wine and a good meal.

As far as standards of living went, there was a certain rivalry between the higher officials and those citizens who had grown rich through trade. The sons of such people were described as 'young gentlemen from well-to-do families' or as 'men of the world' and in the football clubs and other sporting associations, in which they mixed with the humbler employees of the government departments, were surrounded by every kind of hanger-on.

The largest section of urban society was undoubtedly that of the traders. They were organized into guilds and their very clothing distinguished them from the other classes, and even from others among themselves. Thus the incense-sellers wore caps which fell down over their necks, while the pawnbrokers wore a kerchief and a black garment with a special girdle. All the street-traders were distinguished by characteristic head-dresses. The trade-guilds were under a formal obligation to supply the government authorities and were often used by the official corps for compulsory sales. The artisans had to render compulsory service at fixed times and were summoned to the departments as they were required. The payment they received for their work was usually inadequate.

In addition to the city guilds, there were also artisans in the state-factories, most of whom were probably lodged in special enclosed quarters. Their hours of work and leisure were laid down according to the season. In most cases they had to put a personal mark on the finished wares to act as a check on individual output and to prevent sabotage. The guild organization held a large reserve of labour, which could be utilized at any time for special undertakings at no great expense.

A list of some of these craftsmen's associations will give an idea of the extremely varied activities of these groups. Thus there were guilds of jade-cutters, of borers and coilers, of makers of fine combs, belt-makers, goldsmiths and silversmiths, binders, stickers, trimmers of kingfishers' feathers, mounters and paper-workers, makers of small bells, oil and woodworkers, brick-makers, potters, stonemasons, bamboo-workers, lacquer-workers, cutters, candle-makers, paper-makers, makers of burial-gifts and many others besides.

The servants formed another group of urban society, a group composed very largely of women. Thus there were to be found in the houses of the rich, lady's maids, sewing-maids, house-actresses, bath-maids, female lutanists and chess-players and maids for every other conceivable service, including, of course, cooks. The last-named were the most expensive and only the richest could afford them. Among male servants, the most numerous were the waiters in the eating-houses; there were also supervisors in shops and pawnbrokers' establishments, book-keepers and messengers. The officials often employed travelling secretaries, outriders to escort sedan chairs, as well as a Taoist to look after their incense-burners, gardeners, chairmen, house-boys and so on. As has already been noted, all these willing spirits were obtained from certain tea-houses through the agency of a guild elder. These elders also provided carriers and attendants for those making overland journeys. They usually also had guarantors in the servants' native place, whose duty it was, in cases of theft or other crimes against the traveller, to conduct an investigation on the spot.

In addition to those servants who were employed by firm contract, if only for short periods, there were others who earned their living by casual work. They were known, revealingly, as 'occasional men'. Some of these were unmarried men with no regular occupation, but who had a little knowledge of writing, lute-playing, chess and similar arts which they used to make the acquaintance of the sons of rich families. These young men then employed them as guides and companions in their rounds of the city's places of amusement. Or else they made friends with officials newly arrived in the city, or with rich merchants, for whom they acted as go-between with courtesans and the like. Others could imitate all sorts of voices, sing popular tunes and entertain quite a large company with round songs, riddles and suchlike. Others again were good swimmers and boxers and earned their keep among sportsmen. This category also includes the small public entertainers who pitched their tents and staged fights between cocks, quails or crickets.

The courtesans' and singing-girls' attendants also earned money by performing a great variety of services for their ladies' clients. Like their present-day colleagues, they were extremely importunate and always ready to assert their extravagant demands by provoking loud and scandalous quarrels.

Then there were the low-class singing-girls who joined the company unbidden and would not move off until they had been given a little money; and small traders who were so persistent in offering their unwanted wares that in the end somebody would buy them simply to be rid of the nuisance.

As was only to be expected, the cities also sheltered a criminal underworld. It appears, however, that, in contrast to our own times, crimes of violence were rare. Most of the criminals were frauds or swindlers.

There were, for example, people who organized what they called a 'courtesans' performance', in which a cheap prostitute made up as a distinguished and elegant courtesan seduced young people into paying out large sums of money and all manner of bad business. Another very popular form of swindling was the so-called 'bank gaming club'. This was a band of players who rooked their unsuspecting prey by a pre-arranged method. Again other similar elements practised confidence-tricks: by, for example, pretending to all kinds of influential connections in the department in which a case was being handled, they fleeced people who were visiting the city in the hope of influencing officials to give a favourable turn to their lawsuit.

Deception was also prevalent. Thus garments were made of paper or articles of copper and lead so finished as to look like gold or silver. Clay and wood were used to make imitations of sweet-smelling drugs. These deceptions were often so skilful that they were extremely difficult to detect.

Another group went in for theft. They mostly hung about the gates of the bazaars and, at suitable moments, cut open sacks and purloined their contents. There were also housebreakers who made holes in the walls of the houses, often built only of clay, and stole whatever they could carry off.

Successful rogues of this sort were usually supported by a band of accomplices. In writings bearing on the matter, names of the gang-leaders are given as 'Tiger of the Barricades', 'Nine-armed Dragon' and so on.

The city authority was naturally concerned to combat these criminal elements. This was one of the duties of the fire-fighting police stationed in every quarter of the city. They kept a special watch on many of the official buildings and wealthy citizens' houses.

Mention should also be made of the societies which existed in the city. We have already referred to the poets' clubs, to which the highly cultivated members of the official corps belonged, and to the rich merchants' sports clubs. There were many other, religiously based, societies, including, for example, the Taoist Ling-pao society, the members of which subscribed monthly for recitations from certain Taoist sutras. Meetings were also held in veneration of particular Taoist saints. Special celebrations were held for the feast-day of *chung-yüan* on the fifteenth day of the seventh month, at which the 'earth-official' came down from above to judge between good and evil. It coincided with the Buddhist Ullambana feast for the hungry souls in purgatory. Butchers were forbidden to slaughter on that day. Another Taoist society distributed tea and soup to the poor on the days on which the births of their saints were celebrated.

The Golden Lustre (*prabhā*) society was specifically Buddhist. Its members all came of rich families and owned shops in the main streets. They distinguished themselves by rich gifts of thick candles and incense, and of money and rice for the temple. The higher officials' ladies belonged to the Keng-shen society at the meetings of which passages from the *Pūrṇa Buddha Sutra* (*Sutra of the Perfect Enlightenment*) were recited. For these occasions they wore magnificent girdles and costly head-dresses. According to comments made by commoners, their adornments were worn for show, and the aim of their meetings ostentation rather than religious edification.

Boys and girls gathered near a Buddhist pagoda on the eighth day of the fourth month for a 'meeting of the true faithful', and on the first day of the ninth month, on the birthday of the 'earth-spirit, who honours good as its king', children distributed tea and fruit 'so that hearts might turn to truthfulness'. On the eighth day of every month the faithful gathered in all the temples of the city for a special fast and a recitation of sutras. There were many other combined religious and social events organized by the religious bodies for all classes, but it would take too long to list them.

Other extremely important events in the life of the city were, of course, the state religious festivals, the greatest of which were celebrated by the emperor himself on a specially prepared site and altar in the country outside and to the south of the city. The extensive preparations for these celebrations began two months in advance and became a kind of popular amusement. The great sensation was provided by the elephants which took part in the solemn procession and had to be specially trained. They were received as tribute from the south and their sole duty seems to have been to appear on these occasions. A track marked off outside the city walls was used to accustom them to the din of the signalling gongs and drums, the movement of the horse-drawn coaches, the cracking of whips and the fluttering of the banners and flags. The animals, with their mahouts astride their necks, covered the track twice. Finally they were made to move into line and to bow, with their heads turned towards the north. During this display, small figures of elephants made of clay and wood or pictures on paper were sold among the dense crowds and were given away or kept as mementoes. The elephants were also useful for testing the strength of the bridges over which the procession had to pass. In the procession itself they drew a great wagon which carried some ten musicians with drums and wind-instruments.

The emperor's departure for the site of the sacrifice was guarded by mailed riders and troops which formed a cordon down the whole length of the route. The emperor and his suite passed the night in a veritable city of tents pitched for the occasion. The sacrificial ceremony began at about three the next morning. Its central feature was the emperor's approach to the altar which he repeated three times, offering food and drink to the divinities and his associated ancestors assembled there. Each phase of the action was accompanied by choirs of musicians who stood by and below the altar. The end of the ceremony came when the great pile for the burnt-offering at the south of the site was lit and burnt itself out.

Outside and inside the site of the sacrifice the crowds could be counted in tens of thousands as they stood in awestruck silence. The stirring of a light breeze and the tinkling of the girdle ornaments could be heard. A voice cried: 'All participants bow!' All bowed low. The ceremony was over.[12]

The true climax of the whole thing came, however, when the amnesty was announced, though this was usually restricted to certain categories of crime. A mast surmounted by a golden figure of a cock, from which four ropes hung, was erected. Four agile men climbed the ropes and the one who was first to reach the top received a prize. The order announcing the amnesty was brought down from a tower by a gold figure of a phoenix controlled by wires. During the announcement, prisoners at the foot of the tower were relieved of their shackles and set free.

This great sacrifice on the southern outskirts of the city — which might, in certain circumstances, be replaced by other ceremonies, though these will not be mentioned here — was not merely a religious demonstration but, perhaps to an even greater extent, a political one, designed to proclaim internal and external peace and the secure régime of the Chinese empire to the whole eastern world. The amnesty served to demonstrate to his subjects the emperor's graciousness and clemency.

Life in the great city was further punctuated by a number of festivities, among which the new year's celebrations took pride of place. In the capital of K'ai-fêng during the period of the northern Sung dynasty, sports contests and singing and dancing competitions were usually held at the new year. From early morning great crowds surged through the streets, everyone wishing everyone else good luck for the coming year. In the alleys of every quarter, fruit and cakes were laid out for sale.

The dancing and singing contests took place in a large, brightly-coloured tent. The onlookers in their new clothes were carried thither in numerous carriages and chairs. In the evening even the ladies of the upper classes joined in the games organized by the common people and watched the bustling crowd in the places of amusement. They also commonly visited the eating-houses. Even people of the poorest classes now appeared in clean new clothes and entertained one another with food and wine.

A great congratulatory reception was held at the court with

four large, heavily-armoured men stationed in the corners of the audience-chamber. All the envoys from the neighbouring lands and those officials who were permitted to appear at court arrived in festive attire. The representative of the great northern state of the Liao created a stir with his unusual dress and the form of his greeting. Standing on his left foot, he dropped to his right knee and raised both hands to his right shoulder. Everyone else performed his greeting in the Chinese manner, by kneeling down and making a deep bow. The Uighurs were conspicuous in this courtly society for their long beards and the high bridges to their noses. On the next day there was a great archery competition in the imperial park, for which the best marksmen were selected from the city garrison, although foreign visitors, such as the above-mentioned Liao envoy, also took part. The prizes were coats of armour, saddles and other objects used by warriors. The names of the victors were publicly announced in the city.

The spring ceremony was also universally celebrated; it was reckoned according to the solar year and fell on the fifth of February. In the palace and in the regional cities a clay figure of an ox was beaten with coloured wands to hasten the coming of spring.

The feast of lanterns was celebrated on the fifteenth day of the first month. A great scaffolding was erected in the capital, K'ai-fêng, on which coloured pictures of the saints were displayed. Among them would be, for example, the Buddhist, Manjuśrī, riding on a lion and with water spurting from each of his finger-tips. The whole thing was lit by coloured lamps. There were also great figures of dragons made of transparent green material. Lights were placed inside them and they were made to move like snakes, so that when seen from a little distance they looked like living creatures. Large-scale musical and theatrical performances took place in the palace and in front of the official buildings, watched by the common people from a distance.

At the beginning of the third month, one hundred and five days after the winter solstice, the *ch'ing-ming* ('pure and clear') ceremony took place. Cold food was eaten for the three preceding days. During these three days the fires had to be extinguished in every home and were not re-lit until the third day. The new fire was started by means of lucky willow-twigs. Graves were tidied and set in order at the *ch'ing-ming* feast. Incense and paper money were burned for the dead and sacrifices of food offered them.

The birthday of the Buddha was celebrated on the eighth day of the fourth month. The ceremony of Buddha-washing took place in the temples. People gave each other presents of scented water known as Buddha-washing water. This was the season at which the pomegranates flowered and the song of the oriole — sounding rather like *ch'iu-yu* ('seek the friend') — was heard. Near the pavilion by the pale green willows, the swallows could be seen raising their first brood. In this month aubergines and melons arrived in the markets of K'ai-fêng. Brandy was sold in seventy-two licensed taverns.

The succession of feast-days was kept up throughout the year. The mid-autumn festival was celebrated on the fifteenth day of the seventh month because, at this time, the Shepherd (the star Aquila) and the Weaving Girl (the star Lyra), the heavenly lovers, meet for one night. The Buddhists, however, kept it as a sort of mothers' day, on which they recited in the temples the tale of Mu-lien (Maudgalyāyana) recounted in an earlier chapter, or sometimes performed it as a play.

Nobody, of course, worked on these great or lesser feast-days — which played much the same part in the life of the people as do our sabbaths. The official corps, it is true, had a day known as the bath-day every ten days and did not have to go to their offices. The seven-day week was introduced into China only in very recent times, largely under pressure from the growing workers' movement and against opposition from the guilds and employers.

Both as regards their number and their character, the feast-days naturally varied somewhat in different parts of the country. Thus in the southern provinces there was one in the fifth month known as the dragon-boat ceremony, which was supposed to commemorate the suicide of the minister Ch'ü Yüan. On that day little rice-cakes were thrown into the water or lights were floated on the tide. There were also races between boats with dragons' heads.

The last evening of the year was dedicated to driving out evil spirits and unwholesome influences. High and low, rich and poor alike carefully swept their houses on this last day and turned out the rubbish. A portrait of Chung K'uei, the opponent of the demons, and an amulet made of peach-wood were then fastened to the door. In the palace a great ceremony of exorcism took place. The court players in every kind of mask and coloured costume, armed with wooden lances and swords, drove the evil spirits out of the palace to the noisy accompaniment of drums and wind-instruments. Their din could be heard in the farthest quarters of the city. Nobody slept that night; everywhere people sat round the fires waiting for day to break. This was known as seeing the new year in.[13]

5. SUNG PHILOSOPHY

Reference was made at the end of the section on the first great philosophical epoch of the Chan-kuo period to the fact that there was a resurgence of Chinese philosophy during the Sung period. A comprehensive presentation of the subject would, in fact, be more appropriate to a history of Chinese thought and further details might justifiably be omitted from the present book. But since this revival of Chinese speculative philosophy is generally regarded as so characteristic a feature of the period under discussion, a few words at least should be said about it.

The wave of philosophical speculation which arose in the Sung period may be explained by the efforts made by Confucian officialdom to assert itself against the infiltration of foreign ideas. This, of course, applied primarily to Buddhism, which, with its systematically and dialectically organized philosophy, increasingly threatened to draw the educated classes into its sphere of influence.

The reaction of the Sung philosophers against Buddhism was often described by the men themselves as the resumption of a traditional attitude starting with Mêng-tzŭ and carrying on, via Hsün-tzŭ, to their own period. A juster appreciation of the line of development may, however, be gained if we regard this philosophy as the continuation of the Confucianism of the later Han period and the *ch'ing-t'an*. We have noted that, in the first, a strongly rationalised Taoism with the framework of Confucian fundamentals was much in evidence.

The system now expounded by the philosopher Chou Tun-i (1017–1073), also goes back in its basic principles to a Taoist thinker of the Later Han period, and connects directly with the system of a Taoist of the T'ang period. The principle which is its starting-point, namely 'that which is summit-less' (*wu-chi*, i.e. that which can have nothing above it), Chou Tun-i now equates with a positive principle, that of the 'highest summit' (*t'ai-chi*). This is a material principle, the motion and repose of which engenders the two forms of existence, *yin* (dark, female) and *yang* (light, male). From these stem the five breaths or elements, and, finally, heaven and earth. The *I-ching* (*Book of Changes*), however, and the associated mystique of numbers played a prominent part in other similar derivations of this school.

Viewed in broad terms, two important intellectual currents can be observed at the beginning of the Sung period. There was, on the one hand, orthodox Confucianism, the main efforts of which were bent towards opposing and replacing the other leading intellectual movements. This was the continuation of tendencies which we encountered briefly in the section on T'ang literature. On the other hand, there were a number of scholars who, like Chou Tun-i, used Taoist ideas and mystical numerical reckonings to assist them in their search for a systematic development of the universe from a first principle.

In the course of the Sung period these two currents were combined by other thinkers of this circle. The brothers Ch'êng Hao (1032–85) and Ch'êng I (1053–1108), for example, replaced Chou Tun-i's first principle by *li*, which is meant to designate the underlying principle by which 'things are what they are'. 'Each thing has a principle, so that, for example, fire has that which makes it hot and water that which makes it cold.' In order to become familiar with the principles of things, we have to examine each one and discover 'why it is precisely as it is'. This axiom leads on to the *ko-wu* method, the 'examination of individual things', which is often compared with our inductive method. It was chiefly expounded by the leading Sung philosopher, the great scholar and classical commentator, Chu Hsi (1130–1200).

By contrast, Chang Tsai (1020–77) again introduced a material first principle, the breath (*ch'i*) or ether. This is found, for example, in human breath.

Chu Hsi in his philosophy finally combines *li* and *ch'i* when he assumes both a spiritual and material principle as the basis of existence. In this version of neo-Confucian philosophy, *ch'i* (breath) occupies the same position as that of matter in many western philosophical systems.

Opposition came from another school, of which Lu Chiu-yüan (1139–93) was the principal founder. His slogan was 'The universe is my spirit (*hsin* = heart) and my spirit is the universe'. The influence of the doctrine, briefly mentioned above, of the Buddhist Dhyāna (Ch'an) school on this philosophy — often described as having been extremely idealistic or individualist — is unmistakable. Later on, the chief exponent of this trend was Wang Shou-jên or Wang Yang-ming (1472–1529), who was also well-known as a general. He had begun by being a convinced follower of Chu Hsi's doctrine and began to scrutinize every single object — a bamboo, for example — for its inherent principle, but this method brought him no success. Enlightenment came to him, however, in the middle of one night when he recognized that all the wisdom of the sages — which means all the wisdom in existence — is held within the individual mind and the individual nature and that all attempts to search beyond this are vain.

Such, in the broadest possible outline, is the substance of neo-Confucian philosophy as it is generally represented. But if one looks a little more closely, it will be seen that these remarks by no means exhaust all there is to be said about trends in speculative philosophy during the Sung period.

Another of the thinkers of this period is Wang An-shih, whom we encountered earlier on as an economic reformer. He represents a brand of enlightened realism. His argument is roughly as follows:

> Mêng-tzŭ says that man's nature is good. Hsün-tzŭ says it is evil. But the fact is that *t'ai-chi* creates the five elements and

> only then do the beneficial and the harmful come into being. But we cannot say that *t'ai-chi* is (in itself) good or evil. In this I differ from both masters.[15]

He defines what he calls 'human nature' a little more closely:

> Human nature and the emotional impulses are one and the same . . . When joy, anger, sorrow, desire, love and hatred still do not manifest themselves externally but remain locked in the heart, this is human nature . . . This is the root of emotional impulses. These in turn are the functions of nature . . . The emotional impulses become attached to an external object and they are then in motion. When, being in motion, they correspond with a commonsense principle, we have a sage or virtuous man (*hsien*), when not, we have an ordinary man . . .[15]

In contrast to orthodox Confucians, Wang An-shih also expresses the view that natural catastrophes had nothing to do with the behaviour of the emperor and that it was pointless for him to mortify himself when these occurred.

At the time of the southern Sung dynasty there emerged a few thinkers, not highly regarded today, whose philosophy is probably the expression of a different intellectual milieu, the world of the great merchants.

Among these was Yeh Shih (1150–1223), the founder of the so-called Yung-chia school. He represents a radical utilitarianism. 'If they do not lead to concrete benefits, ethics and legality are useless, empty words.' He came finally to a materialism of almost modern appearance:

> When the people's hearts are full but their stomachs are empty, when the body is weak but the will is strong, that they then always yearn for things (which they do not possess) can be understood from their situation. But when conditions are reversed, their external situation leaves them with no desire for things. The saint knows what all the world desires. And, following the (natural) Tao (the Way), he tempers and utilizes (this desire) and thus brings the state organization into being. But Lao-tzŭ

> wishes to force the desires to complete extinction and all he achieves thereby is disorganization.[16]

He also expressed the heretical opinion that the founding emperors of the Han and T'ang dynasties in their struggles for power cared nothing for the salvation of the people but only for their own advantage and personal prestige.

Another who held the same views was Ch'ên Liang (1143–1194). Ch'ên Liang carried on a polemical correspondence with Chu Hsi, in which he primarily opposed the orthodox opinion that in the earliest periods of Chinese history there were only ideal personalities who neither sought personal advantage nor strove for riches and honours. He starts from this assumption: 'Given the manner in which Tao (the Way, the method) is in the world, what thing could be without Tao? Taking a thousand paths and ten-thousand tracks, it creates a rule in the light of a given circumstance.'[17] Only when a man has penetrated to the depths of that which causes action and repose does he recognize the rightness of Confucius's fundamental principle, 'Be true to your own nature and use it with kindliness to others.' He was a convinced opponent of the group of philosophers mentioned briefly above, describing their teachings as unrealistic, useless, decadent and harmful to young people.

6. CHINESE PAINTING

All who have touched upon this subject have drawn attention to the links between painting and writing in China and have underlined the fact that Chinese pictures are not painted in our sense, but 'written'.

An anecdote which tells how one of the emperors commanded an artist to execute a painting of a peony is often used to illustrate this connection. The artist asked for five years' grace in which to produce his work. When, at the end of this ample period, the emperor reminded him of his commission, the painter took a sheet of paper and in a few moments produced a finished rendering of a peony. He then led his astonished patron into his studio and showed him five rooms full of sketches of peonies.

The purpose of this story is, of course, to show that the Chinese painter studies his subject for so long and with such intensity that in the end he can draw it or, as it were, write it down, in a few strokes which yet convey the essential nature of the object. Chinese painting here follows the same line of development as writing, which also began as a series of pictorial renderings; these became increasingly schematic and abbreviated until their resemblance to the drawn object disappeared almost completely and the object — its nature, as one might say, preserved solely in the brush-strokes of the character — became extinguished in the realm of writing.

As time went on, artists learnt to paint, as calligraphers to write, by drawing upon constantly recurring formal types which could be assembled by the individual painter to make pictures. The best and most celebrated work for instructing the budding painter in the application of these forms is the *Chieh-tzŭ yüan hua-chuan* (*The Mustard-Seed Garden Manual of Painting*), which although it did not appear until the seventeenth century, has a line of antecedents. It contains many woodcuts, with accompanying text, which lead the young artist from simple to more and more complicated forms and then on to using them to compose a picture.

It will already be clear that the Chinese painter is basically less concerned to produce a true imitation of nature than to express his artistic inspiration by combinations of conventional forms.

According, at least, to ancient works on painting, the painter should rely more on what he finds within himself and less on what he sees in the world around him. 'A landscape takes shape (unknown to him) in the painter's mind.'[18] It may be said to be the result of the restless, inner, meditative effort of the artist to become one with the nature which surrounds him. 'When he wakes, he portrays it as a picture. There is in it no trace of the things of the world (around him).' The typified forms which he has learned by diligent study serve him as a kind of handwriting.

Chinese pictures, therefore, cannot generally be apprehended by the eye alone but must to some extent be read. They are rather the expression of the mental processes of the artist creating them than representations of external themes. This also means that a Chinese painting is not conceived from an observer's fixed viewpoint, and this in turn obviously means that there is no need for the picture to be built up on our laws of perspective. A Chinese painting, at least in more recent times, consists largely of brushwork and its quality resides to a great extent, if not almost entirely, in the manner in which the brush has been used. Colour, by contrast, occupies a subsidiary position, although, especially in earlier periods, it was much used. It was of prime importance in a particular technique known as 'boneless painting', a style in which the contours were not first drawn in with the brush.

In the earliest treatise on painting, the *Ku hua p'in-lu* (*Old Record of the Classification of Painters*), six principles for the creation of a good painting are listed. They may be rendered as follows:

> The first is: Spirit Resonance (or, Vibration of Vitality) and Life Movement. The second is: Bone Manner (i.e. Structural) Use of the Brush. The third is: Conform with the Objects to Give Likeness. The fourth is: Apply the Colours according to the Characteristics. The fifth is: Plan and Design, Place and Position (i.e. Composition). The sixth is: To Transmit Models by Drawing.[19]

This last principle refers to the 'writing' of pictures, the process briefly described above. Another consequence of this practice was that copies, when they were 'written down' with the power and rapidity of the original, were considered just as valuable as the original itself and were not subject to the same disparagement as is the 'copy' in western art.

This is the point at which to state that Chinese painting, particularly in the earlier phases of its history, did not serve merely decorative or aesthetic purposes but was primarily used for moral edification and as a magical means of warding off evil. Representations of the good rulers of antiquity were designed to spur the observer to good while those of bad rulers served as warnings.

A work on paintings of the T'ang period says:

> Painting is a practice by which moral training is perfected and the social order sustained. It penetrates to the roots of the transmutations of nature as well as of hidden and subtle things. It is equal in merit to the six skills of antiquity (i.e. ritual, music, archery, charioteering, writing and calculating) and moves with the four seasons. It originates in nature itself and not in human invention.

And in another passage we read: 'This shows that paintings are a means of presenting events in such a way that they may serve as examples to the able and deterrents to the evil.' In this sense, therefore, painting was basically a means of propaganda for the public morality which the state required of its citizens.

The pictures of tigers that were fastened to doors, portrayals of subduers of demons and other paintings of this kind, however, were intended to drive off evil influences. In this connection, we should bear in mind the belief that by knowing its name a man acquired power over an object and that this power was even greater if he could write the name. A painted representation is no less efficacious than a written character.

Painting has certainly been practised in China since ancient times but virtually nothing but literary evidence has survived from periods up to and including the Han. The extremely rare examples which have come down to us are insufficient to give us anything like a clear idea of early painting.

Ku K'ai-chih (*c.* 344–405) is the first Chinese painter who emerges as a fairly recognizable person. He came from Wu-hsi in Kiangsu, possessed wide-ranging literary knowledge and had held several secretarial positions. His portraits were particularly celebrated. Having finished one of these, he would often wait several years until, in a moment of special inspiration, he added the pupils of the eyes, for, as he said, in them the spirit was revealed and it was through them that the portrait became a likeness. One of his most celebrated works was the painting of the Buddhist saint, Vimalakīrti. The temple on one of the walls of which it was painted received over a million gold pieces in gifts from visitors. Unfortunately, no original work by this painter has survived, only a few copies by later artists, from which we may gain an approximate idea of the work and manner of the master.

During the period of political separation between the north and the south, lasting from the late fourth to the sixth century, the fine arts show differences that derive from variations in the dominant characteristics of the peoples. While the north was under the influence of the proud, hard, habitually bellicose nomads, the avowed inclination in the south was towards delicacy, beauty and softness. Moreover, as a result of the endless conflicts and disturbances, many sought refuge in the Buddhist monasteries and this, as has already been mentioned, brought about a great flowering of religious arts. Artists painted divinities on temple walls — though probably all these have disappeared with the passage of time. Apart from the wall-paintings in the cave-temples near Tun-huang, which countless publications have made world-famous, virtually nothing has survived.

One of the worst catastrophes to have befallen Chinese painting was the destruction, by the Liang dynasty (502–556), of the great collection of works of art and books belonging to the Buddhist emperor, Wu-ti, in Nanking. 'Some hundreds of cases of paintings from the imperial palace were burnt by the usurper Hou Chi. The rest were removed to Chiang-ling, only to be destroyed there by General Yü Chin of the western Wei dynasty.'

Tsung Ping, a landscape-painter from Nan-yang (in the south of the modern province of Honan), who enjoyed great renown among his contemporaries, was active at this time. In his youth, Tsung Ping loved to roam the hills to the south of the central and lower Yangtze. When advancing years made this impossible, he finally settled in Ching-ling (Hupei) and painted from memory all the landscapes he could no longer visit. His paintings are lost, but he wrote a short introduction to landscape-painting which has survived, and which may be regarded as the earliest work of its kind in China.

If that which the eyes see and the heart feels is the principle (of an object) and the artist seeks its likeness with consummate

> skill, then all other eyes will see it and all other hearts feel it. Through this seeing and feeling the true principle (of an object) is attained. . . .
>
> The mind is not in the first place fixed on anything. But when it applies itself to a form and stimulates a likeness, the principle enters the outline.

Despite the complex mode of expression, we here recognize the typical Chinese conception set out at the beginning of this section.

Tsung Ping was not, however, the first Chinese landscape-painter. This place is accorded to a Lady Chao, sister of one of the ministers of the state of Wu at the time of the Three Kingdoms.

The work *Li-tai ming-hua chi* (*Records of Famous Painters of all Ages*), finished in 847, contains a critical consideration of ancient landscape-paintings, in which their shortcomings are indicated:

> The landscapes are filled with crowded peaks, their effect is like that of filigree ornaments or horn combs. Sometimes the water does not seem to flow, sometimes the figures are larger than the mountains. The views are generally enclosed by trees and stones which stand in a circle on the ground. They look like rows of lifted arms with outspread fingers.[20]

Whereas in the north painting was probably largely confined to the adornment of temple walls, pictures in the south were also painted on screens and on silk and paper rolls. Southern painters chose secular as well as religious subjects. Treatises on painterly technique, the classification of painters and painting were produced in the south only. These are the continuation of the true Chinese cultural tradition, whereas the military and administrative organizations of the newly united empire of the Sui-T'ang, which emerged at the end of this period, were taken over from those of the northern dynasties. These works also show that from about the Han period onwards, a class of independent painters had developed alongside the court artists.

The rulers of the new Sui united empire apparently wished to use Buddhism as an agent to create a parallel unity in the spiritual world. Many of their measures, at least, make it seem probable that this was their intention, and in the process Buddhist painting also, of course, gained a new impetus.

A stylistic innovation occurred at the same time. Whereas until this time, representation had been based essentially on linear outlines, an attempt was now made to give the subjects plasticity and to provide an illusion of truth to life.

The new style, the origins of which can be traced back to the previous era, is characterized in numerous little anecdotes. For example: the hall of a temple was continually being disturbed by pigeons which had taken to nesting on one of the beams. In order to end this nuisance, a well-known artist painted an eagle on the west and a hawk on the east walls of the temple; both were so deceptively true to nature that the pigeons no longer ventured in. It is possible that this naturalism was inspired by painters who went to China from central Asia or from India.

The first Sui emperor was a great lover of the arts. He erected two buildings in Loyang, the eastern capital, one of which was filled with examples of the calligraphy of ancient masters, the other with paintings. He and his descendants also had many palaces built on the Grand Canal between Ch'ang-an and Chiang-tu (in Kiangsu), which were richly decorated with paintings. Unfortunately, most of these treasures were again lost in the disturbances that marked the transition from the Sui to the T'ang. At the beginning of the new dynasty there were only three hundred paintings of the earlier period in the imperial collection.

The second emperor of the T'ang dynasty, however, evinced a great love of painting and bought pictures from private individuals. Even at that time the works of well-known masters brought very high prices. We read that paintings could command between ten and twenty thousand gold pieces.

During the empress Wu's interregnum, all the painters of the empire were brought to the capital of Ch'ang-an to assist in restoring the paintings of the palace collection to their former condition. Each following his own speciality and artistic bent, the artists made copies of all the paintings, drawing on paper and making exact replicas of the originals, so that they could not be distinguished from them. Many of the princes also became famous for their paintings of celebrated personalities of animals, or as calligraphers — another sign that the high T'ang nobility were lovers of art.

During the great rebellion of An Lu-shan some of the artistic treasures of the palace collections were destroyed, while others fell into the hands of private owners. After 805, virtually none remained in existence.

Even before the T'ang period, painting had ceased exclusively, or even primarily, to serve the purposes of the régime and it showed an increasing tendency to free itself from them. The clearest evidence of this development lies in the change of subject-matter. In addition to landscapes, flowers, birds and the like, the themes of the Buddhist and Taoist religions were now employed.

All these subjects may be found in the painting of the T'ang, and although the most prominent position was occupied by religious painting, there were also many works which clearly exemplified the early Chinese custom of using paintings to inculcate ideals of good citizenship.

Among these last are the officially commissioned portraits of distinguished functionaries, envoys from foreign countries and even prisoners-of-war. All these were accompanied by verses composed by the emperor and preserved in a special hall. There were also paintings of the vestments and utensils used at the great state ceremonies, as well as illustrations of the classics.

The emperor also had official events of special importance — such as the return from the Fêng-shan sacrifice offered at T'ai-shan — commemorated in large paintings. In the case of large works like this, the commission was often divided between several artists, of whom one would paint the human figures, another the animals and a third the landscape, according to his speciality.

Wall-painting in the Buddhist and Taoist shrines enjoyed another great period of efflorescence under the T'ang. Famed among these were the two hundred representations of the 'pure land' (*ching-t'u* or paradise in the west) by a Buddhist who called himself the 'great teacher of the good way' (*shan-tao ta-shih*). It is also recorded that the celebrated painter, Wu Tao-tzŭ, executed over three hundred wall-paintings. These paintings were not confined to temples; the imperial palaces and the houses of the high aristocracy and the rich were also decorated in this manner. Nor were the subjects exclusively religious or historical: Wu Tao-tzŭ and Li Ssŭ-hsün together painted the landscape of the Chia-ling river on the walls of the palace of Ta-t'ung.

There is a story which shows the different working-methods of these two great painters. The T'ang emperor, T'ien-pao (742–755), bethought him one day of the beauty of the landscape of the Chia-ling river and sent the two artists there to make studies in preparation for a painting. While Li worked diligently and returned with many sketches, Wu did not produce a single brush-stroke but stored it all 'in his heart'. When he began to paint, however, he took a single day to complete hundreds of miles of the panorama of river and mountain for which the emperor had asked, while his colleague toiled for months on end.

In wall-paintings of this kind one artist often drew in the outlines while another completed the picture.

In addition to the two we have already mentioned, we shall refer briefly to just two more celebrated painters of the period.

One of these is Wang Wei, whom we have already encountered as a poet. He was a slightly younger contemporary of Wu Tao-tzŭ, who died in the year 760, and was typical of the kind of universal artist which may well have represented an ideal in the eyes of the educated classes. In addition to poetry and painting, he practised music, calligraphy and landscape gardening with equal success.

He is often said to have invented a new technique of ink-painting, in which a broad brush and a copious flow of ink were used, and which was later taken over by the so-called Southern school. Unfortunately, however, none of Wang Wei's own work has survived and the copies, on which any impression of his art must rest, do not employ this technique. Later on, certain somewhat eccentric exponents of the technique ceased altogether to apply the ink with a brush and used instead their fingers, the flat of their hands, their hair and even their tongues.

(Although we are anticipating somewhat, we must emphasize that to divide painting into a Northern and a Southern school, as is so often done in histories of art, is a purely arbitrary act of separation and one which is based on an analogy with the division of the Buddhist Ch'an sect into Northern and Southern schools. Although there are certain stylistic affinities which may be said to constitute a 'Southern' school, the so-called 'Northern' school is no more than a repository for those paintings which did not please the critics of the Ming period.)

The second painter of note is Han Kan, whose fame was based on his paintings of horses. Little need be said here about the important part played by the horse among civilizations of the east, especially that of China. Noble horses were among the most highly valued of all the emperor's possessions, and Hsüan-tsung (712–755) of the T'ang dynasty is reputed to have had over forty thousand in his stables, many of which were trained as circus horses. It was natural, therefore, that paintings of horses should have been much treasured also. Han Kan did not go on repeating the traditional stencilled figures, but was the first painter to execute his paintings from exact observation of nature.

Whatever T'ang painting as a whole may have been like, our assessment of it rests primarily on descriptions in later catalogues. Silk and paper were materials too fragile to withstand the passage of centuries.* We have touched on the fate of wall-paintings in temples, but fine ones have been excavated recently from tombs.

Of original works of the T'ang period, probably all that now exist are a few portraits of Buddhist patriarchs which were taken to Japan and are preserved in the Shingon temple of Tōji in Kyoto. Apart from these, any work which is described as a T'ang painting may, at best, be claimed as a near-contemporary copy of the original.

The era of the Five Dynasties (907–960), which followed the T'ang period, was a period of transition, not only in politics but also in painting. It was then that T'ang formalism gave way to the freer stylistic modes of the Sung epoch.

* Except where, as in the sealed library at Tun-huang, they have been preserved by chance.

In the religious sphere, the Ch'an or Dhyāna meditative school came increasingly to the fore. In painting, the monochrome ink technique, which had first been used in the T'ang period, gradually began to dominate the field and the two trends were probably associated. This technique enables the artist to express his vision of a landscape with the lightest possible wash of ink. Brush-strokes and the most diaphanous of shading skilfully disposed over the surface bring mountains, forests, rivers and dwellings to life in the observer's imagination.

Another consequence of the social upheavals of this period was that painting ceased to inhabit exclusively the narrow world of temple and palace and gained a footing among wider circles of the population.

As a result of the political disturbances of the time, art and culture came to centre principally round two comparatively quiet cities: Ch'êng-tu, capital of the Shu state in Szechuan, and Nanking, capital of the southern T'ang, whose last ruler, Li Yü, was himself not only a poet of repute but also a great lover and patron of the arts.

A number of artists, however, worked in K'ai-fêng, later the capital of the Sung dynasty, and their work was the point of departure for the great landscape-paintings of the first Sung period.

Although surviving works of the period of the Five Dynasties are not as rare as those of the T'ang period, they nevertheless represent only an infinitesimal proportion of the works recorded in various literary sources. Here again, those wishing to gain an impression of the state of painting at the time are largely forced back on copies or on later works executed in the style of the old masters.

Notable progress was being made at this time in figure painting. The painter Kuan-hsiu (b. 832) created the type of the Buddhist saint with bushy eyebrows, large eyes, pendulous cheeks and a high-bridged nose, which persisted unchanged into the Yüan period. Other painters, such as Wang Kuan and Wu Tsung-yüan, whose lives extend into the Sung period, adopted the style of Wu Tao-tzŭ and, indeed, markedly improved upon it.

Another branch of painting developed at this time: this was more or less the equivalent of what we call genre painting. It portrayed intimate scenes of court life or scenes from the lives of scholars or of women and children of different social classes.

While genre painting was particularly cultivated at the court of Li Yü in Nanking, flowers, birds and animals were the favourite motifs in Ch'êng-tu. There the celebrated Huang Ch'üan evolved a new style of flower-painting, increasingly eliminating the ink outlines, until finally he was applying only a light wash of colour.

The great flowering of Chinese painting occurred in the Sung period. Indeed, one might almost say that, from the cultural point of view, painting is as much the characteristic feature of this period as is poetry of the T'ang.

By the reign of the first Sung emperor (960–976), an academy had already been founded in the Sung capital. Modelled on the pattern of similar institutions at the courts of the Wu-tai states, it was in many respects comparable with the Académie des Beaux-Arts and other similar European institutions. The artists originally brought together at this academy were mainly those of the defeated Shu and southern T'ang. Before he could be admitted the candidate had to prove his ability in a set painting, usually an illustration to an ancient poem. The catalogue of the great collection of the emperor Hui-tsung (1101–1126) has come down to us and is divided into the following subjects: Taoist and Buddhist saints, other persons, palaces and other buildings, members of native clans, dragons and fishes, landscapes, animals, flowers and birds, bamboos, vegetables and fruits.

The order in which the subjects are placed is — as always, in China — by no means accidental: it indicates that, in theory, the portrayal of human beings and the didactic element were still considered of first importance. In practice, however, the situation had changed so much that nearly half the items in the whole catalogue occur in the section, 'flowers and birds'. Landscapes come second.

This shows that the favourite themes of the Sung painters were flowers — and the small creatures, such as insects and birds, which often went with them — and landscapes. It was these which they brought to perfection and which remain most typical of the period.

The academy in the end became a special department, like medicine, astronomy, music and calligraphy, of the Han-lin state academy. Its great days occurred during the reign of the emperor Hui-tsung, who was himself one of the famous landscape-painters of his period. When the court and government moved to Hang-chou in the south it was re-established there. Within the academy, the artists were graded according to their talents. The highest grade was *tai-chao*, which may be rendered 'court painter'.

As has already been stated, landscape-painting reached an outstandingly high level. A contemporary work states that '. . . among the landscapes there are those fit to walk through, those fit to contemplate, those fit to ramble in and those fit to live in.'[21] The two last were preferred to the first. We also find practical tips on how to compose such pictures. 'Mountains without clouds are not beautiful and without water are uninteresting. Where there is no path there is no movement, where no forest, no life . . .'

Li Ch'êng and Fan K'uan may rightly be regarded as the foremost among these landscape-painters. Li Ch'êng came of a family of scholars from Ch'ang-an. By the beginning of the Sung dynasty, in about 969, he was already a celebrated artist. He lived in comfortable circumstances and was not obliged to struggle for office and income. He did not, indeed, accept money for his paintings. He was also well-known for his taste for wine; like many Chinese painters, it was only when intoxicated that he could attain to the state of ecstasy which enabled him to produce a work of art. He was said to use a thin wash of ink and to paint in a dream-like trance. Even during the Sung period itself his style of painting was so much imitated that a history of painting tells us that there were only two authentic works by Li Ch'êng to over three hundred imitations.

We know little about the life of Fan K'uan. He did not take the examination and therefore never held office. He also loved wine and was drawn to Taoism. As a painter, he began by imitating the manner of Li Ch'êng but soon returned to direct study of the world around him and began to develop his own style. This has been described as follows: 'His paintings give an impression of heroic boldness. But they are dark as a night of waning moon. It is impossible to distinguish the rocks from the earth.' Mi Fu (1051–1107), the best known art-critic of the Sung period, hailed him as the greatest landscape-painter of his time. Of the numerous surviving works attributed to him, only a few may be regarded as originals.

In addition to these artists, both of whom came from the north, mention should also be made of southerners such as Tung Yüan. Tung Yüan's paintings must be viewed from some distance since his coarse brushwork does not produce the right impression from close to. Nevertheless they were in the main true to nature and their effect was 'an inspiration to the poets'.

In addition to landscape-painting, bamboo-painting, which has already been mentioned as a category on its own, must be briefly noted. Painting and writing could scarcely be more closely associated than they are in this genre; indeed, some of the elements of calligraphy are actually used in the composition of the pictures. Herein, however, lay the seeds of decay for Chinese painting. Apart from the work of certain celebrated latecomers of the Sung period, it lost much of its originality and power and gradually became dissipated in the deft, super-subtle brushwork of *littérateurs*. In later years paintings were often judged simply by the number of brush-strokes and the manner in which they were disposed upon the surface. The result was a smooth, unlifelike mannerism: painting had taken a wrong turning, the causes of which were outlined at the beginning of this section.

Thus, since this is a general history of civilization, we may close the chapter on painting with the Sung dynasty and for information on later developments refer the reader to the numerous specialized works, a few of which will be found in the Bibliography at the end.

X

The Chinese Theatre in the Yüan Period

The Sung dynasty was brought down by the Mongols in the year 1280. And any seeds which may have existed in Chinese society and which might in the course of time have ripened into a new social order — perhaps similar to the bourgeois orders of the west, or a bureaucratic state in the Confucian sense—were now destroyed.

The rule of the Mongols, that is the Yüan dynasty, meant a new feudal régime for China set up by an alien nomadic nobility. The whole population was divided into classes, of which the Chinese, particularly the southern Chinese who had been defeated most recently, were the lowest. One of the results of this was that for a long period the examination, by means of which the educated Chinese entered official posts, was suspended. It now became extremely difficult for men of letters to obtain office, particularly high office. This may have been one reason why many of them turned to a different literary genre, that of the drama.

The main cause of its flowering was probably, however, the pleasure taken by the court of the Mongol emperors in musical and theatrical performances. These were the channels through which the culture of the empire they had conquered was communicated to them. From the point of view of the history of Chinese civilization, drama is just as important for this period as verse and the short story were for the T'ang period.

A few indications about the development of the Chinese theatre have been given already. An attempt will now be made to follow them up very briefly and in the most general outline.

Our description of court life under the Han dynasty showed

that theatrical performances were already taking place at that time. An old text furnishes a few more details:

> There was a man from Tung-hai (in present-day Kiangsu) called Huang-kung (Yellow Duke). While still a boy, Huang-kung became an adept at all kinds of arts, he could charm snakes and ride a tiger. He wore a short copper sword at his belt. His hair was bound with a red silk ribbon. When he grew old, his powers diminished and he could no longer practise his arts. Towards the end of the Ch'in dynasty (in about 208 B.C.) a white tiger was seen near Tung-hai and Huang-kung wished to subdue it with his sword. But his art failed and the tiger killed him. The story was taken as a theme for popular theatrical performances. The piece was also given at the imperial court of the Han.[1]

The piece was presumably based on acrobatic combats, dancing and singing and must have enjoyed great popularity at the time.

This passage also casts considerable doubt upon the argument which is frequently advanced that the true sources of the Chinese theatre were the dances and performances of the shamans.

Soon after the Han period short scenes in which the actors wore disguises — a man might, for example, appear as a woman — came into fashion. In this connection, a prince of the northern Ch'i dynasty (551–580) who possessed a markedly feminine cast of feature acquired a certain renown among the people by his habit of wearing a mask when on military campaigns in order to hide his face and create a war-like impression. This brought him great popularity and he and his martial deeds came, moreover, to be extolled in song and dance.[2]

At the beginning of the T'ang period there was also another very popular folk drama. It is impossible to say with certainty whether it was imported from Turkestan or whether it represents a later variant of the tiger play already described.

The action ran much as follows: a young man's father is attacked by a tiger on a wooded mountain-side and killed. The son sets out to find the body. He seeks it in eight ravines and his search is described in eight interpolated songs. The principal actor lets his hair loose, wears mourning garments and has a tear-stained face. Finally he encounters the tiger and kills him.

Another extremely popular folk drama dealt with a man named Su, who is said to have been a real person living under the northern Ch'i dynasty. He had a large nose, and although he never held office, always insisted on being addressed as 'secretary'. He used often to get drunk, when he would beat his wife, who was pretty and had a good voice; on these occasions she would go into the streets and pour out her troubles to the passers-by; and her actions were, of course, represented on the stage by means of songs and dances.[3] This piece was probably already divided into several acts, which may respectively have shown the drunken 'secretary' returning home and ill-treating his wife, his wife bemoaning her plight in the street and her complaint before the district committee. There may also already have been a chorus of neighbours and passers-by to accompany the action.

All the plays of this type are ultimately derived from the old combats and sporting contests of the Han period which have already been briefly described.

Another line of Chinese theatrical development began, probably in the T'ang period, with the so-called 'inspector plays' (*ts'ang-chün hsi*). These may hark back to an historical event said to have occurred during the late Han period, between about A.D. 89 and 104. A granary inspector (*ts'ang-chün*) was guilty of embezzling money. But the emperor valued his talent and allowed him to go unpunished. At every court banquet, however, he had to wear a clinging white garment and submit to the jeers and ridicule of the court comedians.[4]

The story is said to have been revived in the T'ang period and made into a short comedy-like play. It was probably largely taken up by a witty conversation between two actors in costume, one of whom pretended to be rather stupid in order to amuse the audience.

A certain Li K'o-chi earned great renown through performances of this type. Dressed as a learned scholar, he would seat himself on a lecturer's chair and begin a discussion on, for example, the three doctrines (Confucianism, Taoism and Buddhism). Somebody might ask him: 'What sort of man was this Lao-tzŭ?' And he would flummox the audience by replying: 'Lao-tzŭ was a woman.' He would then go on to explain that it does, indeed, say in the *Tao-tê ching*: 'It gives me great sorrow that I have a body, had I no body I should not be sorrowful.' Now 'to have a body' in Chinese also means 'to be pregnant'. And the passage can therefore also be rendered: 'It gives me great sorrow that I am pregnant . . .' and so on. In the same way he shows that both Confucius and Buddha were really women.[5]

During the T'ang period this principal personage, the 'inspector', was often given a servant (*ts'ang-hu*) who sat in a corner and was usually the butt for the mockery of others.

However, since, in this case, it is the inspector who is the butt, it is doubtful whether the *ts'ang-chün* dialogues can be connected with it at all. It is possible that the name derived from the fact that the emperor at some time bestowed the title of 'inspector' on a favourite actor — an action which, in view of the humble standing of actors, would be a distinction. But, when all is said and done, these witty dialogues, in which contemporary personalities and conditions were often ridiculed, may have in fact originated among the common people and have gradually made their way upwards into court society.

It is, however, recorded that the emperor Su-tsung (756–762) made his palace ladies dress up and impersonate his officials; on these occasions they wore green garments and held bamboo tablets in their hands and were called *ts'ang-chün-ch'un* or, roughly speaking, 'staff of inspectors'. From this it would appear, first, that both the name and these performances may have had a different origin; secondly that, in contrast to later periods, actresses were allowed to appear in male costume. Other references to these performances show that songs accompanied by flutes and stringed instruments were sung with them.

This second category of primitive theatrical performance differs from the first-mentioned chiefly in the fact that major prominence is given to ridicule and wit, whereas the former consisted largely of gymnastic contests and tussles. Both these elements remain clearly apparent in the later development of the Chinese theatre.

But even as early as the T'ang period there were pieces in which the two genres were combined. This was particularly true of the so-called 'mixed plays' (*tsa-chü*) of the first Sung period, which derived largely from the *ts'ang-chün* plays and those in which the 'secretary' beat his wife. At a later stage of development they appear in the plays of the Southern Sung period, which are the direct antecedents of the Yüan dramas.

These differ from earlier pieces mainly in the fact that virtuoso acrobatic skill is increasingly relegated to the background while the action or plot becomes the most important element.

A sign that the Chinese theatre was developing in other respects as well lies in the fact that more actors than the few who had taken part in the short pieces described above were now appearing. Whereas in the early days it had been the practice for two characters to conduct a dialogue alone, the productions of the Sung period called for a far larger number of actors who all represented different stock characters. As in *opera buffa*, there was the hero, the clown, the worthy old father, the bandits, the young man, the wife, the concubine, the orphan and so on. Different actors specialized in each of these parts. All the female parts were now played by men. Mimicry of a high order was clearly called for. The actors who played female parts in China achieved such mastery that not only were they indistinguishable on the stage from real women, but many of them, including the celebrated Mei Lanfang, far surpassed them in feminine charm.

As a less enviable result of their artistry, the actors gained the reputation of being perverts and until very recently were included with slaves, prostitutes and ushers among the disreputable classes of society. One of the results of their being so classified was that they were much more severely punished for the crimes they committed than were those who committed crimes against them.

Actors were often bought from their parents while they were still children by an impresario whose slaves they thenceforth became. Companies of actors consisted for the most part of between eight and ten persons. Provincial performances were subject to permission from the local authority, who often insisted that boring and pedantic moral pieces should be put on as well as the popular draws.

I do not know whether permanent stages existed in earlier times for these companies to perform on. But as a rule, no doubt, temporary stages were constructed of bamboo canes and mats. The houses of the rich, however, — and, of course, the palace — contained rooms or halls which were used exclusively for theatrical performances.

Plays intended as propaganda for public morality were mostly subsidized by public funds. Usually, however, before deciding upon a play, the director of the company would organize a collection from the rich people of the neighbourhood so that the finances of the undertaking were guaranteed in advance.

From as early as the T'ang period there were special training places at the court for male — and at that time some female — artistes and actors.

Whatever the nature of these performances of the pre-Yüan period, they represent only the imperfect beginnings of the Chinese theatre. It was only with the drama of the Yüan period that the play became an independent literary form.

Its origins being what they were, it consisted of a combination of spoken and sung text and was always divided into four acts. In addition, there was often a kind of prologue which contained an exposition of the whole piece; in default of a prologue, the first act took over its function. The action was developed in the second and third acts and the dénouement came in the fourth with the unravelling of the plot, punishment of the wrongdoers and so on. As it was in many cases very difficult to accommodate a complicated action in four acts, an *entr'acte* was also often slipped in. Since these interpolations were important only as aids to understanding the action and not from the point of view of the artistic and musical structure of the piece, they were not counted as complete acts. The further division of acts into scenes was less clear-cut than in our theatre. Such divisions were as a rule indicated simply by directions in the text like 'enters' and 'exit'.

Scenery as we know it in Europe did not exist in the early Chinese theatre. The stage was practically empty and was not even separated from the public by a curtain. This fact in itself gives some idea of the exacting demands made on the interpretive skill of the actor, who had by his bearing and gestures to evoke the scenery that was not there and bring it as much alive to the audience as possible.

In contrast to the simplicity of the stage décor, the actors' costumes were often extremely sumptuous and magnificent. It was they which enabled the audience to orientate itself among the characters of the play, the period of the action and so on. Thus generals were always recognizable by the long feathers in their head-dresses and scholars by their fans. There were a number of other actors' conventions: thus when an actor carries a riding-whip the character has arrived on horseback, he raises his leg to show that he is dismounting, persons in black are invisible and so on.

The subject-matter of the Yüan plays is often taken from the humbler literature of the previous periods, such as the short stories of the T'ang era. Sometimes, however, it was taken from history. Complicated crime and love-stories were, of course, very popular. Of these, one of the best known is the story of the beautiful Wang Ch'iang, usually known as Chao-chün, who was received into the women's apartments of the Han emperor Yüan-ti (48–33 B.C.) and then married off to the khan of the Huns.

This popular drama is called *Autumn in the Palace of the Han*. The long summary which follows should give some idea of what it was like. The passages omitted are mainly those which were sung and those in verse. Most of these do little to further the action and only serve to heighten the emotional content of a given situation.

The play opens with a short prologue in which the stock character Chung-mo, that is to say, the actor who plays the third principal male part, enters dressed as the Hun khan and after a few preliminary verses introduces himself:[6]

> I am the Khan Hanyeh, an old inhabitant of the steppes and sole ruler of the northern regions. The chase is our livelihood, warlike attack our chief occupation . . . For seven years my

ancestor Maotun surrounded with his forces the Emperor of the Han until a treaty was concluded giving him a Chinese princess in marriage. Each successive generation of Chinese emperors has sent us princesses. I am therefore a true descendant of the empire of Han. With a hundred thousand armed warriors I have moved south and approached the border to demonstrate the reality of these ancestral ties. Yesterday I sent presents to the court and demanded a princess in alliance. But it is not yet certain that the Emperor of the Han will ratify the treaty . . . (*Exit*).

Enter a masked actor: I am Mao Yen-shou, a minister at the court of Han. By a hundred arts of flattery I have ensnared the Emperor, until he places his whole delight in me and follows my counsel alone. Within the palace and without all bow down and fear me. I shall now see that the Emperor keeps aloof from his wise counsellors and seeks all his pleasures with the women of his palace. Thus will I strengthen my power. But here comes the Emperor.

Enter the principal male actor, attended by menservants and women: I am Yüan-ti, Emperor of the Han . . . The empire is tranquil and at peace, not through my personal influence but as a result of the exertions of my ministers and generals. At the death of my father, the palace ladies were all dispersed. Now all is quiet in the palace. But what was the use?

Mao-Yen-shou: Consider, sir, that after a good harvest even the husbandman may desire to take a new partner. How much more so, then, the Son of Heaven and ruler of the world? Why do you not send commissioners to search throughout the empire for all the most beautiful maidens of whatever rank of the nobility between the ages of fifteen and twenty and people the palace with them?

Emperor: Minister, you say well. I herewith appoint you minister of selection and invest you with written authority. Search out the best in the empire and let me be provided with a portrait of each lady as a means of fixing my choice. On completion of the mission, your reward is certain. (*Exeunt.*)

Act 1

Enter Mao Yen-shou.

Mao Yen-shou: Having received the Emperor's commission to search the empire for the most beautiful damsels, I have selected ninety-nine. Their families have all bestowed rich gifts upon me and I have thus amassed much silver and gold. Yesterday I reached the head town of a certain district and found another girl. She is the daughter of one Wang Ch'ang. Her name is Wang Ch'iang and she is called Chao-chün. She is more beautiful than all the others and surely the most beautiful in the whole world. But unfortunately her father is only a poor peasant without means. I asked for a hundred pieces of gold to secure first place for his daughter. But he said he was too poor and, relying on his daughter's extraordinary beauty, refused payment altogether. I therefore dropped the matter. (*Considers awhile.*) But no! I have a better plan . . . I need only disfigure the girl's portrait somewhat. Then she will never be noticed in the palace and will spend her life in bitterness. I have it now! He is a poor wretch whose hatred is lukewarm! No hero without malice! (*Exit.*)

Enter actress with two female attendants.

Wang Ch'iang: I am Wang Ch'iang, known as Chao-chün, from the neighbourhood of Ch'êng-tu. My father is a simple peasant. My mother dreamed before I was born that the light of the moon shone on her breast, but then fell to the earth. I am now eighteen years old and have been chosen for the imperial palace. But the minister Mao Yen-shou, disappointed of the money which he demanded of me, has disfigured my portrait in such a way that the Emperor will never notice me and I must live in a remote part of the palace. In my parents' house I learned to play stringed instruments and woodwind. Sorrowing in the deep stillness of the night, I will play my flute to dispel my grief. (*Begins to play the flute.*)

Enter Emperor, attended by a Eunuch carrying a light.

Emperor: I, the Han Emperor, have not yet found among the ladies chosen for the palace one on whom to fix my preference. I have been restless today and am roaming the palace, still searching for a lady who may please me. (*Hears the flute.*) Is not that one of the ladies' flutes?

Eunuch: I hasten to advise her of your Majesty's approach.

Emperor: No, discover first to what part of the palace the lady belongs, then bid her come to me; but do not alarm her.

Eunuch: . . . What lady is she who plays the flute? The Emperor is here. Approach and be presented.

Emperor: See, Eunuch, that all the lights burn brightly and let us together watch the lady.

Lady: Had your handmaiden but known it was your Majesty, she would have been less tardy. I deserve punishment.

Emperor: Truly, I behold a very perfect beauty. What is your family?

Lady: Your handmaiden's name is Wang . . . known as Chao-chün. My father is a simple peasant. Therefore I know nothing of the manners that befit a palace.

Emperor: How is it that such beauty has been hidden from me?

Lady: When I was chosen by the minister Mao Yen-shou he demanded money of me. But my family is poor and could pay nothing. He therefore disfigured my portrait by putting a scar under the eyes and so I remained unnoticed in a distant part of the palace.

Emperor: Eunuch, bring me that picture. (*The Emperor sings a song in praise of Chao-chün's beauty.*) (*To the attendant.*) Command the palace guard to behead Mao Yen-shou.

Lady: My parents, sir, are subject to ground-tax in Ch'êng-tu. May I entreat your Majesty to exempt them?

Emperor: That shall readily be done. Approach and hear my pleasure: I appoint you to the position of favourite.

Lady: How unworthy is your handmaiden of such gracious distinction. Never would I have dared to hope to share the Emperor's cushion. (*Exit Emperor.*) The Emperor is gone. Let the attendants close the doors. I will retire to rest.

Act 2

Khan of the Huns: I the Khan of the Huns lately sent an embassy to the court of Han, with a demand for a princess in marriage. But the Emperor has returned a refusal, under the plea that the princess is yet too young. This, of course, I do not believe. He has plenty of ladies in his palace and could easily have found one for me. I will now recall my ambassador with all speed, move my troops south and thus, I fear, break a truce of many years standing.

Enter Mao Yen-shou.

Mao Yen-shou: I extorted money when I was selecting ladies for the palace. I also disfigured the portrait of Chao-chün and banished her thereby to the most distant rooms of the palace. But the Emperor found her, obtained the truth from her and condemned me to death. I contrived to make my escape, though I do not know where to turn. I will now take this portrait of the palace beauty and give it to the Khan, persuading him to demand her in marriage. The Han Emperor will be unable to refuse him. I see now a great concourse of men and horses in the distance. This is the Hun camp. (*Addresses himself to a bystander.*) Officer, inform the Khan that a minister of the empire of Han is come to speak with him.

Khan (*on being informed*): Command him to approach. (*To Mao Yen-shou.*) Who are you?

Mao Yen-shou: I am the minister Mao Yen-shou. In the western palace of the Han court is a lady named Wang Chao-chün who surpasses all others in beauty. When your ambassador came to demand a princess, this lady would have been chosen; but the Emperor of Han cannot bring himself to part with her. I repeatedly exhorted him and asked how he could value a woman so highly as to sacrifice the welfare of two nations to her. For this the Emperor would have beheaded me. I have therefore come to you with the portrait of the lady. Should you send an ambassador with the picture to demand her, she must surely be delivered up. Here is the portrait.

Khan: Has there ever been so beautiful a creature in the world before? If I could only obtain her as a wife all my wishes would be fulfilled. I shall send an ambassador this very day with a letter to the Emperor of Han, demanding Chao-chün as the condition of peace. Should he refuse, I will presently invade the south. Neither hill nor river shall stop me. (*Exit.*)

Enter Lady.

Lady: For ten moons now have I, Chao-chün, enjoyed the Emperor's favours. The Emperor's fondness for me is so great that he has long neglected to hold an audience. I hear he is now gone to the hall of audience. I will therefore ornament myself at my toilet-table and adorn myself to receive him at his return. (*Stands in front of a mirror.*)

Enter Emperor.

Emperor: Since I first met Chao-chün in the western palace I have been as though deranged. A long time has elapsed since I held an audience. But today I held one and could scarcely wait until it was over to return to Chao-chün. (*Perceives Chao-chün.*) I will not alarm her but will observe her in silence.

Enter Secretary of State.

Secretary: I am the secretary Wu-lu Ch'ung-tsung and this is the chamberlain Shih Hsien. Today when the audience was concluded, an ambassador arrived from the barbarians to demand Chao-chün as a guaranty of peace. This is why I have come to the western palace. (*Sees the Emperor.*) I report to your Majesty that the Khan of the Huns sends an ambassador to declare that Mao Yen-shou has presented him with the portrait of Chao-chün and that he demands her as the condition of peace. If refused, he will invade with a great army and nothing will stand in his way.

Emperor: We have maintained the army for a thousand days in order to be able to use it at a given time. Vain are the crowds of officials and officers about the palace! None of them will drive back these barbarians. They are all afraid of the swords and arrows. Because they refuse to join battle themselves, they expect this young girl to secure peace instead of them.

Secretary: The foreigners are saying that the Emperor is

neglecting the affairs of state because of Wang Chao-chün. There will be war if she is not yielded up. I recall that once already in the course of history a dynasty has fallen through a woman's beauty. Our army is weak and we lack brave generals. What will happen if we are defeated? Your Majesty should give up the lady in order to save the empire.

Enter Officer.

Officer: The ambassador of the barbarians waits without for an audience.

Emperor: Let him approach.

Ambassador: The Khan of the Huns sends me to the Emperor of Han. North and south have long been bound in peace. Ambassadors have twice been sent to demand a princess, but the requests have been refused. Now the minister Mao Yen-shou has brought the portrait of a beautiful lady to our Khan. He has sent me to demand the lady as the guaranty of peace. Should your Majesty refuse, the Khan with his great army of brave warriors will forthwith invade the south to try the chances of war. I trust your Majesty will not err in your decision.

Emperor: The ambassador may retire to rest in his lodging. (*Exit Ambassador.*) Let our officials and officers advise me whether the foreign troops can be forced to retire without my giving up Chao-chün. They take advantage of the compliant softness of her temper . . . It would seem that for the future it would be better to use fair women rather than officials and officers to keep the empire in peace.

Chao-chün: Only death can repay your Majesty's gracious bounty. For the sake of peace I will cheerfully enter into this agreement, and so make a name for myself in history. But how can I ever lay aside my affection for your Majesty?

Emperor: And I am just as incapable of ceasing to love you.

Secretary: Your Majesty must sacrifice your love in order to preserve your dynasty. The lady must be sent at once on her way.

Emperor: Let her then today be sent only as far as the ambassador's lodgings. Tomorrow I will take leave of her at the

Pa-ling bridge . . . I will take leave of her in the evening and afterwards return home to hate the traitor Mao-Yen-shou.

Chao-chün: Though I depart for the nation's good yet I can ill bear to part from your Majesty. (*Exeunt.*)

Act 3

Enter Ambassador of the Huns escorting Chao-chün, with a band of musicians.

Chao-chün: I was chosen for the palace and despite the treachery of Mao-Yen-shou, who disfigured my portrait and thereby caused me to be banished to a distant part of the palace, I received his Majesty's favour. But a truer likeness of me was presented to the Khan of the Huns who now comes at the head of an army to demand me. There was no course other than to sacrifice myself for the sake of peace. How shall I endure the wind and cold of the land of the barbarians? It has been said of old that surpassing beauty is often coupled with an unhappy fate.

Enter Emperor.

Emperor: Today we take leave of the lady at the Pa-ling bridge. (*To his ministers.*) Can you not yet devise a way to avert the danger without yielding up Chao-chün? (*Descends from his horse and he and Chao-chün abandon themselves to grief.*) Let my attendants be patient until the lady and I have drained the parting cup.

Hun Ambassador: Lady, let me urge you to make haste. Night is coming on.

Chao-chün: Unhappy maiden that I am, when shall I ever behold your Majesty again? I will take off all my court robes and leave them behind me. So it goes: today in the palace of Han, tomorrow the wife of a barbarian. I could not bring myself to wear these garments from the imperial court and show my beauty to others adorned in them.

Hun Ambassador: Let me urge you again to make haste, Princess. We have delayed too long already.

Emperor: No, oh no! Lady, when you are gone, forbear to think of me with hatred. (*They part. Exeunt Chao-chün and Ambassador.*)

Secretary: Your Majesty must not dwell with such grief upon this matter.

Emperor (*sings*):

> Now she has gone. Devoid of valour,
> The armed men guard the frontier.
> If they but hear the clash of arms,
> They tremble like shy forest beasts.
> Their duty has been done by a maid today.
> How can they now pass for men?

Secretary: I entreat your Majesty to return to the palace. Do not dwell so bitterly upon her departure.

Emperor:

> Not think of her? Should my heart be iron?
> My tears flow in a thousand streams.
> The fair one's likeness shall hang in the palace
> And I will sacrifice to it by the taper's light.

Secretary: I beseech your Majesty to return home. The lady is already far away. (*Exeunt.*)

Enter Khan and clan chieftain, with Chao-chün.

Khan: The Emperor of Han has now in observance of old treaties and for the sake of peace yielded up Wang Chao-chün. I shall make her my queen. There will be peace between our two nations. (*To his leaders.*) Generals, transmit my command to the army. We move north forthwith. (*They march off.*)

Chao-chün: What place is this?

Ambassador: It is the River of the Black Dragon, the frontier between the Han empire and ours.

Chao-chün (*to the Khan*): Great King, I desire a glass of wine that I may turn to the south and pour a last libation to the Han empire. (*Pours the libation.*) Oh, exalted Emperor of Han, your handmaiden's life is finished today. I await you in the next life. (*Throws herself into the river.*)

Khan (*having tried in vain to save her*): Chao-chün was loth to go to our foreign land. She has thrown herself into the stream and drowned. Let her be buried on this river-bank and let the place be called 'the hillock of the verdant grave'. Since the maiden is dead I think our enmity with the court of Han has been in vain. Mao Yen-shou was the author of all this sorrow. (*To an officer.*) Badur,[7] take Mao Yen-shou prisoner and deliver him to the Emperor for punishment. For my part I will renew the old peace-treaty and preserve the uncle-cousin relationship between myself and the Emperor.

Act 4

Emperor: Since the lady was handed over to the barbarians, I have not held an audience for a hundred days. Now I am growing as sad as the melancholy shadows of the night. I will take the portrait of the fair one and suspend it here as some small solace in my grief. (*To the Eunuch.*) The incense in the vessel has burnt out. Replenish it. I am weary and will lie down to rest.

Chao-chün appears before the Emperor in a dream.

Chao-chün: I, the maid Chao-chün, who went north with the barbarians, have escaped them and come home.

A Hun warrior appears in the dream.

Warrior: While I chanced to sleep Chao-chün escaped. In hurried pursuit of her I have reached the Han palace. But there I see her! (*Carries her off. The cry of a wild goose — regarded as a messenger bird in China from ancient times — is heard.*)

Emperor (*waking*): Chao-chün has just returned to me. Why do I suddenly no longer see her? (*Sings a sad ditty.*)

Servant: Your majesty should cease grieving and consider the importance of your person.

Emperor: I cannot do otherwise. I must grieve.

Enter Secretary.

Secretary: This morning, after the audience, an ambassador from the barbarians arrived bringing Mao Yen-shou with him in fetters. He announced that the fellow had deserted his allegiance and occasioned all these calamities. Chao-chün is dead and the Khan wishes for peace and friendship between the two nations. The ambassador awaits your Majesty's sacred command.

Emperor: So be it then. Strike off Mao Yen-shou's head and

present it as an offering to Chao-chün. Let the ambassador be hospitably entertained and provided with food for his journey home.

The end

This example will, I hope, give the reader an adequate idea of the character of the old Yüan drama. The play is not a true representation of historical events: in fact, the marriage between the Hun khan and Chao-chün was by no means unhappy and she is even said to have borne him two daughters.

The author of the play was Ma Chih-yüan of Peking, who held offices in Kiangsu and Chekiang and also enjoyed a certain reputation as a poet.

The real creator of the Yüan drama was, however, Kuan Han-ch'ing. Little is known about the circumstances of his life except that he also came from Peking. In the early days of Mongol rule he withdrew into private life and wrote dramas. The best-known of these is probably *The Wrong done to Tou Ê*. It is a crime story in which a young widow is involved in an act of poisoning, and, though innocent, is accused, condemned and executed. Before her execution, which takes place on a summer's day, she announces that to mark her innocence, heaven will send a fall of snow and decree a three-year drought. Her father, however, a poor scholar who at the beginning sold his daughter to be daughter-in-law to a widowed money-lender but later, after sitting the examination, becomes inspector of justice, atones for the wrong and the guilty parties are punished.

The drama, having reached this stage of development did not, of course, remain static. When the Mongol empire fell, many of the authors of these plays migrated to the south, where they adapted their writing to the local character and their art flowered afresh.

A feature of the drama of this period is that the number of acts had increased enormously, to fifty and more. Whereas the interpolated arias had hitherto been performed by one of the principal actors, a group of male and female actors now sometimes sang a kind of duet. The plays were also considerably better constructed and had acquired greater psychological depth. Some laid greater stress on the musical passages, others on poetical speech or on action.

When Hangchou was laid waste in the Taiping uprising, this type of southern Chinese drama also disappeared, for the actors for these plays were trained there and nowhere else. Its place was taken by the *ching-hsi* (theatre of the capital), which was usually shorter and more dramatic and had loud and rather undistinguished accompanying music. It also contained a larger number of vulgar expressions.

A play was now seldom performed in its entirety. It became customary to put on a selection of acts from different dramas in order to give famous actors the opportunity of showing themselves in the most effective passages of their parts.

Not surprisingly the Chinese theatre has in recent times become more and more modernized and a performance of an old play is just as curious a rarity as is that of a pre-Elizabethan play with us.

Love of the theatre is, however, deeply rooted in the Chinese character and the Communists used performances by travelling companies or little impromptu pieces staged by the local inhabitants to spread their ideas.

Among modern pieces, one achieved special, even international, prominence. This was *The Story of the White-haired Girl*, which was much admired as a play, opera and film in mainland China.

The story, briefly, is that of a young girl, who is engaged to an agricultural worker of about her own age. Her father hands her over to the lascivious landowner in settlement of a debt and he, of course, coerces her into becoming his mistress. The girl, however, finally escapes and takes refuge in a cave, where she gives birth to a stillborn child and drags out her life for so many years that her hair turns white in the darkness. In the meantime her former betrothed has joined the Red Army. One day a detachment comes along, frees the unfortunate girl from her cave-existence and avenges all the wrong that has been done.

Unfortunately, the play is so grossly overloaded with political argument as to obliterate all artistic merit. Moreover, the sentimentality is laid on so thickly that the piece provokes merriment rather than tears.

XI

The Chinese Novel

The evolution of the Chinese novel runs more or less parallel with that of the theatre. It reached its highest level of accomplishment in the Ming period (1368–1643).

We have already encountered the *pien-wên*, those tales in verse and prose told in bazaars for the entertainment of the common people of the T'ang period. Under the Sung dynasty these story-tellers began to use notebooks (*hua-pên*), which contained promptings in the vernacular to remind them of their words.

Notebooks of this type may even then, however, have afforded a welcome source of reading-material among literate people. This was certainly the case after printing had become widely established, especially in the south-eastern provinces in the second period of the Sung dynasty.

Hua-pên material was soon taken up by educated people and made into new stories. One collection of such stories is the well-known *Chin-ku ch'i-kuan* (*Wonderful Sights, Ancient and Modern*), much of which has been translated into European languages.

The *Ch'üan-hsiang p'ing-hua* ('explanations [of history] illustrated in every particular') of the Yüan period represent another step forward. These are storytellers' versions of passages from Chinese history or legends — although they do not adhere closely to historical fact. They are the direct antecedents of the popular novel, in which the *Ch'üan-hsiang p'ing-hua* themes are taken up and elaborated.

It is thus by no means true to say that the Chinese novel is simply an extension of the short story of the T'ang period. It is rather the culmination of another line of development, one which begins with the professional storytellers of the bazaars and temple courtyards.

Their heredity is indicated by, for example, the way in which the narrative breaks off at a particularly exciting point and the reader is referred to the continuation in the next chapter. This derives from the practice of the storytellers who used to interrupt their performances and collect the money at the very moment of greatest tension.

The emergence of the novel in the Ming period is probably also connected with the general political situation. If, in general terms, it is fair to regard the Sung régime as a bureaucracy with a literary background, the Ming dynasty has, in contrast, the air of a totalitarian monarchy. (It should not be forgotten that it was in this period that the ancestral tablet of Mêng-tzŭ was ordered to be removed from the Confucian temple because of the democratic passages in his work.)

Chu Yüan, the founder of the dynasty, whose humble beginnings had doubtless brought him into contact with the unpleasant sides of officialdom, greatly disliked the officials and at once deprived them of their favoured social position. It came to such a point that candidates for official posts were sent from the provinces to the capital like convicts. There they were usually selected for an official position. But they might equally well be condemned to compulsory labour. They could neither refuse a post when it was offered to them nor, once they had taken it, give it up at their own discretion. The common people could make complaints about them direct to the emperor. There was a special inspectorate whose duties were to supervise the administration.

As the dynasty wore on these conditions probably changed, but over against the official corps there now stood another powerful group, namely the eunuchs, those servants who were closest of all to the emperor. They began to assume ascendancy in about 1457. They acquired education and evolved an organization by which they controlled all offices inside and outside the capital. They also ran the secret police with all its ramifications, as well as a vast organization of informers and police spies.

As a further consequence of the curtailment of their power, the officials were forced to devote themselves exclusively to the technical aspects of administration. They were forbidden to discuss the policies of the day. This in its turn resulted in the examination becoming formalized: the 'eight-part essay' (*pa-ku*) — based simply on the commentaries on the classics brought in by Chu Hsi — was introduced. This allowed no more than an impersonal presentation of themes divorced from contemporary life.

It may have been due to this situation that some men of letters turned towards those humbler forms of literature which were otherwise objects of contempt. In fact, the great historical novels of this period, although they recount events of the past, must be regarded as criticism of contemporary conditions and as vehicles of political protest.

The best known of these is probably the *San-kuo-chih yen-i* (*The Romance of the Three Kingdoms*) by a certain Lo Kuan-chung; he is supposed to have been a scholar with no official position, who lived at the beginning of the Ming period.

This work was preceded by a *San-kuo-chih p'ing-hua*. Like the novel after it, this work began with the great rebellion of the Yellow Turbans which brought down the later Han dynasty. The author is not known.

Since the *p'ing-hua* works have not yet been translated into western languages, I should like to give a short extract from one of them, in a very free rendering:

> Sun T'ai-kung's establishment lay in a remote mountain gorge. He had two sons. The elder devoted himself to agriculture, the younger studied in books and was therefore known as the 'scholar'. He suddenly contracted a skin disease which caused all his hair to fall out and his whole body to be covered with blood-stained pus. The smell he gave off was more than his parents could bear. So he went to live in a grass hut at a little distance behind his father's establishment. His wife took him food every day.
>
> One morning she came with his food. It was in the third month of spring. From the moment she reached the door she

was aware that her husband was ill and, unable to bear the smell, she covered her nose and mouth with her hand. Keeping as far away as possible, she handed him the food. Hsüeh-chiu — the name means 'scholar' — sighed and said, 'When they are alive a wife shares a house with her husband and when they are dead they share the outer coffin. If even my wife is disgusted by the sight of me, how much more so must others be. Why should I go on living?' When he said this, his wife left him.

Hsüeh-chiu now decided that it would be best to die. He took his crutches and, wearing his pus-filled shoes, walked a few dozen paces away to the north of the hut. There he noticed a rift in the ground; he dropped his crutches, tore off his shoes and jumped in.

The inside of the cave proved suitable for human habitation. He fell to the ground and lost consciousness. After some time he came to himself. Immediately above him he saw a small strip of sky. He said, 'I sought death but have not found it.'

Gradually he became aware, through the gloom, of a patch of light lying due north and he moved a few paces towards it.

There he saw a staff made of jade and took hold of it. At the same time he noticed a door, set his shoulder against it and opened it.

Behind the door was a cave which was as light as day. In it he saw a stone seat, onto which he dropped.

Exhausted by his efforts, he at last lay down and fell asleep.

As soon as he had stretched himself out, feeling a soft mass on his feet, he took fright and woke up. What did he see?

He saw a large snake unwinding itself and gliding into the cave. Hsüeh-chiu followed it until he lost sight of it. In its place he saw a stone receptacle. He opened it and found that it contained a manuscript roll.

Reading the roll, he found that it explained how four hundred and four diseases could be cured without administering the usual medicines or using the breathing technique. All diseases, whatever their symptoms, could be cured by a bowl of consecrated water . . .

When Hsüeh-chiu read this he rejoiced and, taking the

heavenly message with him, left the cave and sat down again on the stone seat.

At this point the tale takes a fresh twist. Hsüeh-chiu's wife set out to take more food to her husband but was unable to find him and told the family.

Thereupon, they all set out under the leadership of the elder brother, to look for him. They came to the rift in the ground and saw the crutches and shoes lying there. So they stood round in a circle and lamented.

Soon, however, they heard a human voice rising from the rift and, letting down a rope, brought Hsüeh-chiu back to the light of day.

His father saw him and wept. When the violence of his tears had abated Hsüeh-chiu said:

'Calm yourself, father. I have received a message from heaven with which I can cure my disease.'

Then they all went home together.

There Hsüeh-chiu took a bowl of pure water, consecrated it and drank it. His fever diminished and his hair and skin returned to their pristine state.

Sick people now began to come to him from far and wide and he cured them all. In this way he soon grew rich and had nearly five hundred pupils who used his method to work cures.

Among them was a man named Chang Chio.

One day Chang Chio took leave of Hsüeh-chiu, saying: 'I have an aged mother at home, I beg to take leave of you so that I may look after her.'

Hsüeh replied, 'When you go I will give you a roll containing some celebrated recipes. There is no need to return it to me.'

And indeed he gave the roll to Chang Chio on the condition that he should cure all the diseases in the world but accept no money for his pains.

So Chang Chio left his master and returned home. Wherever he went, he healed diseases and took no money. But he passed the watchword: 'If my cures have proved successful, let all young and strong men become my followers and come with me, but let the old stay at home.'

So Chang Chio traversed the country and whenever his following numbered ten thousand men he had their names, addresses and dates of birth recorded and gave them these instructions: 'When I need you, you will receive a letter from me. You must then come without the least delay and assemble according to provinces. If a man fails to come, he will die. Whoever disobeys me will come to harm.'

Then one day the Yellow Turbans rose against the Han state. This was due to Chang Chio's letters, which were circulating through the length and breadth of the empire . . .

Chang Chio had two cousins who had themselves elected generals by the assembled crowd, ordered strips to be torn from great bundles of yellow material and had them distributed as badges among their followers.

Chang Chio gave the watchword: 'Today the Han dynasty falls and we rise. If one day I become emperor, the leaders among you will be made princes, those immediately below them dukes and the others officials.' And with that the gathering broke up.

They had at first nothing but turbans and sticks. But, under the leadership of Chang Chio and his two cousins, they took Yang-chou, where every kind of implement of war fell into their hands.

Thus within a few days the Yellow Turbans built up an army and, working from Yang-chou, took village after village and district after district, until finally they had conquered many regions.

Wherever they went they plundered the country. Anyone who did not follow them was killed or enslaved. Three-quarters of the Han empire was in their hands and they numbered three hundred and sixty thousand.

If this particular passage be compared with the corresponding passage in the *San-kuo-chih yen-i*, it emerges that it contains additions which do not occur there. The *San-kuo-chih yen-i* is, however, much closer to the historical texts than the *p'ing-hua*.

It is, on the whole, fairly true to say that this novel, the *San-*

kuo-chih yen-i, represents a specific group of the widely popular professional storytellers' tales which have been brought together to form a single work.

In addition to these tales of the period of the Three Kingdoms, stories of other troubled times in history circulated freely. In the end almost all such ages found literary expression, until there was scarcely a single phase of Chinese history which did not appear in novel form.

Another group of folk-tales found expression in the novel, *Shui-hu chuan* (*Story of the Water Margin*). The locality described afforded refuge to a band of malcontents in revolt against the corrupt administration at the end of the first Sung period. After many heroic deeds and adventures, they finally returned to the service of the régime and were even employed to put down the dangerous rebellion of Fang La. The tales which make up this work have, however, nothing to do with recorded history, but are pure products of the writer's imagination.

Lo Kuan-chung is named once again as the author of the *Shui-hu chuan*. But the novel is held to be based on an earlier draft by Shih Nai-an, who is otherwise unknown. Of all the novels of the Ming period, the *Shui-hu chuan* certainly deserves to be regarded as the best. It has been translated into English by Pearl Buck, under the title *All Men are Brothers*.

The *Chin-p'ing-mei* is a work of yet another kind. Because of its partly pornographic nature, it is widely known and has been translated into all the major oriental and western languages. The tale of a wealthy libertine and his amours, it gives an extremely realistic picture of life in a period of decadence. It is also the first Chinese novel in which the female characters are not mere empty lay figures but are really informed with an existence of their own. The story ends with the downfall of the spoilt pleasure-seeker and his concubines which fully accords with the Buddhist and Taoist doctrine of retribution. Although, in itself, this novel is only the continuation of an episode in the *Shui-hu chuan* and is therefore set in the Sung period, it in fact reflects corruption under the Ming dynasty.

Another celebrated novel of the period is the *Hsi-yu chi* (*The*

Journey to the West). This is the tale of the well-known Buddhist, Hsüan-tsang, who brought religious texts from India, and is embellished with fantastic, supernatural adventures.

Mention should also be made, in this connection, of the *Fêng-shên yen-i* (*The Investiture of the Gods*), an account, tricked out with many mythical features, of the destruction of the last tyrannical king of the Yin dynasty by Wu-wang, founder of the Chou; also of the *P'ing-yao chuan*, which takes as its subject the rebellion of Wang Tsê (1047), but is so overladen with mystical and magical elements that the historical facts only occasionally show through.

The *Chin-p'ing-mei* inspired a series of love-stories of increasingly sentimental tenor set within the family group, which culminated in the *Hung-lou mêng* (*Dream of the Red Chamber*). The author of this work is Ts'ao Chan (d. 1763), the scion of a rich family from Nanking, which had been ruined in 1728 as a result of huge debts incurred in an extravagant mode of life. The family, which comprised a hundred and fourteen persons, was transferred to Peking, where they lived a wretched existence dependent upon imperial favour.

These are the events which form the substance of the novel. It describes how the carelessness, extravagance and negligence of a rich family lead to its downfall; while the story of the love of the extremely youthful Chia Pao-yü — in all probability a self-portrait of the author — and his cousin Lin Tai-yü, an orphan girl adopted by the family, occupies a central position in the action.

Because of Tai-yü's delicate health, Pao-yü was later married to his robust cousin Pao-ch'ai. Believing herself abandoned by her lover, Tai-yü dies on his wedding night.

The whole novel is a masterly picture of the life of a Chinese family group, whose destiny is faithfully reflected in its characters. It was finally completed not by Ts'ao himself, but by Kao Ê, and was published in about 1792.

While the old Chinese marriage customs were criticized in the *Hung-lou mêng*, other novels attacked the corruption of the officials, which was no less marked in the Ch'ing dynasty than in previous periods.

The best known of these are the *Ju-lin wai-shih* (*Unauthorized*

Tales of Confucian Officialdom) by Wu Ching-tzŭ (1701–1754), and the *Kuan-ch'ang hsien-hsing chi* (*Records of the Condition of Officialdom*), by Li Pao-chia (1867–1906).

As European influence grew, this branch of Chinese literature came increasingly under its sway and reflected each current as it came into vogue in the west. This is, of course, particularly true of the literature which emerged after about 1920, when the colloquial language (*pai-hua*) was adopted as the literary language as well.

Modern Chinese literature soon became very largely a weapon in the battle for social change and almost always evinces a markedly nationalist tendency. It is barely necessary to state that in the most recent times all writing in mainland China has been given a Marxist-Leninist slant.

The most celebrated modern writer was Chou Shu-jên who became internationally famous under his pseudonym, Lu Hsün. He was born in 1881 in Shao-hsing (Chekiang), and died in October 1936 in Shanghai. A government scholarship enabled him to study medicine in Tokyo. He was dismayed, however, at the indifference of his compatriots to the Russo-Japanese war, which was being fought out on Chinese soil, and turned to writing as a means of rousing political involvement.

In his works, Lu Hsün espouses the cause of the right of every individual to life, food and shelter and the right of each man to develop his own gifts without restriction. 'Everything which stands in the way of these three basic rights must be removed and destroyed, whether it be ancient religions or modern whims.' He was equally opposed to both the scholars of the old classical schools and the highly qualified students who returned home from England and America with ideas of moderation and compromise.

The work by which he is best known is *The Story of Ah Q*. It ridicules the revolution of 1911 and exposes what Lu Hsün regarded as the most contemptuous weaknesses of the Chinese national character: the tendency of people to use philosophical explanations to accommodate themselves to unpleasant and dangerous situations, to interpret painful defeats as victories, and to vent their spleen on weaker peoples when they themselves are oppressed by stronger, instead of rising against their oppressors.

Ah Q is a poor casual labourer in a village. He has no name and when he imprudently assumes the name of the rich and powerful local family of Chao, he ends up with his ears being boxed and having to pay appeasement money to the local police. He finally vents his wrath on a little Buddhist nun whom he makes ridiculous and cruelly wrongs.

When he makes an immoral proposal to a girl in the Chao house, he loses his job in the village and goes to the town, where in some mysterious way he acquires a largeish sum of money. As it were by mistake, he becomes a revolutionary, although he does not even remotely understand the significance of the revolution, which in any event has changed nothing in his own surroundings. In the end he is executed for plundering, although he was innocent of the crime.

It is unfortunately impossible to describe here all the typically Chinese elements of the story (such as Ah Q's personal taboos which constantly involve him in brawls and quarrels). No other work of modern Chinese literature — not even *The Story of the White-haired Girl* — can equal *The Story of Ah Q* in popularity and importance for the modern age. It has already been translated into all the major languages and has become in the true sense part of world-literature. The brilliance of the work lies in the way in which the quintessence of the Chinese world and its history has been concentrated into the destiny of one man.

XII

The Chinese Intellectuals and the Impact of Europe

Any author would be justified in ending his history of Chinese civilization with the Ming period. This limit has been adopted by Joseph Needham, for example, in his massive work *Science and Civilisation in China*.

The following passage is from Needham's introduction:

> After the coming of the Jesuits, Chinese science fused with universal world science, and though its rise may have been slow during the 18th and 19th centuries, inhibited by the same factors in Chinese society which had hindered it through all earlier history, it is no longer easy to distinguish any particular style in the contributions made by Chinese thinkers and observers. The work of liaison begun by the Jesuits in the 17th century was continued by the Protestants of the 19th, until in our own time China took her place among all other nations as participant in the world community of science.[8]

Prime among these inhibiting factors is undoubtedly the sharp division between the literary men of the cultivated classes on the one hand, and the peasants, artisans and traders on the other.

Our whole knowedge of ancient China has come down to us solely from literary records left by the cultivated classes; it was they who, during almost the whole course of Chinese history, held the high offices, became the landowners and used the ramifications of a linked clan system to become the real power in the land. They spread like an unbreakable net over the millions of humbler folk, whose own existence came to light only in an occasional uprising or in rare records of folk-songs, plays and stories.

Whoever, as time went on, came into conflict with the interests of this class, whether it were the nobility, the eunuchs or a reformer such as Wang An-shih, the historical records defamed their memory — when they did not simply pass them over in silence.

This class maintained a monopoly, especially in all that concerned education. It recovered its position comparatively quickly and completely after the first great attack it suffered at the impact of Buddhism, but was seriously shaken for the first time by the arrival of the missionaries from the west.

It was now threatened by the representatives of a highly developed civilization, which, although geographically remote, was able, thanks to superior military techniques, to give far greater weight to its invasion than Buddhism, whose weapons had been purely spiritual. The Opium War of 1840–43, which for the first time revealed China's military weakness, is therefore one of the most important events in this conflict of civilizations.

It was obviously as a consequence of this threat to the educational monopoly, that blind fanatics like Yang Kuang-hsien (1597–1669) and, later, the Mongol, Wo-jên (1804–1871), opposed any innovation originating from abroad, even when, as in the case of the calendar and applied science, its superiority was proven. Wo-jên made a statement to the effect that mathematics and astronomy were incapable of saving a nation from ruin and of reinvigorating it. 'The issue is decided by the mental attitude of the people, not by technical tricks.' In his opinion, western civilization was merely a conglomeration of technical skills and contemptible, morally damaging heresies.[9]

This antagonism extended downwards into rural life. Many a poor scholar dwelt in the country and earned his living by teaching the children of prosperous landowners reading, writing and the rudiments of education in the light of the classics. Now, however, they were faced with the missionaries who not only taught subjects which were much more useful in the changed circumstances, but whose instruction was free into the bargain. As a result, the scholars naturally used all means in their power to fan hatred of foreigners to the point of fanaticism among the lower classes to whom they had for centuries stood guardian.

However much justification there may be for Needham's view, there still occurred in the period from the seventeenth to the twentieth century, a resounding clash and a dialogue between two civilizations unique, so far as I know, in all history. Every contributory factor, on either side and down to the last detail, is vouched for by documentary evidence. It is therefore astonishing that in our time, when there is supposed to be a burning interest in cultural questions and precedents, this historical event has attracted comparatively little interest. As far as I am aware, the attempt has not yet been made to recount or to analyse this clash of civilizations in its context or in all its ramifications, though there is no doubt that such a study would in many respects greatly advance the science of civilization.

Unfortunately, we still lack many of the preliminary studies for so comprehensive a work, among them a complete bibliography of European and American works translated into Chinese since about the seventeenth century. Such a compilation would reveal, for example, the precise form in which western civilization has been presented to the Chinese and what it is that they regard as its quintessence.

We might then understand why the Chinese, so far from allowing western civilization to be imposed upon them, were, on the contrary, strengthened in their age-old pride in their own civilization and their traditional sense of its superiority. They regarded this confrontation primarily as an ethical problem and believed that the strength of a civilization was revealed first and foremost in the firm moral stand of its advocates.

But the Chinese, unfortunately, also had to learn that technical rather than ideological superiority wins the day; and that Chinese civilization — or whatever today goes by that name — owes its existence mainly to the circumstance that the western powers were too greatly divided among themselves to accomplish a final division and colonization of China.

We have noted several times already that this was not the first cultural invasion suffered by China. The incursion of Buddhism was just as penetrating as that of Europe. And it has also been suggested that, in both cases, certain sections of the population welcomed the new element as the vehicle of 'liberation'. As regards the Buddhist invasion, liberation was felt to be from the old, rigid forms of ritual. That accomplished by Europe largely affected the lower, working classes — including, apparently, women, almost as much as men.

The position of women in old China was a truly unhappy one. They were the servants of their husbands and the slaves of their parents-in-law, all of whom had the right of chastisement. The mothers-in-law were particularly cruel and their inhuman treatment drove many a young woman to her grave. Almost the only means available to her of improving her lot was to give birth to the much desired son and heir. Nor were young people free to choose their own spouse. Marriage was an agreement made by the clan elders. The wishes of the persons concerned were scarcely ever consulted.

Not until the beginning of the twentieth century did young people of the intelligentsia, mostly those who had studied abroad and married a non-Chinese, begin to break away from the tutelage of the family. They lived mostly in the coastal cities, which were strongly subject to foreign influence, and conducted their married lives according to the European pattern. Marriage reform, which the Communists were probably the first actually to enforce, dealt the most powerful blow of all to the traditional clan system.

But even before this, we hear of events which show that women were chafing against their centuries-old lot of inequality and oppression. Thus the prostitutes from one of the towns on the Yangtze are said to have staged a demonstration aimed at improving their condition, in the course of which some of them marched naked — as it were, in their working attire — at the head of a procession — an enterprise which would have been entirely unthinkable in old China.

Drastic protests like this were not confined to the lower classes but were matched in educated circles, where, for example, girl-students at the high schools are supposed to have founded clubs which made deflowering compulsory for their members. I myself, in 1934, heard Chinese ladies of good families freely discussing contraception in my presence, whereas before they would not have been allowed even to be seen in the company of a foreigner.

It was, of course, the attitude of the intelligentsia which primarily reflected Chinese reaction to the foreign culture that was infiltrating into their country. And the history of the incursion of European civilization is, to a great extent, the history of the Chinese intelligentsia, their absorption and modification of the new element. Unfortunately this history can only be told in the broadest possible outline and with every reservation, since, as has already been said, the preliminary works on which it would need to be based have not been written.

We have already mentioned that section of the Chinese intelligentsia which rejected everything new with a fanatical hatred and confined itself to orthodox interpretation of the classics. It should be added that this was the intellectual attitude fostered and promoted by the Manchu, who had conquered China in the year 1644, and, themselves an almost imperceptible minority, governed a population of millions. Orthodox Confucianism was the spiritual instrument of their régime.

The opposition of the Chinese intelligentsia to the hated rule of these foreigners from the north, therefore, first showed itself in their subjection of the classics to an increasingly critical examination and a new interpretation. This trend was already apparent in such a personality as Ku Yen-wu (1613–1682), who, although he lived the greater part of his life under the Manchu, never wavered in his loyalty to the Ming. He was a convinced opponent of the neo-Confucian philosophy, which at that time still dominated the spiritual life of the educated classes and their interpretation of the classics — the subject of the state examination — to the exclusion of all others. Ku Yen-wu's efforts were, however, directed towards reviving the textual and critical studies of the classics in the form in which scholars had conducted them in the Han period, in order to rid them of all the accepted general interpretations current among the Sung Confucians. He thus contrasted the 'Han' and 'Sung' theories, asserting also that the former period was considerably closer than the latter to the time when the classics had been written.

His studies provided the stimulus for the modern linguistic analysis of Chinese and for textual criticism, which, though at first concentrated on the classics, soon came to include all surviving branches of the old literature and today dominates the field of sinological research.

The line of study initiated by Ku finally came into the open with K'ang Yu-wei (1858–1927), who achieved celebrity largely as a result of his leading role in the ill-fated 'Hundred Days Reform' of the year 1898. In his work *Hsin-hsüeh wei-ching k'ao* (*Modern scientific examination of the authenticity of the classics*), he holds up Confucius as a political reformer and founder of a Confucian religion who clothed his ideas in the form of a legendary prehistory. He seeks to establish a parallel between Confucius and Jesus Christ, whose teachings he wrongly regards as the basis of western government. He finally advocates a kind of 'world community' (*ta t'ung*), which to a certain extent represents the ideal democracy, in which a universal 'sense of community' pervades the world and a world government unites all nations. Some of the principles he advanced to this end seem ultramodern indeed. Thus he says that an association between a man and a woman should never last for more than one year, after which each should enter a new partnership. Pregnant women should go to a school for pre-natal instruction, children should be brought up in children's homes. The dead, however, should all be burnt and their ashes scattered on the fields as fertilizer.[10]

This, of course, represented a radical challenge to the reigning clan system and was completely unacceptable. K'ang Yu-wei's reform, which was primarily directed against the examination system and therefore immediately involved all candidates who had been successful under that system, was thus condemned from the outset to rapid frustration.

A further section of the Chinese intelligentsia was represented by the personalities behind the so-called Self-Strengthening Movement. Of these I will here mention only Li Hung-chang (1823–1901) and Chang Chih-tung (1837–1909).

Li Hung-chang left a highly significant account of the impression made upon him by the French and British war potential:

> I was on board the vessels of the British and French admirals and ascertained that their guns were extremely efficient and standardized and that the munitions for them are excellent. The troops look like fighters and the discipline is good. The foreigners are superior to us in all these matters . . .[11]

The Self-Strengthening Movement, accordingly, set out to adopt foreign techniques, especially weapons, as quickly as possible. Otherwise, however, the members of this movement held fast to the opinion that in all other matters — such as administration, organization and training — China was superior to other countries. Chang Chih-tung, who did so much to promote the building of railways and installations for heavy industry, went to the other extreme: as a counter-measure to the modernist aspirations of certain other schools, he founded a school for the special study of the ancient Chinese classical and historical writers.

The Self-Strengthening Movement was brought to an end by the unhappy war against Japan in the year 1894; this showed that superficial imitation of foreign technical methods was insufficient. Without the attitude of mind and changed social order that went with it, it became mere ineffectual blundering.

It was now, however, that the era began of sending students to Japan, Europe and America, while at home modern universities and colleges were founded and the chairs often given to overpaid foreign lecturers. Education was, in effect, being purchased on a grand scale.

The students returning from abroad soon proved an indigestible element, for they were full of ideas which could not be implemented because even the most rudimentary conditions were lacking. Furthermore, they were usually quite without the backing necessary to assert themselves against the conservative cliques in the ministries. Many of them, unable any longer to fit into the old way of life, settled in the coastal cities and took up various kinds of literary occupation. It was not until the 1920's that their influence began, via the universities, to make itself increasingly felt.

One student who had studied abroad was Sun Yat-sen (1866–1925), who went to a mission school in Hawaii and later studied medicine. Sun Yat-sen was a principal figure in the revolution of 1911 which brought down the Manchu dynasty; he conducted it largely with money contributed by expatriate Chinese and by employing secret societies. After many set-backs, he made an alliance with the Communists in 1923. But this soon led to more or less open rivalry within the Kuomintang, which he himself had founded and which the Soviets sought to use as an instrument in the struggle for supremacy in China against the generals, who were supported by other interested powers. The conflict was resolved in 1927 when Chiang Kai-shek, with the assistance of the secret societies, finally put down the Communistically inclined workers' unions in Shanghai. The Kuomintang then drew closer once more to the old Chinese reactionary policy and to Confucianism. Chiang's authority was ultimately based on a clan system of the old pattern.

In this connection, mention should also be made of the Taiping rebels, whose uprising (1850–1865) must surely be regarded as one of the principal causes of the downfall of the Manchu dynasty. Its true causes, however, are probably to be found rather in the rapid increase in population during the eighteenth century and in the corruption rife in high places.

The Taiping are like a foreign body in the Chinese way of life. It is well known that their leader, Hung Hsiu-ch'üan, was influenced by Christian ideas and described himself as the 'younger brother of Christ'. He devised a political organization based on religious principles, in which the political, military and social order became one. There was theoretical equality under the Taiping, particularly where relations between the sexes were concerned. Women were allowed to serve in the army, to sit the examination and so on. Marriage was compulsory, but there was freedom in the choice of partner. In order to prevent the population from increasing too fast, men and women were segregated and only permitted to unite occasionally. It appears that the same tactics were later adopted by the Communists in the first, primitive phase of the communes. The Taiping also championed the building of steam-ships, railways and factories. They also for the first time introduced the seven-day week into China. Everyone was made to attend religious service on Sundays, when workers were publicly praised for good work and reproved for idleness. The Taiping rebellion came to grief largely on account of internal dissension and because its leaders did not themselves observe the rules they laid down for the people at large.

A line of development can, however, be drawn from the Taiping to the final section of the Chinese intelligentsia to be mentioned here, a section largely represented by the Marxist-Leninists.

The Chinese Communists, too, began as a small group of typical university intellectuals as remote from the great mass of the population as were, by tradition, the members of the educated classes. It was the experiences gained when a Chinese labour corps was sent to France during the First World War, and participation in the movement of the 4th May 1919, that first changed this state of affairs.

This movement was a protest by Peking students against the Versailles Peace Conference, at which Tsingtao was given to Japan. The movement found a vigorous response among the workers, who were thus for the first time brought by common action into close sympathy with the students. The next move was that the students abandoned their studies and devoted their whole time to propaganda among the working classes.

In the same year — also for the first time — groups of students were sent as workers to France in order to earn money to carry on their studies at a foreign university. Although the success of this enterprise was minimal, members of the Chinese intelligentsia did thereby for the first time become aware of the crude facts of physical labour and came into direct contact with workers, even though they were foreign. The result was that when they returned to China they established immediate contact with the workers of their own country.

Thus there finally grew up an intelligentsia which had moved onto an equal footing with manual workers, behaved and moved like workers and even spoke as they did. Having once adopted the workers' way of life and thought, the intellectuals then became leaders of the masses and champions of the Communist ideas. One of them was Mao Tsê-tung.

Even before 1927, when the workers' movement, which had begun in about 1919–20, was put down by Chiang Kai-shek in Shanghai, Mao Tsê-tung was devoting his energies to preaching the revolution to the peasants and by this time already had a following of approximately two million. It was this peasant movement that, after severe conflict and many reverses, finally carried the day and forced the Kuomintang régime to withdraw to Formosa.

Today the two Chinas stand in mutual opposition: Formosa representing the China of tradition modified to fit into the world of today; mainland China under the sway of Marxism transposed into the Chinese mode. It is already clear that the gulf between the two is widening — not only culturally, but even in the realm of language itself.

Notes

CHAPTERS I TO III (pp. 21 to 42)

1. Han Fei Tzŭ. *The Complete Works. A Classic of Chinese Political Science*, trans. from the Chinese, with introduction, notes, glossary, and index by W. K. Liao (2 vols.; London, 1939–59), chap. 49, p. 276.

2. Mo Ti (Mo-tzŭ), *The Ethical and Political Works of Motse*, trans. from the original Chinese text by Yi-Pao Mei (1929), chap. 6, 'Indulgence in Excess'.

3. Han Fei Tzŭ, *op. cit.*, chap. 49, p. 275.

4. *Li Chi* (*Records of Rites*): Max F. Müller (ed.), *Lî, Kî* trans. by James Legge (2 vols.; New York: Dover, 1967); *Lî Kî*, trans. by James Legge, *Sacred Books of the East*, XXVII–XXVIII (London, 1885): Book VII, The Lî Yun, Section I, 2, Part III.

5. *Lü-shih ch'un-ch'iu* (*Spring and Autumn Annals of Lü Pu-wei*), chap. 20, 'Shih-chün'.

6. Cf. Wang Yü-chê, *Chung-kuo shang ku shih-kang*, pp. 42–43.

7. Ssŭ-ma Ch'ien, *Shih-chi* (*Records of the Historian*), chap. 3, 'Yin pên-chi'.

8. *Shih Ching* (*Book of Songs*): *Shu King*, trans. by James Legge, *The Chinese Classics*, IV (1871): Part IV, Book III, Ode III.

9. *Shu Ching* (*Book of History*): Max F. Müller (ed.), *Shu King*, trans. by James Legge (2 vols.; New York: Dover, 1967); *Shu King*, trans. by James Legge, *The Chinese Classics*, III (1865): Part IV, The Books of Shang, Book I: The Speech of Thang, Part I.

10. Mêng-tzŭ (Mencius), *Works*, trans. by Leonard A. Lyall (London, 1932), Book VI, chap. 5, p. 90.

11. This and the following example are from Hu Hou-Hsüan,

Chia-ku-hsüeh Shang-shi lun-ts'ung (1944), on which my treatment of the subject is largely based. I have not in this context taken into account the work of Chêng Tê-k'un, *Archaeology in China* (Toronto, Ontario: University of Toronto Press, 1960), II: *Shang China*. This is chiefly notable for a comprehensive exposition of the Shang system of ancestor worship.

12. *Küo-yu* (*Conversations from the States*), II, 10.

CHAPTERS IV AND V (pp. 43 to 121)

1. Ssŭ-ma Chien, *op. cit.*, chap. 4, 'Chou pên-chi'.
2. *Ibid.*, chap. 3, 'Yin pên-chi.'
3. According to Chêng Tê-k'un, *op. cit.*, p. 225 (see note 11 to chaps. I–III), these concepts already existed in the Shang period.
4. *Li Chi* (*Records of Rites*): Müller, *Lî Kî*: Book I: Khü Lî, Book I, Section I, Part IV, §§ 10, 50–51.
5. *Ibid.*, Book XXIX: *Piâo Kî*, § 30.
6. Cf. also Chêng Tê-k'un, *op. cit.*, pp. 216–17 (see note 11 to chaps I–III). According to him the beginnings of the Chou organization are already to be found under the last Shang rulers.
7. Confucius, *K'ung-tzŭ chia-yü* (*The School Sayings of Confucius*), chaps. 30, 42
8. *The Book of Songs*, trans. by Arthur Waley (1937, 2nd impression 1954), Nos. 194, 195.
9. Wan Yü-chê, *op. cit.*, pp. 148–52.
10. *Shih Ching* (*Book of Songs*), Part IV, Book I (i), Ode X.
11. *Shu Ching* (*Book of History*): Müller, *Shu King*: Part IV, Book VII: The Pan-Kang, § 1.
12. *Li Chi*: Müller, *Lî Kî*: Book XX: Kî Fâ, § 5.
13. *Tso Chuan*: *The Ch'un Ts'ew, with the Tso Chuen*, trans. by James Legge, *The Chinese Classics*, V (1872): Book X: Duke Ch'aou, Year VII.
14. *The Book of Songs*, No. 203.
15. *Shih Ching*, Part III, Book II, Ode III.
16. *Kung-hang chuan*, *Hsüan-kung*, 8th year.
17. *Li Chi*: Müller, *Lî Kî*: Book XXI: Kî I, §§ 1. 2.

18. *Ibid.*, Book XX: Kî Fâ.
19. *Shih Ching*, Part III, Book III, Ode V.
20. *Tso Chuan*, Book IV: Duke Min, Year II.
21. *Shu Ching*: Müller, *Shu King*: Part V: The Books of Kâu, Book XII: Announcement of the Duke of Shâo.
22. *Tso Chuan*, Kuo-yü, Chou-yü, 1.
23. *Shih Ching*, Part II, Book VI, Ode I.
24. *The Book of Songs*, No. 156.
25. *Tso Chuan*, Book X: Duke Ch'aou, Year VII.
26. *The Book of Songs*, No. 35.
27. *Ibid.*, No. 111.
27a. *Ibid.*, No. 72.
28. *Ibid.*, No. 86.
29. Hou Wai-lu, *Chung-kuo ku-tai shê-hui-shih lun* (*Review of the Social History of Ancient China*) (Peking, 1955).
30. Sun Tzŭ, *The Art of War*, trans. with an Introduction by Samuel B. Griffith (Oxford and New York, 1963), chap. 2.
31. *Tso Chuan*, Book X: Duke Ch'aou, Year XVI.
32. *Shih Ching*, Part III, Book III, Ode IV.
33. *Shih Ching*, Part I, Book V, Ode I, quoted in the *Tso Chuan*, *Chao-kung*, 16th year.
34. Confucius, *Lun Yü* (*The Analects*), trans. and annotated by Arthur Waley (London, 1938; New York, n.d.; paperback edition, New York (Vintage), n.d.), Book I, 7, p. 84.
35. Confucius, *K'ung-tzŭ chia-yü*, chap. 2, 2. (See *K'ung-tzŭ chia-yü. The School Sayings of Confucius*. Introduction, translation of §§ 1–10; Proefschrift . . . door R. P. Kramers (Leiden, 1949).)
36. Confucius, *Lun Yü* (*The Analects*), Book XVII, 11, p. 212.
37. *Ibid.*, Book XII, 1, p. 162.
38. *Ibid.*, Book XVI, 2, p. 204.
39. *Ibid.*, Book XIII, 4.
40. *Ibid.*, Book XIV, 7, p. 180.
41. Han Fei Tzŭ, *The Complete Works*, Book XIII, chap. 34, p. 93.
42. Confucius, *Lun Yü* (*The Analects*), Book XII, 4, p. 163.
43. *Ibid.*, Book XVII, 19, p. 214.

44. *Ibid.*, Book XX, 3, p. 233. But there is good reason to believe that this Book is a later interpolation.

45. *Ibid.*, Book XI, 11, p. 155.

46. *Ibid.*, Book VIII, 19, p. 136.

47. Mo Ti, *The Ethical and Political Works*, chap. 49, 'Lu's Question'.

48. *Ibid.*, chap. 9, 'Exaltation of the Virtuous', II.

49. *Chuang-tzŭ*: chap. 33, 'T'ien-hsia'.

50. *Huai-nan Tzŭ*, chap. 20.

51. Mo Ti, *op. cit.*, chap. 48, 'Kung-Mêng'.

52. *Ibid.*

53. *Ibid.*, chap. 27, 'The Will of Heaven', II.

54. *Ibid.*, chap. 4, 'On the Necessity of Standards.'

55. *Ibid.*, chap. 15, 'Universal Love', II.

56. *Ibid.*, chap. 14, 'Universal Love', I.

57. *Ibid.*

58. *Ibid.*, chap. 32, 'Condemnation of Music, I.'

59. *Ibid.*, chap. 48, 'Kung-Mêng'.

60. *Ibid.*, chap. 28, 'Will of Heaven', III.

61. Arthur Waley, *The Way and Its Power: A Study of the Tao Tê Ching and Its Place in Chinese Thought* (London, 1934; New York, 1956), chap. 13, p. 157.

62. Chuang-tzŭ, chap 4; *Chuang Tzŭ: Mystic, Moralist, and Social Reformer*, trans. from the Chinese by Herbert A. Giles (London, 1889), chap. 4, p. 54.

63. Kuo Mo-jo, *Shih p'i-p'an shu* (1954), p. 152.

64. *Kuan-tzŭ*, chaps. 37, 'Hsin-shu', and 38, 'Pai-hsin'. The translation is here partly taken from MS. 107005 in the library of the School of Oriental and African Studies, University of London. (*Kuan-tzŭ*, chaps. 37, 49, and 55; translation, interpretation, and notes by the late Professor Gustav Haloun. Lecture notes taken down by G. W. Bonsall (Cambridge).)

65. Chuang-tzŭ, chap. 2; *Chuang Tzŭ: Taoist Philosopher and Chinese Mystic*, trans. from the Chinese by Herbert L. Giles (London, 1961), chap. 2, 'Ch'i-wu Lun'.

66. *Ibid.*, chap. 1, 'Hsiao-yao yu'.

67. *Ibid.*, chap. 18, 'Chih-yüeh', p. 174.

68. *Ibid.*, chap. 17, 'Ch'iu-shui' (Autumn Floods), p. 170.
69. *Ibid.*, chap. 22, 'Chih-pei yu'.
70. *Ibid.*, chap. 6, 'Ta-tsung shih' (The Great Supreme), p. 76.
71. *Ibid.*, chap. 7, 'Ying ti wang' (How to Govern), p. 87.
72. *Ibid.*, chap. 3, 'Yang-shêng chu' (Nourishment of the Soul), p. 49.
73. *Ibid.*, chap. 9, 'Ma-t'i' (Horses' Hoofs), p. 97.
74. *Ibid.*, chap. 10, 'Ch'ü-ch'ieh' (Opening Trunks), p. 100.
75. *Ibid.*, p. 101.
76. Arthur Waley, *The Way and Its Power*, chap. 76, p. 236.
77. *Ibid.*, chap. 78, p. 238.
78. *Ibid.*, chap. 28, p. 178.
79. *Ibid.*, chap. 52, p. 206.
80. *Ibid.*, chap. 40, p. 192.
81. *Ibid.*, chap. 38, pp. 189–90.
82. *Ibid.*, chap. 22, p. 171.
83. *Ibid.*, chap. 67, p. 224.
84. *Ibid.*
85. *Ibid.*, chap. 57, p. 211.
85a. Tzŭ-ssŭ, *The Great Learning and the Mean-in-Action*, newly trans. from the Chinese, with an introductory essay on the history of Chinese philosophy by E. R. Hughes (London, 1942), section I, chap. 1, p. 106.
86. Confucius, *Lun Yü* (*The Analects*), Book VI, 27, pp. 121–22.
87. Mêng-tzŭ, *Works*, Book VII, chap. 4, p. 104.
88. *Ibid.*, Book XIII, chap. 15, p. 207.
89. *Ibid.*, Book XIII, chap. 1, p. 202.
90. *Ibid.*, Book XIV, chap. 14, p. 228.
91. *Ibid.*, Book IV, chap. 13, p. 66.
92. Hsüntze, *Works*, trans. from the Chinese, with notes, by Homer H. Dubs (London, 1928), Book V, p. 73.
93. *Ibid.*, Book XVII, p. 175.
94. *Ibid.*, Book XXIII, p. 302.
95. Mêng-tzŭ, *op. cit.*, Book II, chap. 1, p. 16.
96. David Hawkes (ed.), *Ch'u Tz'ŭ: The Songs of the South* (Oxford and New York, 1959: paperback edition, Boston (Beacon Press), 1962).

CHAPTER VI (pp. 122 to 163)

1. *Chan-kuo ts'ê* (*Intrigues of the Warring States*), 'Tung-chou ts'ê'; *Han Shu* (*History of the Former Han Dynasty*), 'Kou-hsü chih'.

2. *Lü-shih ch'un-ch'iu* (*Spring and Autumn Annals of Lü Pu-wei*), XIII, 5, and VII, 3.

3. Ssŭ-ma Ch'ien, *Shih Chi* (*Records of the Historian*), chap. 6.

4. *Ch'in-hui-yao*, p. 118.

5. Ssŭ-ma Ch'ien, *loc. cit.*

6. *T'ai-ping yü-lan* (*Anthology and Digest of Reference Works of the Six and T'ang Dynasties*), chap. 690.

7. For one version see Ssŭ-ma Kuang, *Tz'ŭ-chih t'ung-chien* (*The Mirror of Good Government*), trans. and annotated by Achilles Fang (Cambridge, Mass., 1952), chap. 14, Year 177 B.C.

8. *Hui-yao* (Edition Chung-hua shu-chü, 1955), chap. 7, p. 62.

9. *Ibid.*

10. *Ibid.*, p. 63.

11. *Ibid.*

12. *Ibid.*, p. 67.

13. *Ibid.*, p. 76.

14. *Lü-shih ch'un-ch'iu* (*Spring and Autumn Annals of Lü Pu-wei*), V, 2.

15. *Li Chi*: Müller, *Lî Kî*: Book VII, the Lî Yun, § IV, 4.

16. Cf. contribution by W. Eichhorn to the *Festschrift* for E. Erkes.

17. From the *Wên-hsüan* by Chang Hêng.

18. *Ibid.*

19. *Hui-yao*, chap. 49, p. 505.

20. For one version see Ssŭ-ma Kuang, *Tzŭ-chih t'ung-chien* (*The Mirror of Good Government*), chap. 34, Year 3 B.C.

21. *A Hundred and Seventy Chinese Poems*, trans. by Arthur Waley (1918), 'Old poem', p. 32.

22. *Ibid.*, 'Fighting south of the castle', pp. 33–34.

23. *Chung-kuo wên-hsüeh shih* (1959), vol. I, p. 176. Another translation into English: Robert Payne (ed.), *The White Pony: An*

Anthology of Chinese Poetry (London, 1949; paperback edition, New York (New American Library), n.d.), 'South of the river we gather lotus', p. 122.

24. *Ibid.*, 'Old song', p. 122.

25. Ssŭ-ma Kuang, *op. cit.*, chaps. 69–78, 'The Chronicle of the Three Kingdoms' (A.D. 220–265), p. 13.

26. Ssŭ-ma Chien, *op. cit.*, chap. 86.

27. *Ibid.*, chap. 122.

CHAPTER VII (pp. 164 to 199)

1. T'ang Yung-t'ung, *Han, Wei, Liang-Ch'in, Nan-pei-ch'ao Fo-chiao-shih* (*History of Buddhism in the Han, Wei, Ch'in and Nan-pei-ch'ao Periods*), (1938), p. 72.

2. *Ibid.*, p. 39.

3. *Jên-wu chih* (Peking, 1955), p. 1.

4. Wang Pi commentary on the *Tao-tê ching*, chap. 1.

5. Ko Hung, *Pao-p'u tzŭ, Wai-pien*, chap. 25.

6. *Ibid.*, chap. 26.

7. W. Eichhorn in *Zeitschrift der Deutsch-Morgenländischen Gesellschaft*, 94 (1940), No. 1, 47–48.

8. Joseph Needham, *Science and Civilisation in China* (Cambridge and New York, 1954–65) III, p. 217.

9. Ko Hung, *op. cit.*, chap. 25.

10. K'ou Ch'ien-chih, *Wei-shu*, 114 (Shih-Lao). Also the biographies of K'ou Ch'ien-chih and Ts'ui Hao.

11. T'ang Ch'ang-ju, *Wei, Ch'in, Nan-pei-chao shih lun-ts'ung* (*Collected Essays Towards the History of the Wei, Ch'in, and Nan-pei-ch'ao Periods*) (Peking, 1955), pp. 340 ff. The following quotations are also from this work. The section is also based on the relevant sections in Lü Chên-yü, *Chung-kuo chêng-chih ssŭ-hsiang shih* (*History of Political Theories in China*) (Peking, 1953), and on other works by modern Chinese historians.

12. *T'ang hui-yao* (Edition Chung-hua shu-chü), chap. 49, p. 861.

CHAPTER VIII (pp. 200 to 249)

1. Tanabe, Hsiao. Quoted in Lü Ssŭ-mien, *Sui, T'ang, Wu-tai shih (History of the Sui, T'ang, and Period of the Five Dynasties)* (Peking, 1959), p. 1344.

2. These and similar details are taken both from sources cited in the list of Works Consulted and from the relevant chapters of the *T'ang Hui-yao*.

3. Wei Cheng, *Sui-shu (History of the Sui Dynasty)*, 'Shih-huo chih'.

4. *Chiu T'ang-shu (Old T'ang Dynastic History)*, chapter on economics.

5. Quoted by Lü Ssŭ-mien, *op. cit.* (see note 1 in this chapter), p. 950.

6. Quoted by Tung Shu-yeh and Shih Hsüeh-t'ung, *Chung-kuo tz'ŭ-ch'i shih lun-ts'ung (Essays Towards a History of Chinese Porcelain)* (Shanghai, 1958), p. 23.

7. Confucius, *Lun Yü (The Analects)*, Book XIX, 4, p. 225.

8. This short story and — where no other source is given — those following it are to be found in the work of Liu Kai-jung, *T'ang-tai hsiao-shuo yen-chiu (Research into the Short Story of the T'ang Period)* (Shanghai, 1955), and in *Chung-kuo wen-hsüeh shih (History of Chinese Literature)* (1959), prepared by the Faculty of Literature, University of Peking.

9. Cf. *T'ai-p'ing kuang-chi*, chap. 427.

10. Quoted by Liu Ts'un-jen, *Chung-kuo wen-hsüeh shih* (1959), p. 105.

11. A. R. Davis (ed.), *The Penguin Book of Chinese Verse*, trans. by B. M. Kotewall and Norman L. Smith (Harmondsworth and Baltimore, Md., 1962), p. 23.

12. Payne, *The White Pony*, 'Living in the Country', trans. by Yang Yeh-tzu, p. 138.

13. *Ibid.*, 'The Ancients', p. 149.

14. The date 781 given in the *Chung-kuo li-tai shih-hsüan*, p. 373, as the year of Wang Wei's death must be a mistake.

15. Payne, *op. cit.*, 'In a bamboo grove', p. 151.

16. *Ibid.*, 'Verses', p. 151.

17. Quoted in *Ch'üan T'ang shih*, Peking, 1960.

18. Tu Fu, *Tu Fu: The Autobiography of a Chinese Poet A.D. 712–770*, trans. by Florence Ayscough (2 vols., London, 1929–34), I, pp. 315–16.

CHAPTER IX (pp. 250 to 294)

1. *Hsü tzŭ-chih t'ung-chien* (Peking, 1957), p. 32.

2. Ssŭ-ma Kuang, *Su shui chi-wên* (Edition Ts'ung-shu chi-ch'êng), p. 62.

3. Lo Ts'ung-yeh, *Lo Yü-chang hsien-shêng chi*, chap. 2, 'Tsun Yao lu'; see also *Sung shih*, chap. 291, 'Sung Shou chuan'.

4. *Hsü Tzŭ-chih t'ung-chien ch'ang-pien*, chap. 132.

5. Quotation from *Su hsüeh-shih chi* in Ch'i Hsia, *Wang An-shih pien-fa* (*Wang An-shih's Changes in the Laws*) (Shanghai, 1959), p. 24.

6. *Ibid.*, p. 53.

7. *Ibid.*, p. 56.

8. *Ibid.*, pp. 57–58.

9. *Ibid.*, p. 60.

10. Chang Chia-chü, *Liang Sung ching-chi chung-hsin ti nan-i* (*Shift of the Economic Centre of Gravity to the South Under the Sung Dynasty*) (Wuhan, 1957), p. 8.

11. Ku Yen-wu, *Ku-chung sui pi* (Edition Ching-chi t'ang ts'ung-shu).

12. *Tung-ching mêng-hua lu*, chap. 10.

13. *Mêng-liang lu* (*Description of the Capital of the Southern Sung*), (Edition *Chih-pu-tsu-chai ts'ung-shu*), chap. 6, p. 72.

14. Lü Chen-yü, *Chung-kuo chêng-chih ssŭ-hsiang shih* (*History of Political Theories in China*) (Peking, 1953), p. 498.

15. *Ibid.*, p. 497.

16. *Ibid.*, p. 506.

17. *Ibid.*, p. 516.

18. The quotations in this section are taken from works cited in the list of 'Works Consulted', especially from Yü Chien-hua, *Chung-kuo hui-hua shih* (*History of Chinese Painting*) (Shanghai, 1959).

19. Osvald Sirén, *The Chinese on the Art of Painting* (Peiping, 1936; New York, 1963), p. 19.

20. Cf. J. F. Cahill, 'Confucian elements in the theory of painting', *The Confucian Persuasion* (Stanford, California, 1960), pp. 115 ff.

21. Sirén, *op. cit.*, p. 30.

22. Kuo Ssŭ, *Lin Ch'üan Kao Chih* (*The Great Message of Forests and Streams*), quoted by Sirén, *op. cit.*, p. 44.

Chapters X to XII (pp. 295 to 332)

1. Chou I-po, *Chung-kuo hsi-ch'ü lun-chi* (*Collected Essays on the Chinese Theatre*) (1960), p. 10.

2. *Chiu T'ang-shu* (*Old T'ang Dynastic History*), 'Yin-yüeh chih'.

3. Also mentioned by Liu Ts'un-jên: *Chung-kuo wên-hsüeh shih* (*History of Chinese Literature*) (Peking, 1959), pp. 215–16.

4. Chou I-po, *op. cit.*, p. 19.

5. *Ibid.*, p. 20.

6. The following synopsis is made from the original Chinese, in conjunction with the translation of John Francis Davis, *Hān Koong Tsew, or The Sorrows of Han: A Chinese Tragedy*, trans. from the original, with notes (London, 1829). Another English translation: Donald Keene in *Anthology of Chinese Literature*, edited by C. Birch (New York, 1965; Harmondsworth, Penguin Books, 1967).

7. *Badur*, a Mongolian officer's title.

8. Needham, *op. cit.*, I, p. 149.

9. Chang Hao, 'Anti-foreignist role of Wo-jên', *Papers on China*, XIV, p. 9.

10. Liang Ch'i-ch'ao, *Intellectual Trends of the Ch'ing Period*, edited and trans. by Immanuel C. Y. Hsü (Cambridge, Mass., 1959), p. 97.

11. Unpublished work by Jerome Chên on the movement, at the School of Oriental and African Studies, University of London.

Bibliography

An Tso-chang. *Han-shih ch'u-t'an* (Attempt at a History of the Han Dynasty). Shanghai, 1955.

Bary, William T. de, Jr., Wing-tsit Chan, and Watson, Burton. *Sources of Chinese Tradition.* With contributions by Yi-pao Mei, T'ung-tsu Ch'u, Chester Tan and John Meskill. Columbia University Press, New York, 1960; paperback edition, 2 vols., 1964.

Carter, Thomas F., and Goodrich, L. C. *The Invention of Printing in China and Its Spread Westward.* Columbia University Press, New York, 1925. 2nd ed. Ronald Press, New York, 1955.

Chang Chia-chü. *Liang-Sung ching-chi chung-hsin ti nan-i* (Shift of the Economic Centre of Gravity to the South Under the Sung Dynasty). Wuhan, 1957.

Chang Wu-hui. *Chung-kuo li-shih yao-chi chieh-shao* (Recommended Works for the Study of Chinese History). Hupei, 1956.

Chavannes, E., and Peliot, P. *Un traité manichéen retrouvé en Chine.* Paris, 1913.

Chên Shou-yi. *Chinese Literature: A Historical Introduction.* Ronald Press, New York, 1961.

Ch'en, Kenneth K. S. *Buddhism in China: A Historical Survey.* Princeton University Press, Princeton, N.J., 1964.

Ch'i Hsia. *Wang An-shih pien-fa* (Wang An-shih's Changes in the Laws). Shanghai, 1959.

Chou I-po. *Chung-kuo hsi-ch'ü lun-chi* (Collected Essays on the Chinese Theatre). 1960.

Chu Ch'an. *The Sutra of 42 Sections and Other Scriptures of the Mahayana School*. The Buddhist Society, London, 1947.

Chu Chieh-ch'in. *Ch'in-Han mei-shu shih* (History of the Art of the Ch'in and Han Periods). Shanghai, 1936.

Feng Ming-chih. *Chung-kuo min-chien wên-hsüeh chiang-hua* (Lectures on Chinese Popular Literature). Hong Kong, 1957.

Gernet, J. *La vie quotidienne en Chine*: Paris, 1959. *Daily Life in China on the Eve of the Mongol Invasion 1250–1276*: trans. H. M. Wright, Allen and Unwin, London, 1962.

Graham, Angus Charles. *Two Chinese Philosophers: Ch'êng Ming-tao and Ch'êng Yi-chuan*. Lund Humphries, London, 1958.

Hao Chien-liang and Pan Shu-ko. *Chung-kuo li-shih yao-chi chieh-shao chi hsüan-tu* (Selected Examples of Chinese Historical Writing). Shanghai, 1957.

Hightower, James R. *Topics in Chinese Literature: Outlines and Bibliographies*. Harvard University Press, Cambridge, Mass., 1950: revised ed. 1953.

Hou Wai-lu. *Chung-kuo ku-tai shê-hui-shih lun* (Review of the Social History of Ancient China). Peking, 1955.

Hsiao-T'ung. *Die Chinesische Anthologie* (übersetzt von E. von Zach), 1958. *Wên-hsüan* (Chinese text), Hong Kong, 1959.

Hsü Fu. *Ch'in hui-yao ting-pu* (Historical Materials of the Ch'in Dynasty). Shanghai, 1955.

Hsü T'ien-lin. *Hsi-Han hui-yao* (Historical Materials of the Han Dynasty). Shanghai, 1955.

Hummel, Arthur William (ed.). *Eminent Chinese of the Ch'ing Period (1644–1912)*. U.S. Government Printing Office, Washington, D.C., 1943–44.

Kiangsi Province Centre for Porcelain Research. *Ching-tê-chên t'ao-tz'ŭ shih kao* (Draft of a History of the Ching-tê-chên Porcelain). Peking, 1959.

Liang Ch'i-ch'ao. *Intellectual Trends of the Ch'ing Period*. Edited and translated by Immanuel C. Y. Hsü. Harvard University Press, Cambridge, Mass., 1959.

Liu, James J. Y. *The Art of Chinese Poetry*. Routledge and Kegan Paul, London, 1962. University of Chicago Press, Chicago, Illinois, 1962.

Liu Kai-jung. *T'ang-tai hsiao-shuo yen-chiu* (Research into the Short Story of the T'ang Period). Shanghai, 1955.

Liu Kuo-chün. *Chung-kuo shu-shih chien-pien* (Popular History of the Chinese Book). Peking, 1958.

Lü Chên-yü. *Chung-kuo chêng-chih ssŭ-hsiang shih* (History of Political Theories in China). Peking, 1953.

Lu Ssû-mien. *Sui, T'ang, Wu-tai shih* (History of the Sui, T'ang, and Period of the Five Dynasties). Peking, 1959.

Nagasawa, Kikuya. *Geschichte der chinesischen Literatur* (übersetzt von P. E. Feifel). Hildesheim, 1959.

Nöthen, R. *'Das Yang Shih Nü Sha Ch'üan Fu', ein Drama der Mongolenzeit* (thesis). Munich, 1960.

Peking University, Faculty of Literature, *Chung-kuo wên-hsüeh shih* (History of Chinese Literature). Peking, 1959.

Rotours, Robert des. *Le traité des examens*. Paris, 1932.

Sirén, Osvald. *The Chinese on the Art of Painting*. Peiping, 1936. Schocken Books, New York, 1963.

T'ang Ch'ang-ju. *Wei, Ch'in, Nan-pei-chao shih lun-ts'ung* (Collected Essays Towards the History of the Wei, Ch'in, and Nan-pei-ch'ao Periods). Peking, 1955.

T'ang Yung-t'ung. *Han, Wei, Liang-Ch'in, Nan-pei-ch'ao Fo-chiao-shih* (History of Buddhism in the Han, Wei, Ch'in and Nan-pai-ch'ao Periods), 1938; Shanghai, 1955.

Têng Chih-ch'êng. *Chung-hua êrh-ch'ien-nien shih* (The Two-Thousand-Year History of China). Peking, 1954

Tung-ching mêng-hua lu (Description of the Capital of the Northern Sung). Shanghai, 1956. *Mêng-liang lu* (Description of the Capital of the Southern Sung).

Tung Shu-yeh and Shih Hsüeh-t'ung. *Chung-kuo tz'ŭ-ch'i shih lun-ts'ung* (Essays Towards a History of Chinese Porcelain). Shanghai, 1958.

Waley, Arthur. *The Book of Songs, Translations from the Chinese.* Allen & Unwin, London, 1937; second impression 1954. Alfred A. Knopf, New York, 1955.

Waley, Arthur. *The Life and Times of Po Chü-i, 772–846 A.D.* Allen & Unwin, London, 1949. Hillary House, New York, n.d.

Wang Chih-hsin. *Chung-kuo ts'ung-chiao ssŭ-hsiang shihta-kang* (Short History of Chinese Religion and Thought). 1933.

Watson, Burton. *Early Chinese Literature.* Columbia University Press, New York and London, 1962.

Willetts, William. *Foundations of Chinese Art.* McGraw-Hill, New York, 1965.

Yang Jung-kuo. *Chung-kuo ku-tai ssŭ-hsiang shih* (Intellectual History of Ancient China). Peking, 1955.

Yang K'uan. *Chan-kuo shih* (History of the Warring States). Shanghai, 1955.

Yü Chien-hua. *Chung-kuo hui-hua shih* (History of Chinese Painting). Shanghai, 1959.

Yü Han-chieh. *Han, Wei, Liu-ch'ao min-ko hsüan-i* (Folksongs of the Han, Wei and Liu-ch'ao Periods). Hong Kong, 1959.

Zaehner, Robert C. (ed.). *The Concise Encyclopaedia of Living Faiths.* Hutchinson, London, 1959. Hawthorn Books, New York, 1959.

Zürcher, E. *The Buddhist Conquest of China.* 1955.

Histories of Chinese Civilization

Fitzgerald, C. P. *China: A Short Cultural History*. Cresset Press, London, 1935 and 1954. Frederick A. Praeger, New York, 1961.

Grousset, René. *The Civilisations of the East*. Translated from the French by Catherine Alison Phillips. Hamish Hamilton, London, 1934. Vol. III: *China*. Alfred A. Knopf, New York, 1934.

Reischauer, Edwin O., and Fairbank, John K. *East Asia: The Great Tradition*. Houghton Mifflin, Boston, n.d.

Tsui, Chi. *A Short History of Chinese Civilisation*. Gollancz, London, 1942.

Wilhelm, R. *A Short History of Chinese Civilization*. Translated from the German by Joan Joshua, with an Introduction by Lionel Giles. G. G. Harrap, London, 1929.

*List of Author's Writings on Related Subjects**

'T'ung-sŭ des Čeu-tsi' (with W. Grube), *Asia Major*, Leipzig, 1932.

'Chou Tun-i, ein chinesisches Gelehrtenleben aus dem 11. Jahrhundert', *Abhandlungen der Deutsch-Morgenländischen Gesellschaft*, Leipzig, 1936.

'Die Westinschrift des Chang Tsai', *Abhandlungen der Deutsch-Morgenländischen Gesellschaft*, Leipzig, 1937.

'Zur Kulturgeschichte des 4. und 5. Jahrh.', *Zeitschrift der Deutsch-Morgenländischen Gesellschaft*, 1937.

Chinesisches Bauernleben, drei Dramen, Tokyo, 1938.

'Kolonialkämpfe der Chinesen in Turkestan während der Periode Ch'ien-lung', *Zeitschrift der Deutsch-Morgenländischen Gesellschaft*, 1942.

'Zur Vorgeschichte der chinesischen Arbeiterbewegung', *Saeculum*, XII.

'Bemerkungen zum Aufstand des Chang Chio und zum Staate des Chang Lu', *Mitteilungen des Instituts für Orientforschung*, 1955.

'T'ai-p'ing und T'aip'ing-Religion', *Mitteilungen des Instituts für Orientforschung*, 1957.

'Taoism', in *Living Faiths*, ed. R. C. Zaehner, London and New York, 1959.

* See also pp. 338 and 339.

Index